WESTWOOD LAKE CHRONICLES

Lawrence Winkler

Note for Librarians: A cataloguing record for this book is available from Library and Archives Canada at www.collectionscanada.ca/amicus/index-e.html

ISBN – 978-0-99169-415-0

Printed in Canada
on recycled paper

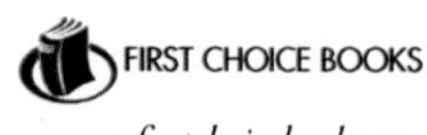

www.firstchoicebooks.ca
Victoria, BC

10 9 8 7 6 5 4 3 2 1

The Chronicles

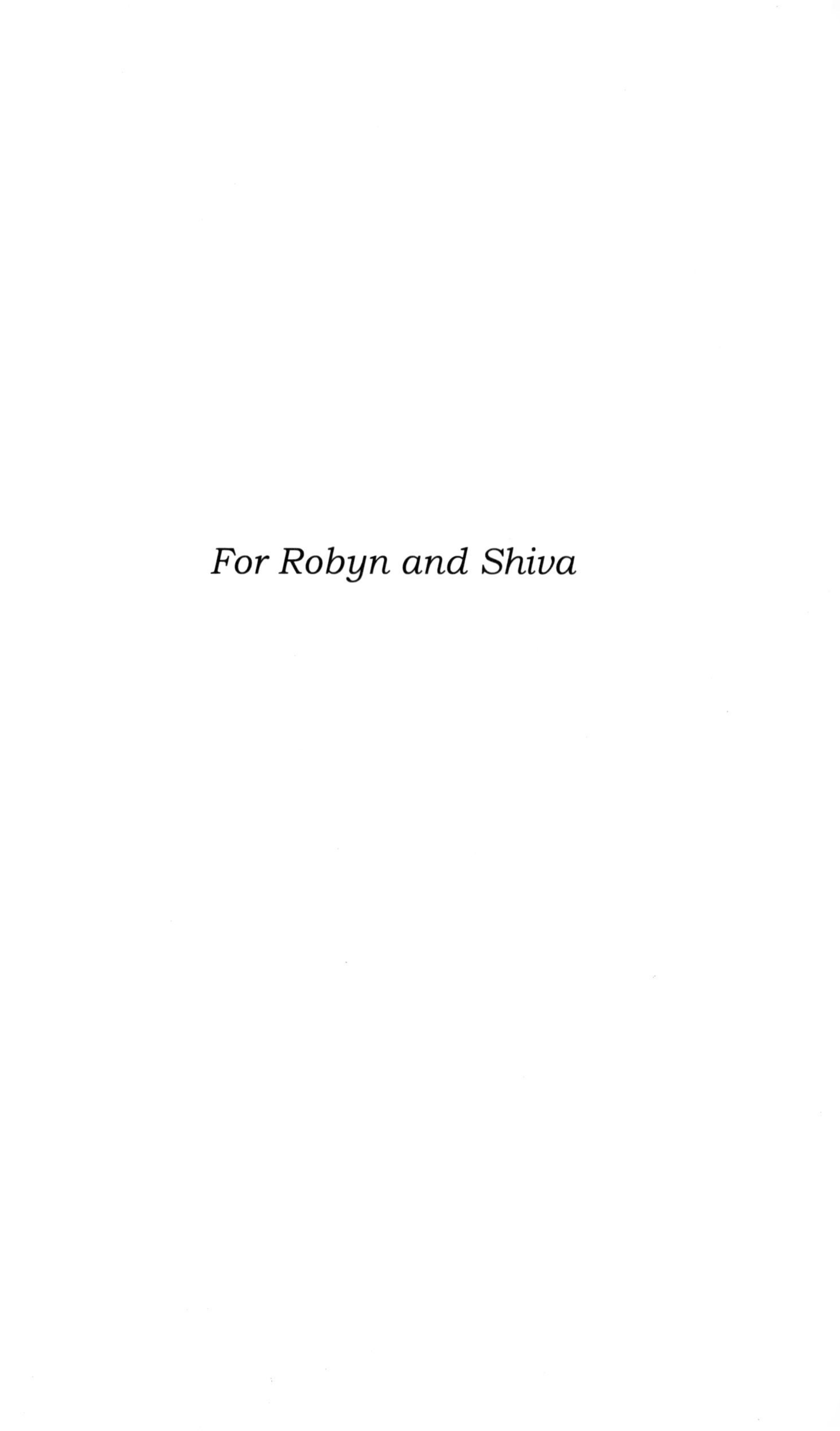

For Robyn and Shiva

Foreword

It's early morning on the *Queen of Alberni* ferry. Mount Benson is receding behind heavy black clouds. Against the whitecaps on the Strait of Georgia, it is a study in charcoal.

I want to bring you a sense of the natural (and some unnatural) history of a place in time. A special place but not, I fear, for much longer. Beyond the brooding storm, at the base of the mountain, lies Westwood Lake.

Twenty-five years ago Robyn and I bought a wooded homestead there, on the water's edge. We brought home a Lab Akita puppy eight years later. Her name is Shiva.

This is a chronicle of the seasons on Westwood, told in photosynthesis, heartbeats, and prevailing winds. Pitched battles of love and terror are in play here. Slowly the chainsaws and developers are extinguishing the life forces of what makes this place unique, but the pages ahead of you are still a safe refuge.

This is for you to remember us by. The tree frogs and swamp lanterns are here. So is a Tai chi set in the vineyard's snowdrifts, and a glide down through the thigh high ferns on the ridges. Robyn and Shiva and I will carry you. Have a pleasant journey.

Amphibitheatre 13 April

"If we can discover the meaning in the trilling of a frog, perhaps we may understand why it is for us not merely noise but a song of poetry and emotion."

Adrian Forsythe

We have big old teak front doors that jam shut in late October and can only be reopened on one night in early spring. I don't know why the timing is so precise, but it seems to have something to do with temperature, humidity, barometric pressure and twilight. I also know that, like other resurrections of biblical scale, we await the sliding apart of the heavy gates with no small spiritual intensity. For over five months we have to go through the garage to access our living spaces. Then suddenly, one fated spring evening, the doors open, and frogs begin to sing. The teak responds to a secret Ali Baba amphibious harmonic. Unlike Arabian nights, however, the treasure is outside the cave.

Our Pacific Chorus frogs *(Pseudacris regilla)* live and breed in *ephemeral* wetlands, racing against the clock to make amphibabies, before the water runs out. *Ready for love.* They are adapted in three ways, to hop over the foreplay. First, the boys are dressed to the nines. Chorus frogs have a dark stripe, extending from their nostrils, past their ears, and through their eyes wide shut. Every guest at this masked ball is able to change the colour of their dinner jacket, from light to dark, and back again. Secondly, unlike the other amphibians in their geographical range, Chorus frogs have toepads, for grip. If you happen to be in a hurry, and smaller than your intended paramour, hanging on tight is a procreative advantage. It has a name, *amplex*, and looks an awful lot like a half nelson. The males get so worked up, they will mate with any amphibian that doesn't make a noise. They will wrestle roadkill. Time's fun when you're having flies. Any salamander, taking a shortcut home, is nervous. The final adaptation that Chorus frogs possess can be deduced from their appellation. They can sing.

Every vernal equinox, the two seasonal ponds in our back yard are home to a Stravinsky extravaganza of boombox ventriloquists. Chorus frogs can throw their voices into the next pond. For creatures so tiny, they sound like rifle fire, cracking in a tunnel. In mating season, from the first night our teak doors spring free, their usual *c-r-r-ick* transforms into a Herculean ***Krek-ek***, laden with urgency and anticipation. But the balance between survival and competing for girl frogs in the dark, has turned them into a choir with an invisible collective conductor. When one of them perceives approaching danger, all of them stop on a dime. When the bravest one decides that the threat has passed, he will cautiously utter a first tentative *Krek-ek* and, if no tragedy befalls him, other less courageous competitors will ramp up the chorus, until the pond becomes a cacophonic amphibitheatre of bouncing braggadocio. We often try to see how close we can get to a pond, while the Rite of Spring concert is in full bombast. We never arrive. When they stomp on that dime, there is only deafening silence.

And the reason they are all chorusing in the first place? Opinions vary. Some think that it is artifactual, the noisy result of a bunch of selfish boys trying to out-*Krek* the other guys' vocalizations. The most prevalent theory involves a collective benefit that comes from calling together. A *Nash equilibrium* model, like hunting in packs. What could be the benefit? It may be to confuse predators (although I think it has more to do with attracting the ladies). The individual calls of the tropical treefrog, *Smilisca sila,* intentionally overlap each other, confusing the echolocation abilities of their principal threat, a species of frog-eating bat.

Our own Pacific Chorus frogs are also *antiphonal* callers. In the spring of 1964, a Berkeley professor, Woodbridge Foster, was the first biologist to parse the structure of their chorus. He found that it was composed of small groups of male duets or trios. A few years later, Frank Awbrey, at San Diego State, noted that individual callers adjusted the timing of their calls to avoid overlapping recorded calls that were played to them. He found that the lead frog acted as a pacemaker, a "choir master", who signalled the beginning and end of each night's singing, and that the frogs spaced themselves out, so two or three neighbors could call, without interfering with each other's singing. Another California biologist, Doug Allan of UC Irvine, reported that Chorus frogs use trills at the beginning of a calling session to precisely establish the 'hostility spacing' between males.

There are three other call types in the chorus frog vocabulary. A monophasic call is uttered by a female approaching a calling male. *Hey, big fella.* The release call is the response of a male which has been amplexed by another male. *Get off!.* Finally, there is the biphasic advertisement call, the *'Krek-ek,'* or *'Ribbit.' I'm here!.* All the movies, that come out of Hollywood, use the call of our Pacific Chorus frog as the standard background remote nature mood music, regardless of whatever geography or climate the film is supposed to be set in.

I'd like to think that it is that first brave little guy to *Krek-ek* and not get eaten, who wins the prettiest lady's round toe pads, and if Darwinian theory is correct, he likely is. Unfortunately, Charles would probably also bet that he will ultimately lose everything to *Rana catesbiana*, the American Bullfrog, that we humans, in our greed for novel protein (and our management arrogance) have introduced. Compared to *Pseudacris regilla, Rana catesbiana* is the Mike Tyson of the Wetlands. He can grow to 1.5 pounds. He will eat anything he can fit in his mouth, including the ducklings that are increasingly disappearing from some of our local lakes. Whereas the Pacific Chorus frog will lay 10 to 70 eggs, the American Bullfrog will spawn up to 20,000. The lifespan of this nocturnal ambush territorial carnivore is up to nine years. When the Chorus frog colonists first hear the baritone Jug-o-Rum army on the move, they will feel like Frodo at the gates of Mordor.

But all is not lost. The American Bullfrog needs perpetual, not ephemeral, wetland, so our little friends still have a chance. As well, the same species that introduced this monster to our neighbourhood has no interest in catching and eating the legs of Pacific Chorus frogs.

Local natives once believed that there was a Chorus frog for every person on Earth. If there is hope, it will always be on that one special night every year when the front doors finally open, and we hear the first *Krek-ek* swell into the Rite of Spring for the little guy. If, on some shimmering evening in the future, the doors don't throw wide, or no chorus greets us, we'll know that the property developers and weed-whackers will have won. It's not easy being green.

"We are born princes and the civilizing process makes us frogs."

Publilius Syrus

Shiva and the Turkey Vulture 19 April

"Vultures are one of the few bird species that are afraid of their own dead. But only if they're hung at the roost site If you hang them anywhere else then they'll eat them."

Martin Lowney

On most days off, I take my dog up across the Ridges behind Westwood Lake. When Shiva sees my heavy socks come out, she starts bouncing around on the cedar deck like a drunken wallaby, in canine appreciation that we will soon be off on another special pilgrimage. I pack my water bottle, Italian rosewood mushroom knife, and a Milkbone into my daypack, and open the garage door. Shiva careens around the truck, and I have to fend her off from licking the nose off my face, while I try to tie up the laces on my hiking boots. She does this little rotational dance, first in one direction then another, like a honey bee waggle dance, chiding me, in more and more urgent vocalizations, to hurry up. Time is short if you have so many odours waiting, and every year is really seven.

By the time I stand up again and reach for my walking stick, she is nearly apoplectic with anticipation. On some later occasion I'll tell you even more about Shiva. Eventually I'll also take you more slowly along the Ridges. Today, you need to know about the vulture.

We first encountered the vulture (or maybe he found us) one early spring day, while trekking across the second Ridge. The trailhead was an hour behind us. The manzanita was in full bloom, with pink and white bell flowers, and the sun was throwing emeralds on the wet moss lining the rock path, in a grove of rusty arbutus trees. For a brief moment the light cut out, and we heard a hiss of pinion feathers slide above us. I looked up and was suddenly blinded by the brightness coming back on. And then I saw it, first as a slowly-sailing coffin-size shadow in my peripheral vision, and then as it really was, a carrion airship, thermal-riding down to eye level with Shiva, who sat motionless, returning the interest. The monster bird wobbled from side to side, like Shiva did in the garage. I wondered what kind of exchange was really happening at a molecular level, between my dog's twitching black nose and the olfactory messages reaching into the Turkey vulture's brain, most of which is devoted only to finding death. It was the mother of all mass spectroscopic battles. Shiva has 220 million olfactory receptors compared to my 5 million. The Turkey vulture (*Cathartesis aura meridionalis*) is able to detect dead animals below a forest canopy, by finding just a whiff of *ethyl mercapten*, a foul breakdown gas of putrefaction. And I do mean a whiff. If humans are able to perceive 2.8 parts per billion in air (which is why it is injected into propane and butane to make container leaks more detectable), imagine what our six-foot-wide hovering hyena can smell. Small amounts of ethyl mercapten are also components of normal human breath, the knowledge of which certainly made me want to hold mine. Ethyl mercapten also prevents the growth of tuberculosis bacteria, a handy thing to have around, if most of your *primi piatti* are rotten beyond recognition. The Turkey vultures' bald heads enable them to enjoy this carrion collation from the inside out, without anything adhering to their unfeathered scalps. If their digestion is disturbed, what they regurgitate is so acidic it can be used as a defensive weapon. Even the babies are able to projectile vulture vomit a full 6 feet. Just to complete the cuteness imagery, Turkey vultures defecate on their own legs, to cool them down in hot weather. This also coats them with uric acid, a fine antiseptic.

Their most brilliant adaptation, however, is the ability to fly so effortlessly. They can float for six hours without a single wing flap. Aircraft pilots have reported them at 20,000 feet. When they migrate from Vancouver Island to Central America they often cover 300 kilometers a day (and survive in environments ranging from deserts to jungles). They can dive at 100 kilometres per hour. All this comes out of a three-pound airmail package with a six-foot wingspan. A colleague of mine is metaphor mad about soaring with eagles, but he doesn't get it. Eagles are not only less well adapted, they are known to follow Turkey vultures to take advantage of where they find the thermals. Besides, vultures have much more interesting social interactions, among themselves and with us. As solitary as we usually find them, they do come together in various vulture venues. A *wake* is a group of perched vultures, so named for their heads hung down as if in mourning. At dawn you can find them all with their wings spread out in the 'horaltic pose' (after the Egyptian god of the morning sun, *Horus*). It was thought that this posture was designed to increase their body temperature after cool nights, but it is more likely that the vultures are sensing winds and currents, checking their instruments pre-flight. When they finally take off collectively into the thermal updrafts, vultures form *kettles*, spiralling upward into clusters, like water boiling in a pot.

The vulture's most prominent interaction with humans, of course, is in death. It's scientific name, *Cathartesis aura*, is Latin for 'cleansing breeze' (from the Greek *cathartes*, meaning 'purifier'). Our ancestral observation, that a human corpse can be completely stripped by vultures within two hours, has evolved into a practice of ritual exposure in at least two Asian cultures. The Tibetans have a long tradition of *sky burial.* They believe that vultures are angels or *Dakinis* (sky dancers). Heaven is thought to be a windswept landscape, where souls wait for reincarnation into their next lives. The sky burial is an act of Buddhist generosity (*jhator*), a gift of human flesh to vultures that might otherwise have eaten other, smaller lives. This virtue was apparently demonstrated by Buddha, who once fed a hawk with a piece of his own leg, to save the life of a pigeon. When a Tibetan dies, monks chant around the body for three days. *Om mane padme hum.* The day before his sky burial, his corpse is cleaned, wrapped in white cloth, and bent into the fetal position he was born in. Before dawn the next morning, lamas chant in procession to the charnel ground, leading the soul of the dead with their intonations. Body breakers unwrap the gift. Hatchets and cleavers are brought out quickly, to crush bones and cut up organs and flesh into small pieces. Juniper incense is lit, and the remains of the deceased, mixed with *tsampa* barley porridge, are spread out over the ground. When the vultures are finally allowed to land, they are, in the proper order, fed the splintered bone mixture, the organs, and then the flesh, to assure ascent of the soul into Heaven.

The other religion that employs vultures to recycle its dead came out of ancient Persia, now Iran. Zoroastrians considered earth, water and fire sacred, and not to be defiled by the dearly departed. High in their Towers of Silence, these communities of fire-worshippers practiced their *Dakhma* ritual exposure to the vultures. Iranian adherants had been persecuted by the Islamic expansion but Zoroastrian colonies still exist in India, especially around Mumbai. Unfortunately for the ritual, most of the vultures have been killed off by inadvertent poisoning with *diclofenac* (an anti-inflammatory used in treating sick livestock), to which their kidneys are exquisitely sensitive. Even with the influx of snakes and crows and the use of solar panels to aid decomposition, Parsi caracasses are piling up.

> *"Our last act of charity was with the vulture. That's the tradition that we have grown up to follow and that tradition has come under threat. When you look at most cultures, the vulture's seen as a scavenger, in a very negative light, whereas to us the vulture's a religious bird because it's...performing a religious service."*
>
> Khojeste Mistree

Shiva also has connections to death. Robyn and I have always named our dogs after Hindu deities (they would at least see the humour in it). Kali was our first dog, Shiva the second. She is called after *Nataraja*, the cosmic dancer who performs a divine dance to destroy a weary universe, and prepare the path for the process of creation. The dance releases the souls of men from the snare of illusion. In Judaism, Shiva (*seven*) is a week-long period of grief and mourning for the seven first-degree relatives- father, mother, son, daughter, brother, sister, and spouse. Like Jewish mourners, our Shiva has her food supplied and does not bathe for pleasure, an observation to which anyone that has tried to approach her with a hose will attest (an understatement).

Every Spring, we look for the Vulture when we're on the second ridge. When it happens, Shiva and I always feel his presence before we see him soar by. Once he landed and sat for a moment beside us, spread-winged and magnificent; if he'd had sunglasses on, he could have been the Jack Nicholson of Turkey Vultures. Eagles would have bowed and averted their eyes. Shiva lay down with her head between her front paws. For just a snapshot in time, there was a glimmer of interspecies recognition passing on an evolutionary offramp. They looked, locked, and looked away. The vulture dropped off the ridge. Shiva and I were suddenly alone again, on the top of the world.

"Part of me is noting the shallow V of the wings, the dihedral position that distinguishes the Turkey Vulture, even from miles away. Part of me is wondering what great dead animal this flock was settled upon a few minutes ago. Part of me is curious where the birds are off to, whether to roost in the trees by the river or nest in the shelter of the hills. But most of me is just standing here under a near-dark moon, watching what ought to be an omen of death and gloom, with a great big grin on my face. Their eyes shining in the dim light, their voices the fierce whispers of childhood delight, my sons are with me. I bird. They bird. We bird."

Peter Cashwel

The Red Bomber of Westwood 27 April

"Living is no laughing matter: you must live with great seriousness like a squirrel for example--I mean without looking for something beyond and above living. I mean living must be your whole occupation."

Nazom Hikmet

It rained on a sunlit morning one day last fall. The noise hit us first with a 'thwak' of bouncing wood on metal. The tin fascia on our master bedroom cried out in pain. The echoes grew more frequent and faster, as they reverberated through the house. We ran upstairs to discover that it was hailing on the mossy soffit, outside our bedroom window. Pine cones. Faster than you could count them. We charged out to the upper deck and squinted up into the fir trees. At first we only saw pine cones. Then we felt them. It appeared that we had become a target. As we retreated for a moment, back inside, the trajectory of the automatic fire migrated back to the midden of pine cones mounding up on the original spot. We ventured out the door again and we were once more pelted. Bastard. The downpour stopped briefly, as the bomber paused to see where the insult had come from.

On a branch, about twenty feet above our heads, a Red Squirrel stood twitching like he'd been tasered. Suddenly he let out a verbal barrage of *ChikChik-ChikChurrrr* that, in squirrel slang, certainly trumped my insult. The message was clear. This was his territory, these were his pine cones, he wasn't going anywhere, and we had been warned. The bravado of this air rat's insolence was infuriating. It got especially aggravating when he didn't let up until almost nightfall. It became intolerable when he fired up his fir food factory again at five o'clock the next morning. And the morning after that, until this particular tree ran out of cones.

What were we to do? Shiva the Wonder Dog couldn't fly or climb trees (although you could tell by the expression on her face that she would have traded her legs for wings, just for one shot at it). Firearms were out of the question. I have a semiautomatic paintball gun, but the idea of having to explain a yellow Red Squirrel to law enforcement was just too terrible to contemplate. Thoreau's comment about the squirrel you kill in jest dying in earnest, lingered on the air he flew through. We decided that the answer was in another form of dissuasion. We hid the pile of pine cones, when he wasn't looking. This was a bad move. As his white eye rings converged on the now empty space, the rest of his face transformed into pure panic. He scratched his head. They were here just a minute ago. No matter. He simply shrugged his little squirrel shoulders, opened the heavens more deliberately than before, and started all over again. We were licked.

The Red Squirrel (*Tamiasciurus hudsonicus*) is as territorial as he is, because she is too. Both males and females have their own turf, about a hectare each. Boundary disputes are, therefore, twice as common. Girl squirrels come into heat one day a year in March or April. On that day the Red Bomber has to fight off other suitors, and successfully chase a female into reproductive frolic, while she tries to elude him, in three dimensions and with gravitational consequences. As well, he has to simultaneously defend his own real estate, because he'll still need it after the pursuit, whether or not he mates. The doe throws him off the property the minute the fun is over. In the autumn, he has to fend off all the young punks, who are also looking for prime airspace (juveniles without their own territory or midden, a full eighty per cent, do not survive their first winter). Our Red Bomber has to be eternally vigilant for predators- cougars and domestic cats, goshawks and owls, and us. On the one hand, humans cut down his old growth habitat while, with the other, they rob his cone caches of seeds for tree replanting. In Finland, before coins were in circulation, squirrel pelts were currency, as they were among the young boys at my elementary school in Northwestern Ontario. He doesn't even know about his big ugly gray cousins yet. Because of all this, and the fact that the Red Bomber only lives for three years at the most, you can't blame him for being half tail and half attitude.

I can blame him for invading my birdfeeder, and stuffing it full of non-bird squirrel food. Or making his nest in my basement (with my insulation), or not cleaning up the mess he makes, some of which is a metre deep. He apparently doesn't know when to stop collecting. None of his actions were deliberately subversive, but some were unnecessarily barbaric. Relief finally came with the winter snows.

But we were also strangely enchanted to see the Red Bomber again this spring, sitting on the very edge of the topmost fascia beam. We walked onto the top deck to greet him and, for a moment, he almost seemed glad to see us too. Then he pushed off into thin air, trusting to his instincts and leaving two gasps behind. He made it across the void to a Douglas fir, scurried up to a branch above our heads, and began to curse us shamelessly. Bastard.

> *"If we had a keen vision of all that is ordinary in human life, it would be like hearing the grass grow or the squirrel's heart beat, and we should die of that roar which is the other side of silence."*
>
> George Eliot

And You Blaze 04 May

"From scarlet to powdered gold, to blazing yellow,
to the rare ashen emerald,
to the orange and black velvet of your shimmering
corselet, out to the tip that like as amber thorn begins
you, small, superlative being, you are a miracle, and you
blaze."

Pablo Neruda, *Ode to a Hummingbird*

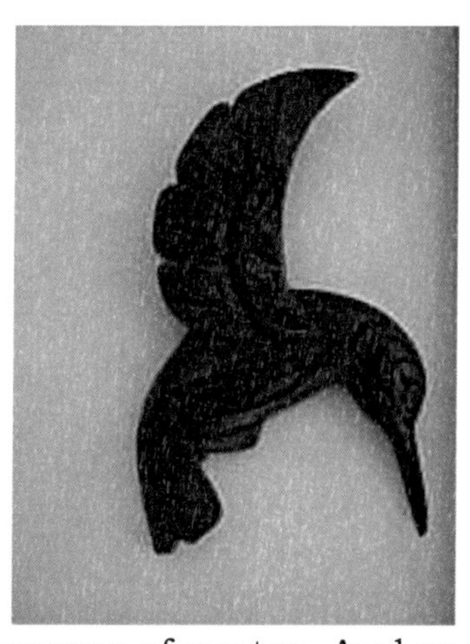

It was in my right ear. I had just stood up from between the raised beds, and the Doppler shifting roar came at me like a chainsaw. For an instant, both startled, I looked up at the receding frozen frame stutter of a Rufous Hummingbird (*Selasphorus rufus*), clearly embarrassed for mistaking my aural appendage for a quick source of nectar. And speed was this mirage's middle name. He flew backwards in a vast reverse parabola of whining whoosh, braked at sixty feet above the berry run, and then accelerated to 50 miles per hour, into a diving arc of emerald and ruby refracted iridescence. For just a few milliseconds, at the lowest point and highest G forces of this power dive, he splayed his tail feathers and fired off a chirping wing whistle *'biz-biz-biz-zing,'* which ricocheted off everything unafraid and still standing. Then he did the whole thing over again. Five times. Not for my benefit, you understand. This was, after 2000 miles of single-minded migration (600 miles of which was nonstop across the Gulf of Mexico), courtship. Mr Razzle Dazzle fancypants.

Rufous is a metabolic Maserati. He is 30 per cent flight muscle. His heart must pump 1250 beats per minute, so his wings can flap at 50 beats per second. He breathes 250 times a minute. Not only will he visit a thousand flowers a day, and feed every 10 minutes to maintain his fuel consumption, but he will also suck up every insect and spider in his path for additional protein and calories. His journey is precisely timed to hit his favorite food sources. The blossoms project out. They know he is in a hurry. Rufous's 'field metabolic rate' is eight times what it is when he is not migrating. His oxygen consumption is ten times that of the most elite human athlete. If your blood sugar ran as high as his, you would be in a coma. He is 40 per cent fat when he leaves Panama in the Spring, and this is what he burns to make it back to Westwood Lake. And, when he has found true love (or several, as he loves the one he's with), Rufous will turn around and make the trip back in the Fall. To complement these amphetamine poster boy abilities, hummers have the adaptive ability to power down when they need to. In situations of cold, hunger or both, they can enter a state of *torpor*, where their body temperature drops up to 20 degrees, and their heart rate down to 50 beats per minute. They can stop breathing. If that doesn't work, they can die.

Hummingbirds first appeared in the primordial rain forests of South America, several million years ago. Of the three hundred varieties that have evolved there, one inspired an ancient Peruvian artist to create a Nazca image so large as to be recognizable 1000 feet overhead. Further north, the Mayas believed that one of their gods created the first two hummingbirds from small feather scraps left over from the construction of other birds. He was so proud of his work, that he held an elaborate wedding ceremony, to celebrate their incarnation. Butterflies marked out a room, flower petals fell into a carpet, spiders spun webs into a bridal path, and the Sun sent beams to illuminate the ceremony with dazzling greens and reds. When the hummers turned away from the Sun, they became as drab as the original grey feathers they were made from.

In pre-Columbian Mexico, children ensnared hummingbirds with slug slime, smeared on twigs near flowers. The captives were fastened to a string through their nose or eyes as live toys. Romantic amulets were made from dead hummingbirds, and their hearts are still dried and ground as the principal ingredient in some modern Latin love potions.

The northern Paiute Indians have a myth about a hummingbird that filled his pants with seeds, to see what lay beyond the sun. Even though he only ate one seed a day, he still had to turn back.

Hummingbirds were unknown outside the Western Hemisphere, until the arrival of European ships. Columbus wrote about them in his diary. Cortez met Aztec kings wearing cloaks of hummingbird skins. The Pilgrims first encountered Native emissaries with hummingbird earrings. The bejewelled parabolic rainbow buzz was on. Fantastic stories of hummingbirds migrating in the neck feathers of geese, or sticking their beaks into trees in the autumn to die and then reviving in the spring, were told in the coffee houses across the Atlantic.

By the middle of the nineteenth century, millions of hummingbirds were being killed in South America, and their skins were being shipped to Europe to make dusters, artificial flowers and other ornaments. Their influence in Western Art began with the trade in their cadavers. By 1832, Lesson had published a three-volume monograph with color plates. Fifteen years later, John Gould had produced five volumes of 360 hand-colored lithographs of hummingbirds, all from stuffed specimens. In 1857, Gould traveled to the US and saw his first live one.

When American bird artist, John James Audubon, referred to hummingbirds as *'glittering garments of the rainbow'*, the picture become prose. When Emily Dickenson wrote *A Route of Evanescence*, the prose became poetry:

> *"He never stops, but slackens Above the Ripest Rose-*
> *Partakes without alighting And praises as he goes,*
> *Till every spice is tasted --He, the best Logician, Refers*
> *my clumsy eye --To just vibrating Blossoms! An Exquisite*
> *Reply! ...With a revolving Wheel-A Resonance of Emerald-*
> *A Rush of Cochineal-And every Blossom on the Bush*
> *Adjusts its tumbled Head-The mail from Tunis probably*
> *An easy Morning's ride".*

Several years ago, Robyn and I flew to Juan Fernandez, the shipwreck island of Alexander Selkirk, and the inspiration for *Robinson Crusoe*. The pilot was an old man who handed out sandwiches to us and two Spanish couples, who also made the 670 kilometer trip, in an old Cessna 170. He let us know when our fuel gauge indicated the point of no return as, sometimes, he can't find the place, for whatever reason.

When we finally broke through the fogbank, we saw an island cut in half by climate, with a totally dry, rust-coloured windward side, and a verdant forest-clad eastern part. We landed in the desert, swung the tail around just in time so as not to fall over the cliff at the furthest edge of the runway, and taxied up beside another plane that hadn't quite made it. We waited at the bottom of a trail with a group of Juan Fernandez fur seals clearly unimpressed with our arrival, until a boat driven by a lobsterman came to fetch us around to the prettier side of the island.

Over the next week we settled in and, one day, decided to walk up the trail that Selkirk hiked every day of his confinement, to see if there were any ships on the horizon. Half way up the mountain, our serenity was shattered by a V1 buzzbomb. This thing sounded like a kazoo on steroids. It hove into view with an undercarriage, an attitude, and the most royal rust red plumage I've ever seen. It was a Juan Fernandez firecrown, the world's largest hummingbird, the Gulliver bumblebird football of the South Pacific. There were only two hundred left.

Sip the sweet moments. Let your true colors glow. Don't get your feathers ruffled over little things. Just wing it. Take yourself lightly. Keep your visits short and sweet. The Spaniards who explored the Coast called our Rufous hummers '*joyas volardores*', flying jewels. So long as these small, superlative beings of neon fire dance in my garden in the spring, I will blaze too.

> *"Gentle day's flower – The hummingbird competes*
> *With the stillness of the air"*
>
> Chogyam Trungpa

Ridgeline Headbanger 07 May

"She'll be makin' her way to a higher high"

Headbanger's Ball

I awoke early this morning around five am. The back part of my brain punched in. This was my half day off. If I left now, I could walk around Westwood Lake before work, and still dig in the garden this afternoon. Shiva and I slid out the side door quietly, so as not to wake Robyn, off into the shadows before dawn. As we powered around the second turn through the fir-covered forest beyond the public beach, we came upon a whitish mound in the middle of the path. Something lay motionless inside a soiled sleeping bag, a tripod of face and knees. It had been a bad night of false revelry. I had a foreboding. The last time I came by this place this early, I ran smack into the wizardly faces of two Great horned owls peering down, eyebrows raised. Today, Shiva and I sneaked by this indiscrete lumpy interloper, eyes lowered. Whither Westwood, we wondered.

After hiking around the far side of the lake, we came onto the long, darker stretch, just ahead of the first few sunbeams that streamed in behind us. Emerging from the tree tunnel into a clearing, we were greeted by a painful staccato *rat-a-tat-a-tat,* from the metal flashing nailed high up on a powerpole to our left. It was a Hairy Woodpecker (*Picoides vellosis*), drumming and resting, and drumming and drumming, for all he was worth. The sound was loud and leaden. Jeezuz, that must hurt, I thought. Apparently nobody knows but the woodpecker.

The impact deceleration, generated by the Woodpecker's beak slamming into the flashing, can exceed a thousand times the force of gravity. This would take your head clean off. Bonzo does this 500 times per minute, eight times a second, at thirteen miles per hour. Like you running headlong into a tree. As fast as you can. Five hundred times a minute. Obviously, Bonzo has aquired some evolutionary adaptations. Yes, he has. His skull is surrounded by spongier bone, and this acts as a dashpot. His brain is relatively small, and packed tightly inside his skull cavity. It has a high surface area for its weight (like a zeppelin), without our convoluted raised wavy haircut. 'Tis better to give than to receive. No concussions. His tongue wraps around his brain for even more elasticity, twice as long as his head. His eyes are held tightly in place and he closes them with every peck. Head muscles contract a millisecond prior to each impact. No detached retinas. He is also a tripod. Not of face and knees, but of tail and feet. His short feet are strong, with two *zygodactyl* toes facing forward and two facing back. You can figure out the Newtonian physics. Finally, he hammers in a dead straight line. Or he breaks his neck.

Our particular woodpecker this morning was a dashing maestro of the Jackhammer, a regular Buddy Rich of the Ridgeline. "Here I am", he said. Here I am, with a little heavy metal hormonal amplification. A girl woodpecker tentatively landed on one of the power pole crossbars below him. Bonzo jumped down, did a little dance, hopped vertically back up to his shiny cymbal, and drummed out some more Led Zeppelin. When he hopped back down to the female, it was all over in a heartbeat. She immediately flew off, three flaps, one glide, three flaps, one glide. Bonzo bounced back up to his chrome perch, gave himself an admiring glance in the mirror and, looking both ways, resumed drumming. Greedy little pecker-head.

Shiva and I lowered our eyes and continued our walk around the lake. I made it to work with time to spare.

The next afternoon we saw a Ridgeline truck muscle over the speedbumps into the Public Beach entrance of the Park, Hip Hop thumping from every window.

"Here I am," said the driver. Here I am, with a little heavy metal hormonal amplification.

Dogs, Gods, and Destructive Diseases 11 May

"High o'er all the early floral train
Where softness all the arching sky resumes
The dogwood dancing to the wind's refrain
In stainless glory spreads its snowy blooms"

George Marion McClellan *1860-1934*

We have a Pacific Dogwood (*Cornus nuttallii*) living beside our garage. For most of the year I don't even notice him, but for two weeks every spring, he explodes into a mountain of white popcorn. During this time, I smile warmly inside, as I check my rear view mirror driving to work in the morning, and again when I come around the last turn in our driveway at the end of the day. He is a magnificent sight. In the Fall he shows a different brilliance, with his prickly reddish-orange golf ball ladybug fruit clusters, but I love him in the Springtime more. Especially this unusually cold Spring. It's called a *dogwood winter.*

The Pacific dogwood has been the official floral emblem of British Columbia since 1956. Prior to that, during WWII, the sale of dogwood lapel pins helped purchase wool for the soldiers. Franco-Columbians have a dogwood blossom on their flag. Two of them, the notorious Renault Brothers in *Twin Peaks*, hung out at *One-Eyed Jacks*, a kind of dogwood flower.

In Chaucer's day, the dogwood was known as a *whippletree*. It was also called *bloodtwig*, because of its autumn coloration. By 1548, it was called the *dog-tree* and by 1614 we finally had the dogwood. It was also referred to as the *Hound's tree*, and the berries, *dogberries* or *houndberries*. Dogs were washed in a frothy brew of its bark in the early 1800's, as treatment for fleas or mange.

Dogwoods were also originally named *dag-woods*, because the excellent hard nature of the wood was perfect for making *dags*, or daggers. It is as hard as horn, from whence its name *Cornus* first originated. Also referred to as *prick timber*, dogwood was utilized in the fabrication of pitchforks, knives, and toothpicks. Victorian watchmakers cleaned their delicate mechanisms with its slivers.

Dogwoods have also been used to make loom shuttles, cogwheels, tool handles, bows and arrows (by the English, and B.C. First Nations), winepress screws, tennis rackets, piano keys, New World printing blocks for engravings.

The Coast Salish used them to make knitting needles. What yarn did they originally knit? The Coast Salish Wool Dog was a special breed kept by the women of the village. It looked like a Pomeranian, and was kept separately from the tribe's coyote-like hunting dogs. The white ones were so specially valued, they were kept on islands in gated caves or fenced pits. They were fed raw and cooked salmon and, sometimes, elk tallow and liver to make their coats shinier. In the Springtime, when the fleece was sheared off with a mussel knife, it was so thick that Captain Vancouver noted he could lift it up by one corner, like a mat.

The dogs were not seen very far north of Vancouver Island for two reasons. First, they were deliberately bred to express the *Malamute Factor,* that set of recessive genes responsible for the lavish underfur growing longer than the outer protective guard hairs. This meant that snow, ice and mud could get in, next to the dog's skin. This, in turn, meant the death of the dog in harsher climates.

The second reason is biologically incredible. The dogs further north were also killed by a prehistoric bacteria living in a flatworm, using a snail as a temporary home, and then penetrating the skin of the salmon that was ultimately fed to the dogs. Let me do that again. *Neorickettsia helminthoeca* is an obligate parasite of all life stages of the flatworm, *Nanophyetes salmincola.* The eggs of the flatworm incubate in freshwater streams for three to seven months and then hatch as *miracidia,* tiny larval Cousin Itts that find and burrow into snails. There, they form baby flatworms called *cercariae.* When they exit the snail, they have two days to find a frog or a fish, penetrate its tissue in less than two minutes, and take up residence in its muscles, kidneys or fins. When an otter, dog, or other canid eats the salmon, the fluke encysts in the host's intestinal wall, and its life cycle comes full circle. But the dog dies horribly, of a distemper-like disease.

All this, added to what we provided to their masters (sheep wool blankets and smallpox, sometimes together), resulted in the Coast Salish Wool Dog becoming extinct as a breed, about the time of the gold rush in 1860. The last one died in 1940.

The Dogwood is also Godwood (no dyslexic pun intended). The 'flower' is a cross-like construction of 4 white bracts, each bearing a rusty indentation. There is a central crown of thorns, a Westwood Lake

Passion flower. The fruit is blood coloured. The Dogwood flower motif was a popular tombstone ornament with immigrants of the last century, symbolizing death but hope, as well. There is a Christian legend that the cross used to crucify Jesus was made of Dogwood. The tree was the strongest and tallest tree in Israel (or so goes the myth). When Christ rolled back the rock, he apparently turned the high and mighty dogwood into the twisted slender tree we know today. At the time, Jesus was apparently having a little difficulty just being Jesus. Houndberries are also a name for black nightshade fruit, alluding to *Hecate's hounds*. Hecate is represented by the Greek cross as the Goddess of Crossroads. The Cherokee believed that a race of little brown people lived among the dogwood, and were sent to teach us how to live in harmony. That didn't work out very well either.

The real horror is just ahead for the Pacific Dogwood. In 1976, a fungus called *Discula destructiva* began killing healthy trees from Washington State on up. We have lost anywhere from 20 per cent to all of our dogwood stands, depending on where you live in the Pacific Northwest. Two years later the identical fungus hit Connecticut and New York's *Cornus florida* dogwoods. This tells us that the disease that it causes, *Anthracnose*, has been introduced, likely by nurseries, although here's where the amazing biology comes into play again. It spreads in two ways: directly by water splash and, remotely, in the feces of *Hippodamia convergens*, our ladybug.

The Lady beetle got her name in the Middle ages, after the Virgin Mary was thought to have sent millions of these little saviours to eat crop pests, during an infestation. The red wings are supposed to represent Mary's cloak and the black spots, her joys and sorrows. There doesn't seem to be very much joy for the dogwood, whenever it comes in contact with this family. The astonishing part is, like the life cycles of the coastal canid parasites, there are fleas on fleas here as well. *Discula destructiva* is infected with two double stranded RNA viruses, the net effect of which is still unknown. Like the tropical Panic grass infested by a fungus, in turn infected by a virus that allows the grass to grow in areas where it would otherwise die of heat.

So it seems there are dogs, gods, and destructive diseases associated with the unassuming tree beside my garage. There is also just a little romance. In the American western frontier, a young girl would wear a white dogwood flower when going out walking; the first man she met with a white hat was supposed to have the same first name as the man she would eventually marry. White hat sales were undoubtedly good.

Anne Morrow Lindberg once said "I don't see why I'm always asking for private individual selfish miracles when every year there are miracles like white dogwood". For those special two weeks in the Spring, I feel it every time I come down my driveway.

Little Apples 17 May

"Que rica esta la manzana
Que cuelga de la ramita
Se esta callendo de buena
Por que ya esta madurita"

Los Tigres del Norte, *Manzanita*

There are three times three dimensions that Shiva and I climb through to get to the Little Apples. The first is the physical hike to a critical altitude above the lake. The second contains the sensory and visceral experiences along the trail. Finally, there is that explosion of awareness upon arriving. Each ascent confers a little more strength, pleasure and meaning. Every worldly weight lifts away as we cross beyond the finish line into our favorite copse of contorted hedges. Deer slip fast and ethereal through this grove, but cougars, dogs, and humans are snag-trapped by its long, stiff and crooked twisting branches. The bushes are zen-like, with beautiful smooth auburn bark, sage green ovate leaves and, when they're in flower, little pink cream to ivory transluscent Japanese lanterns. This is

Manzanita (*Arctostaphylos manzanita*), the elegant Spanish heather of Westwood ridges.

The Mexican sandfly-bitten Spaniards of San Blas gave their own personal names (*Alberni, Cortes, Galiano, Malaspina, Quadra, Texada, Zeballos,* etc.) to our island places. These same Iberian explorers christened this subalpine shrub *Manzanita* ("little apples") because, well, that's what the berries look like. The sweet unfermented cider that was traditionally made from them was sucked from a plume of hawk tail feathers by the Miwok of Yosemite. The leaves were used as natural medicine for stomach maladies and urinary infections. They contain compounds called *arbutins,* one of which is hydroquinone. This chemical can convert silver halides to elemental silver, can be used as a human skin whitener (but with an associated high cancer risk, Michael), and is one of the two primary reagents in the defensive glands of the Bombardier Beetle. The other beetle reservoir contains hydrogen peroxide. Like a rocket engine, when the bug is threatened, it opens up both tanks into a thick-walled combustion chamber, an exothermic chemical reaction occurs, and a flash-vaporized, boiling hot, foul-smelling corrosive explodes onto its attacker. With a loud 'pop'. Seventy times, very rapidly. Dead attacker.

The plants are highly drought-tolerant evergreens that prefer a sunlit, well-drained habitat, but the year before last it was so dry on the ridges, that we lost more than a few. The ravages of two-wheeled Mount Benson thrill riders, with or without two-stroke engines are killing more yet. Souvenir hunters take the wood for furniture and artwork, aquarium and garden decoration ('mountain driftwood'), parrot perches and pipestems. It burns so hot it can crack cast iron stoves, and cause chimney fires. A five-foot-tall Manzanita can generate a forty-foot flame. Seeds usually need fire to germinate. They are severely threatened. Some subspecies are almost extinct.

In 1951 there was only one *Raven's Manzanita* left in existence. It was found on the grounds of the *Presidio* in San Francisco. Its location is still a closely-guarded secret. There are 8 clones alive now, and a proposal to cut down 75 acres of other trees in an attempt to bring it back.

Strangely, my own love for Manzanita has come with increasing familiarity. I first encountered it, in name only, while working at NASA Ames one summer, when I stayed in *Manzanita Park* at Stanford. I didn't know what a Manzanita was, and I wouldn't have cared. My first real connection occurred when I left my shoebox medical office across from the hospital, after seventeen years. I needed a new landlord. I took a sabbatical year of sorts, working in Intensive Care Units and clinics around the Island, and hiking the ridges with Shiva, revelling in the seasonal changing beauty of Mount Benson, and the three dimensional freedom I experienced up there with every climb. When I finally found a building in the Old City of Nanaimo and reopened my own office, I needed a moniker. Other medical clinics in town were named after large trees (*Arbutus, Alder,* and the filbert *Caledonian*) but I was one lone rocket scientist with a Macbook, a single drought-tolerant Little Apple practitioner. *Manzanita Medical* was born.

I am sometimes conflicted when I share the location of special inspirations. The concern is that, like the founders of *Lonely Planet* discovered, one can destroy a place, simply by introducing it to others. If you want to experience Manzanita, you must climb, not ride, up through the three times three dimensions, beyond the finish line, into the Little Apples.

One Particular Arbour 19 May

"But there's this one particular Arbour
So far but yet so near
When I see the days as they fade away
And finally disappear"

To Jimmy Buffett (with apologies)

I love waking up to the violet-green swallows, swooping and loop-de-looping over the lake, at sunrise in the Spring. The sun-light flash dances on the white underbellies of hundreds of open-mouthed acrobats from below, as they soar over the dawn shimmer.

I rise, feed Shiva, and enjoy a tranquil weekend morning coffee with Robyn. We have the first warm day of the season; it was promised to us by the weather police, and we are holding them to it. The garden call is strong today, and I obey.

Shiva is already waiting for me in the garage. You can see the disappointment in her eyes, when I reach for my *Tevas* instead of my hiking boots. But she's happy enough just to have me at home, and we head off to the arbour.

When we first put in the garden, Robyn and I assembled a complex of seven cedar raised beds, on each side of a long central grape and kiwifruit arbour. It served us well, initially, until the predation began. The Gooseberry sawfly found the gooseberries (how and from where I have no idea), the wasps and powdery mildew found the grapes, the rabbits found the ground crops, and the deer found everything else except the cedar. The sowbugs found that. We started with small gentle organic protective manoeuvres (hand picking caterpillars, planting marigolds, reciting incantations). Years later we had degenerated to a fenced and netted armed encampment, replete with chemical weaponry that Saddam Hussein could only have wished for. The Mother of all Maginot lines. We had seen everything, and we had every angle covered.

Except this one, maybe. When I opened the netting entrance to the arbour, I got an immediate loud and panicked ear bashing from an American Robin (*Turdus migratorius*). Her usual *'cheerily cheer up, cheer up'* had morphed into *'PEEK tut tut tut'* to a horse whinny *'he he he'*. She was not happy. Ahead of me on the second crossbar of the arbour, was a nest, with three big juvenile robins, sitting perfectly still with eyes fixed sideways. The mother had made over 180 trips a day just to construct her nest. She was on the threshold of losing all three reasons why she'd gone to the effort. I was dive-bombed. Repeatedly. By the father as well. The mother shrieked at me, as she tail-flicked and deliberately kicked cherry blossoms from a tree, to distract my attention from her brood.

I decided to just go about my business, and began weeding one of the raised beds. It didn't work. One of the juveniles fell, was pushed, or jumped from the nest and the game was rejoined. Other robins showed up, and the hysteria intensified. A Stellar's Jay *crow-cawing* showed up. He was not here to bolster, but to breakfast. The second adolescent jumped out of the nest. The third wasn't going to be left behind, and scurried after his brother, under the netting, and into the underbrush beyond the berry run.

It was all over, although the adult robins went on wailing at the loss for several hours. Cherry blossoms fell. They knew that only twenty-five per cent of new-born robins would see the Autumn of their first year. This first bird of Spring, this first bird song of the morning and the last at night, had found themselves on the sad side of the statistics. I felt their pain.

But then I thought about it. This was the second time in two years that these robins had constructed their nest in the exact same place in the arbour. With the exact same outcome. There is no procreative or survival benefit in repeating an evolutionary suicidal mistake. Einstein defined insanity as doing the same thing over and over again, and expecting different results.

We will just have to see what happens in the future. Propagation potential aside, I still hope they return next spring. Because the eggs, the eggs, my friend, are the most beautiful robin's egg blue visual gifts of nature you can imagine.

Honk if You Love 26 May

"Tonight I heard the wild goose cry
Wingin' north in the lonely sky
Tried to sleep, it warn't no use
'Cause I am a brother to the old wild goose"

Terry Gilkyson, *Cry of the Wild Goose*

It's usually around five am on an early spring day, when they drop from the sky, in perfect 'V' formation. The racket wakes you bolt upright. *'Ahonk-hink, ahonk-ahink, ahonk-hink.'* Only when you hear the decelerating swooshing water landings, do the lights come on. The geese are back.

These Canada Geese (*Branta Canadensis*) are this excited because they are returning to their birthplace. They are returning after migrating up to a thousand miles a day. And night. They are returning to mate, likely in the same nest the female's parents used.

The fact that they are returning at all is no small miracle. They were hunted by European settlers for food, feathers, and 'goose grease', which was blended with turpentine and used as a chest cold liniment.

They were hunted for recreation. The population was down to 1.1 million birds in 1947, and some subspecies (there are eleven) were hunted to near extinction.

Even when the *Migratory Bird Treaty Act of 1918* was passed in the American Congress, continued shooting kept them scarce. They were often used as 'live' decoys, flight feathers clipped and feet tied to underwater weights, sad witness to the demise of their honking brethren.

When a goose is shot out of the formation, two geese automatically peel off from the group, to follow the wounded bird down, and offer help and protection. They will stay until recovery or death, and only then join up with another migrating flock. That's also why hunters usually bagged three geese at a time. Even now, their olive yellow chicks are still stalked by ravens, crows, owls, hawks, gulls, racoons, dogs and many other predatory appetites. This is likely why they're born *precocial*, eyes open, down-covered, and mobile, unlike, say, *altricial* robins, who come into this world blind, naked and helpless.

Overall, however, the geese are back. There are now about eight million. They are back because of, well, Suburbia- parks, golf courses, agricultural land, and airports. Between 1991 and 1997 there were 16,949 civilian airstrikes reported to the FAA. There are another 3000 US Air Force strikes per year. The worst accident killed 24 people at Elmendorf Air Force Base, Alaska, in 1995. The problem is made worse because geese are usually hit below two thousand feet, when flight crews, preoccupied with takeoff or landing, don't have much time or space to react.

Canada Geese are considered menacing pests in other ways as well. They are aggressive, and will give hissing chase and nasty pecks to anything that they feel is threatening their goslings. They are traffic jam noisy, man, are they noisy. They overgraze lawns and landscaping and produce Herculean amounts of clay pipe-stem goose guano, up to 1.5 pounds a day, by some estimates. Multiply that by the numbers of geese that used to inhabit Westwood Lake, and you can understand why human parents thought twice about bringing their children to play on the beach. Goose droppings contain a panoply of infectious microbes (*E.coli, Salmonella, Cryptosporidium, Giardia*), although some goose lovers have maintained that there are more dangerous pathogens in the feces of songbirds that visit your backyard feeder. There are no 24-pound songbirds, of course, and this argument has limitations, but it is true that there are no case reports of human illness transmitted from geese.

The nitrogen and phosphorus content of goose poop, however, is something else again, especially now that we have an increasingly permanent resident Canada goose population around the world. The reason for this is that goslings stay with their parents for a full year after they're fledged. To learn. They learn how to migrate. This is not ingrained. With the massive ecological degradation we've imposed on this continent, converting forest and wetlands to turf, it is no surprise that Canada geese can now fly right over their parent's nest, and not recognize it. It's also no incentive to keep moving. They're already at the Honker Hilton.

In 1994, Bill Lishman undertook *Operation Migration* when, with the aid of goose calls and an ultralite, he took a flock of nonmigratory geese from Ontario to Virginia, a feat that was documented in the film *Fly Away Home.* The problem is, of course, that there are just not enough ultralites to change the magnitude of this type of adaptive behaviour, and convert residents back to migrants.

Canada Geese have taken up citizenship from Scandinavia to Kamchatka and China and Japan. King James II added them to his waterfowl collection in the late 17th century, and they added him to theirs. Teddy Roosevelt bequeathed Canada Geese to New Zealand in 1876, and the farmers in the Wairarapa haven't forgiven him since. Five hundred thousand years ago, Canada Geese moved to Hawaii all by themselves and gradually evolved into the now extinct *Nene*, the flightless crossword puzzle goose.

Resident or not, they still have a *moult migration* in late May to early June, when they fly north to change all their feathers all at once. This makes them very susceptible to predators during this flightless time. The James Bay Cree celebrate '*Goose Break*,' when they leave their settlements, like the French leave Paris in August, to fill themselves with *Shigabon*, goose roasted over an open fire. Their difficulty is that, with the ice melting earlier each year, it is becoming more dangerous to take that snowmobile out of the driveway during Goose Break.

Eating the geese is being considered as a population control method in other jurisdictions as well. In January, the good farmers of Masterton, NZ held their first annual *'Time the Goose was Cooked BBQ'*. The *St. Clair Shores, Michigan Waterfront Committee* has volunteered their geese to participate in Detroit area soup Kitchens. Maybe this is better than the Puget Sound *Final Solution,* which used to involve herding them into hot metal truck boxes and gassing them with carbon monoxide.

George W. Bush had the most expensive innovation last year when, during the 25th test trial of his missile defense system, over Wenatchee WA, he vaporized an errant Canada Goose, instead of an intercontinental ballistic missile. It was claimed that there are similarities. More humane now to addle the eggs with

corn oil, or spray *methyl anthranilate* (the key flavour ingredient in grape soda) in areas where geese will find it a mucosal irritant and, hopefully, leave.
But not too aggressively I hope. These birds have qualities we would do well to emulate. They are monogamous, and mate for life. They look after each other, raising their young together in crèches. When they migrate, all that honking comes from the back of the bus, geese that are calling encouragement to the lead gander; when he tires, and falls off, another takes his place. If one drifts slightly out of the slip-stream formed by his mates in front of him, he is quickly reminded of how much more difficult it is to fly alone, 71% more difficult to be precise. We could stand by each other like that. Two peeling off for the wounded one. Generosity of the Spirit, too much missing in today's pretension of Society. If we wanted to.

Who doesn't pause to look up at dusk, whenever a V-shaped silhouetted flock of these majestic cadets, with their white chinstraps, flies over so close that you can hear the swishing air whispering over their six-foot wingspans? Whose marrow doesn't shiver just a little when they honk?

The Bear at the Top of the Knoll 28 May

"The world has room to make a bear feel free"

Robert Frost, *The Bear*

Shiva and I went out to look for oyster mushrooms this morning. The sky hung limp with dark clouds, and made muffled brooding sounds. Rain was coming. We hurried through the Public Beach area, up into the forest towards the knoll. The thought of finding a moribund alder, pierced with shelves of delicate anise-scented fungi, drove us on. As we rounded the last curved path at the top, a shiny black mass tumbled away, beside us. Shiva's nose went vertical, and she began to prance. I peeked over the huckleberries, to meet two brown eyes looking back. Only for a moment, and then they were gone.

This was not the first Black bear (*Ursus americanus*) that I've tripped over on my walks. I met the last one during a fishing trip to Winter Harbour, this time last year. My companions were kicking back in the cabin, after limiting out on Spring Salmon earlier that morning, when I announced that I was going into 'town' (population 20), on an optimistic mission to find condiments for that evening's dinner. The trail was a boardwalk that weaved along the wooded shore.

On the way, I emerged into a clearing, and to the sound of a creek running into the ocean. It's hard to know which one of us was more surprised, but the bear (and a big boar at that), made it from my side of the stream, to beyond the trees on the other bank, in three of my heartbeats. And they were fast. I continued over the bridge at a determined pace, singing '*Bare Necessities,*' like John Philip Sousa would have written it. Loudly marching, forward ho.

Later that afternoon, I began my return trek to the cabin, carrying a bag of food in each hand. When I arrived at the bridge, Smokey was standing in the middle of it. This time he didn't move. For far too long, he stood nearly motionless, sniffing the air, and sizing up this recalcitrant intruder. And then, for no apparent reason, he ambled away, feigning disinterest or truly bored.

Contrary to their mainstream reputation, black bears are timid, and easily frightened. You're more likely to be electrocuted by your toaster, than to be mauled by one. However, when they do stand their ground, or charge, there are a few bear facts that may contribute to your survival. They can move at thirty-five miles an hour. If you shoot one at fifty metres, he still has enough heartbeats to get to you. They are excellent swimmers, so that idea doesn't work either. One reportedly swam a distance of nine miles, in the Gulf of Mexico.

Their sense of smell is seven times greater than that of a bloodhound, which already has forty times more olfactory receptors than you do. Bears can detect your scent a full fourteen hours after you have passed along the trail. They can smell a dead deer carcass three miles way. They have colour vision, and although a little near sighted, they have a reflective lining at the back of their eyeballs (*tapetum lucidum*) that reflects light onto retinal rods a second time, so they have night vision.

It's probable that bears can also hear better than you can, although this is still a matter of debate. They are intelligent. They are born weighing 8-12 ounces, but their average adult weight is 250 pounds. The largest recorded wild black bear tipped the scales at 902 pounds. Despite their size, they can deftly handle small objects.

When they hibernate (they are not true hibernators but enter a state of *torpor*), they maintain their muscle tissue by converting the urea in their urine back to muscle mass. They live off their fat reserves, and can lose 40 per cent of their weight (and still gain muscularity). They may go a hundred days without urinating, defecating, or eating, and give birth to two to three blue-eyed cubs at the same time.

The word 'berserk' is from the Viking *bear-sark*, a bear skin shirt treated with oils and herbs, and reputed to provide the warrior wearer with a frenzied power to bite through enemy shields, or walk through fire. Just think of them as giant, agile, powerful, unpredictable, indestructible bloodhounds, with claws and teeth, and night vision goggles.

But all this adaptive ability may still not be enough for the black bears. There used to be half a million roaming North America prior to Europeans arriving. Their habitat is now disappearing, as developers proliferate, and forests are cleared around Westwood Lake, and beyond. Most bears, however, die because they are shot. For sport, in the name of public safety, lazy trigger-happiness or, most recently and perniciously, for their gall bladders. They seem to have survived the Europeans, but they may not survive the Asians. The 'Abalone of the Alders,' at up to $4000 each, is easily worthwhile smuggling- a single gall bladder in a box of dates, and you're the richest guy on the block. Confucianism is a powerful force, but it's about my family, not your world. It is interesting that the sought after ingredient in bear bile, *ursodeoxycholic acid (UDCA)*, prevents the formation of gallstones during hibernation. We use it in Western medicine to dissolve human gallstones, and it can also relieve itching in patients with bile stasis disorders. The Asians are definitely onto something. but it is their insistence on a 'natural' source for UDCA that is killing bears like flies, despite the fact that UDCA can also be obtained, in quantity, from domestic cows. Bears can live for over 25 years in the wild, but there are very few wild ones left. Bears know this. If you put a wild coyote in a bear cage, the bear will ignore it. If you put in a dog, the bear will kill it instantly.

The names various tribal peoples have given bears are instructive. The Ainu called them '*The Divine One that Rules Mountains*,' the Cree '*The Angry One*,' but also '*Good Tempered Beast*', the Lapps '*Wise Man*,' '*Winter-Sleeper*,' '*Step Widener*,' '*Master of the Forest*,' and '*Holy One*', and the Siberians '*Owner of the Earth*.' These themes are repeated in cultures on opposite sides of the world, and they all involve bigness, darkness, wisdom, divinity, strength, elusiveness, honey, mountains, and gold.

Several years ago, while I was on call one very early morning (or one very late night), I was driving home from the Hospital around three a.m., in a torpor of my own, I had acquired a reputation for bringing home road kill (mostly rabbits), that I had inadvertently grazed with my old Honda Civic, in the predawn rush to catch a few minutes of sleep, before it started all over again. I had recipes, and we occasionally ate well. On this particular night, as I turned onto Westwood Lake Road, standing totally still, across the width of the pavement, was the biggest black bear I had ever seen. He was at least five hundred pounds, and he didn't even look in my direction, as I cautiously approached, and stopped. I looked out at the bear. I looked down at the Honda. Clearly, this was not going to happen. I waited. I waited for a long time. Finally, out of feigned disinterest or total boredom, the Owner of the Earth ambled away, back to his honey, mountains, and gold.

Watch Your Top Knot 01 June

"The song-birds leave us at the summer's close,
Only the empty nests are left behind,
And pipings of the quail among the sheaves."

Henry Wadsworth Longfellow, *The Harvest Moon*

Weaving through the hazelnuts, and around the second pond beside the chardonnay vineyard, I heard him first. *'Cu-CA-cow, cu-CA-cow, cu-CA-cow'* came up from the ground between the budding vines. Standing still, in all his Middle Guard finery, was a small, portly, Napoleonic Fusilier-Chasseur, complete with a black teardrop-shaped plume, protruding like a forward comma out of his hat. I was fascinated by how his little top knot quiver-waggled, with every quick head movement. He was somewhat less impressed with me. Suddenly, he scurried across several raised rows of grapevines and, with an explosion of wing-engine noise, blasted over the deer fence into the undergrowth, to safety.

California quail (*Callipepla californica*) are not a species native to Vancouver Island but, since we lost Precious the Cat several years ago, they have made the blackberry-lined driveway along our vineyard their home. They make their nests in shallow scrapes in the ground, lined with grass. They lay up to seventeen, golden-brown, spotted, creamy-white eggs, just about now. In twenty-three days, with a good deal of luck, countless tiny balls of down, animated between big eyes and big feet, will quiver-waggle all over the vineyard. The good deal is nailed to the luck, because fifty per cent or more of the nests are destroyed by squirrels, snakes, racoons, feral cats and, if it rains, hypothermia. Only one bird in several thousand will live to be five years old. Because of hunting (over two million a year), environmental chemical contamination, and habitat loss, they are declining. In addition, some chicks are rejected by their parents, for reasons that are still unclear. We know that it has something to do with the later seasonal formation of a covey, that gregarious communal brood of about fifty quiver-waggle top knots that fills up our driveway in late Summer and Fall. It's basically a quail picnic ground, complete with dust baths, mothers chatting over (and under) the fence, white eye-striped black-faced father sentries, and quail children pecking at their parent's excrement, so as to acquire the protozoa necessary to help them digest their food. For some bizarre reason, despite the twelve miles an hour that a single adult bird is capable of running, or fifty miles per hour flying, when I approach on foot, or when I come up the driveway in my car, on the way to work, nobody in the covey is at all bothered to move an inch. Not a chick. Even when I slow down to a crawl, to let them know I'm concerned enough to reduce my usual Mach One driving speed, there is only intense nonverbal signalling that I am imposing on their festivities. This is frustrating for both parties.

It is the top knot, however, which is still the most captivating aspect of these birds. The origin of the name 'top knot' is also obscure, but likely came from the queues worn by Chinese workers imported to construct the railways. A Manchu-modified Qing dynasty original hairdo, the British had called them '*pig-tails*,' not just a little pejorative. The Terra Cotta warriors in Xining have top knots. The Koreans, Thai, and some Japanese, wore them. There was an old American Western farewell expression, 'Watch your top knot.' Watch your head. Don't get scalped. Native Americans used the California quail feathered top knots for clothing and basket decoration. This further evolutionary nonadaptation reinforces the most intriguing question of all. What possible survival advantage could this six-feathered plume bestow on the quail?

In 1792, Archibald Menzies captured a California condor feeding, along with several Grizzly bears, on a beached whale. He sent the condor and a California quail to England, where they were given their common appellations. Since receiving their names, the quail have been transplanted to numerous other countries in both hemispheres around the world.

Last year, Robyn and I bought a farm, with an old 1930's villa, in New Zealand, sight unseen over the Internet (it's not as bad as you think- we had friends who inspected it thoroughly). Several months later, in the cold dead of winter, we flew down over the Pacific, to the *Land of the Great White Cloud.* After visiting with family for a week, we picked up a rental car in Auckland, and drove all day. When we finally arrived down our gravel road, on a late afternoon, the silence was wonderful. We ran, exploring like children, landing in the waning sun on a new planet, with palm trees and olives, and the smell of the ocean on the breeze. When we came back around the front of the house, a young Maori was standing in the circular drive.

"You the new fellas?" he inquired. We made introductions.

"Where's your lounge suite?" he asked. We told him that we didn't have one.

"No lounge suite. Mhuh. Where's your bed?" Same answer.

"Where's your TV?" The concern began to show on his face. For every "Where's your...," all we had was a shoulder shrug.

"Well, what have you got?" he finally asked, very disturbed by all of this scarcity, we being his new neighbours and all.

"We have a quiche, a bottle of wine, and sleeping bags," I said. He jumped back into his truck, and was gone.

"Maybe we're travelling a little light," Robyn said. Fifteen minutes later, he returned with a trailer, full of all those missing things he had asked if we had. We were invited to dinner. There was corned beef and cabbage, a quiche, and a bottle of wine, and great new neighbours. We were home.

The next morning, I wakened early to the birdsong dawn chorus outside our bedroom window. I tiptoed down the hallway to make some coffee. The two dogs that belonged to the farmer across the road were asleep on our front deck. As I plugged in the thermonuclear 'jug' that is *de rigeur* in every appointed Kiwi kitchen, I was knocked off my perch. *"Cu-CA-cow, cu-CA-cow, cu-CA-cow"* rang out in SurroundSound. I peered through the kitchen windows. All over the circular drive, dust-bathing their little hearts out, were a grand multitude of portly California quail, top knots quiver-waggling in the sunrise.

"The people asked, and he brought quails, and satisfied them with the bread of heaven."

Psalms 105:40

Four Roses 08 June

"Rose is a rose is a rose is a rose"

Gertrude Stein, *Sacred Emily*

There are four kinds of roses at our place on Westwood Lake, only three of which are visible. The first is the wild rose (*Rosa acicularis*), floral emblem of Alberta, and the prickly perfumed thicket, that guards the fencelines of the hazelnut orchard and raised-bed garden. During the hottest dog days of the Summer, mellifluous scents waft through the shimmerhaze, like the open door of a New Delhi sweet shop. By late Fall, there are thousands of rosehip Vitamin C buzzbombs waiting for nimble fingers, teapots and jam jars. During WWII, English children were sent out to the hedgerows on rosehipping adventures, to collect the syrup substrate which sustained the health of the nation during a time when no citrus fruit was available (they also saved the seeds, from which they made an 'itch powder' to dump down the dresses of unsuspecting girls). B.C. aboriginal peoples had many culinary and medicinal uses for all parts of the wild rose. They made arrows from its shafts and smoked its inner bark, to what effect I don't know.

Our second rose is the native black hawthorn tree (*Crataegus douglasii*), living alongside the amphibitheatre of the small vineyard pond. Unlike the sensuous milled French soap smell of the wild roses on the other side of the mound, the odour of the white, flat, five-petalled clusters of the Hawthorn is distinctly unpleasant- much like the Anglo-Saxon thorny cattle enclosures for which they were used and named after. Its Latin name, *Crataegus*, means 'hardness'. No delicate wild rose applications here. The hard hawthorn was used for hard tasks- fishhooks, ear-piercers, boil-lancers, tool-handles, fence posts, and for mixing its burning ash with grease to make black face paint. Witches were supposed to be able to turn themselves into hawthorns on the Wiccan holiday of *Beltane*. Merlin was eternally ensnared in one by *Nimue*, the greatest of all Witch goddesses. In Serbian folklore, hawthorn wood stakes were used to impale the corpses of suspected vampires. Hawthorns were to wild roses what orcs were to elves. The English word, *haw,* meant 'hedge,' thorny in particular. The *British General Enclosures Act of 1845* saw the countrywide appearance of a rapid running-stitch of impenetrable hedgerows, angering rustics no longer allowed to enter lands they had previously roamed at will. Medieval French peasants believed that the hawthorn uttered groans every Good Friday, as the unwilling source of Christ's *Crown of Thorns*. It was bad luck to dig it up or to bring any part of it across the threshold into any house. The Germans called it '*Christdorn*.' They used it to construct funeral pyres in Teutonic Death Rituals, believing that its smoke carried souls into the afterlife.

But the hawthorn was not only a symbol of death and destruction. It was an ancient emblem of hope. Moses' burning bush was allegedly a hawthorn. In Arab erotic literature, its smell is that of an aroused woman. The Greeks carried its burning branches in their wedding processions, for the same reason. The Celts thought it capable of healing a broken heart, and called it '*faerie thorn.*' When hawthorn blooms, it is as if lit from below by a dazzling white light. It was also known as the *Mayflower,* like the boat named after it. An old Scottish highland saying '*Ne'er cast a cloot til Mey's oot*', an exhortation not to discard any clothing until the mayflower was in full bloom. According to legend, Joseph of Arimathea, an uncle of Jesus, was a tin merchant who had brought him to Avalon as a young boy. After the crucifixion, Joseph collected a few drops of Christ's blood, returned to England, and planted his hawthorn staff upon landing ashore. The stick grew into the *Glastonbury Thorn*, a sign that Christianity would flourish in Britain. Somewhere near where Joseph built the first English church, he is alleged to have hidden the Holy Grail.

The House of Tudor adopted the hawthorn, after the crown of Richard III was found in one at the Battle of Bosworth in 1485, and placed on Henry's head. The richness of hawthorn folklore, myth, and poetry goes on and on. My earliest encounter was as an impoverished medical student, when I found a little market in Kingston, Ontario, that sold packages of Chinese haw flake pastilles, for a penny apiece. I loved their astringent sweet crab apple tartness, and would easily peel off and eat an entire deck of round discs, not realizing their potential for causing heart rhythm disturbances. Perhaps the Celts were wrong.

The third rose lives next to the path by the first pond. I really don't know what kind of rose it is. It's just Lila's rose. Fragile and beautiful, Lila's rose is not a native here, but she blooms every year with dependable indispensability. She is dwarfed by the surrounding trees. Lila was my mother, and this rose is her still smiling. We planted it after she died from thyroid cancer.

Finally, there is the rose that is not here. She was my Grandmother on my father's side, Baba Rose. One of seven daughters from an old Austro-Hungarian farmer's family (I still have an Old World photograph which shows the broken spirit in the face of the father farmer), she immigrated to Canada (not on the *Mayflower*), married my grandfather, and worked unbelievably hard, through and beyond the Depression, just to eat. She had a Germanic stolid view of life but, underneath the Teutonic death rituals, she had a generosity of spirit, and humour and warmth. She was eighty-one when I last saw her. I was heading out to hitchhike around the world for five years, seeking my own Holy Grail, and I went to visit her, just before I left. We both knew this would be the last time we would see each other. In this family, with its history of immigrant travails, hitchhiking around the world was not the done thing. My visit was awkward. I got homemade cookies, milk (I was twenty-six at the time), raised eyebrows and, as usual, very little in the way of conversation.

"So. Your parents tell me you're going to... hitchhike... around the world." It was a question, actually about half a dozen questions.
"That's right." I said. Silence. I was waiting for it. I was sure it was coming. But it didn't. Instead, she got up and slowly shuffled into her other room. Five minutes later, that seemed like forever, she returned with something in her hand. It was a one-dollar bill. She signed her name on it.
"Bring this back to me in five years." It was a half a dozen answers.

Baba Rose died during my third year on the road. I cried for hours when I got the news in her old hometown, behind what was then the Iron Curtain. I had lost the dollar bill, or it had been stolen, I can't remember which. I do remember the label, on the bottle of contraband bourbon that a local Romanian farmer poured into my glass that night. He was speaking in broken German about life and death and myth and poetry. But I just stared at the Four Roses.

"The rose and the thorn, and sorrow and gladness are linked together."

Saadi

Blackberry Cobbler 12 June

"The vines replied, 'And didst thou deem
No wisdom to our berries went?'"

Ralph Waldo Emerson, *Berrying*

We are having the worst Spring weather in decades and, between the rain and the cold, there has been only the rain and the cold. The hazelnuts and potatoes are having a festival. Everything else is having second thoughts. Yet today a Bolshoi ballet of thin vines *scurry runs* delicate white flowers along the fenced border of their wine grape cousins' enclosure. From this dewberry necklace will shine black cap gems of intense musky briar fruit essence, when the sunbeams finally come on. I can already feel the tug of tiny berries pulling off, as I gently half twist them into my bucket. I am salivating blackberry juice as I write. It takes an awful lot of these little fruits to fill anything but your mouth. Big bear mouths require even more, but they seek after these minute blackberry explosions madly, as its Latin name, *Rubus ursinus*, suggests. If you're running from these bears, be careful that your ankles aren't shredded by its diamond-saw vinous ground cover.

Also known as the Trailing Pacific Blackberry, it has served as the wild patriarch of other, more civilized cultivars. All kinds of Californian ghosts haunt it's domestication. After Judge H. J. Logan introduced the Loganberry in 1880, he bought the Grover Lumber Mill, and transformed it into *Brookdale Lodge*. His niece, Sarah Logan, drowned in the creek that runs right through the middle of the dining hall. On some Summer evenings, her spectral image is still reported, levitating over a bridge crossing that does not exist. The scent of gardenias whirls alongside the orchestral music that echoes through the place, even though there are no gardenias nor orchestras on the property.

When Walter Knott revived some of Rudolph Boysen's vines and began to sell his wife's Boysenberry preserves and pies out of his roadside stand in Buena Park, California, he had no idea that, with the addition of her fried chicken dinners, he would become the magnate of *Knott's Berry Farm*, the quintessential American Agricultural Amusement Park. Walter Knott began to hang out with Walter Disney, from a different California theme park. In 1951, he bought the real silver mining ghost town of Calico, California in the Mojave desert. The miners' ghosts were apparently not impressed with the purchase. They were prescient. Today there is an admission charge.

Much of early American blackberry hybridization was done by Luther Burbank, the self-described Californian 'infidel,' fond of the paranormal, and who made the biggest blackberry booboo in history. His actions eclipse even those of Captain Walter Grant (a third-rate Walter), who planted three shrubs of Scotch Broom (*Cytisus scoparius*) at his home on Vancouver

Island in 1850. Nice one, Walter. What did Luther do that was worse? Luther developed more than 800 strains and varieties of plants over a fifty-five year career, among which were included the Shasta daisy, Fire Poppy, Santa Rosa plum, and the Russet Burbank potato, the spud that mitigated the Irish Potato Famine and now provides the ten million pounds of McDonald's French fries every year. In 1885 Luther 'discovered' a blackberry cultivar, in a catalog of an unidentified seed exchange in India. He introduced it as *'Himalaya Giant.'* He was wrong about it's origin (it was actually from Armenia, traveling to Germany around 1835, and then eventually from England to India, New Zealand, and around the world). He was right about the 'Giant' bit.

Rubus armeniacus Focke is a Leviathan. The first plant to appear on scorched earth after a fire, arched dense thickets of extravagantly thorn-spiked canes appear overnight, green parabolic plumes propelled skyward. After apogee, falling under their own weight, the cane tips eventually rest on distant soil and new root systems emerge, radiate and stabilize their tentacles. If H.G. Wells had been colourblind, he would have written about *Armeniacus* instead of Martians. The invasion continues rapidly by underground subway root and surface sucker propagation. Birds drop seeds made more viable by passing through their digestion. Native plant regrowth doesn't get a look-in. The Armenian takes over entire stream channels and ditch banks, often smothering sensitive wetland habitat. We find it along roadsides and railroad tracks, in clearcuts and Old Growth, and even in city alleyways. Its spread was facilitated by dairymen and cattle farmers, planting brambles around seepage ponds and along riverbanks, to keep their herds from falling in and drowning. Light, shade, damp, drought, rich soil, poor soil, doesn't matter. Once established, good luck Jack. Armeniacus is a greenbelt black art combatant. Pull it out of the ground and you'll break off a regenerative root. Cut down the canes, and come back in a week. Burn them and they'll love you all the more for it. Hit them with *glyphosate* or other chemicals, and Rasputin rolls back the Rock on the third day. They don't seem to be actively participating in the natural world, but they are monitoring the situation. It was Sleeping Beauty's castle and countryside that was supposedly overgrown with these impenetrable thorny briars. The Ancient Greeks used it as a remedy for gout. Michaelmas Day (September 29th) is the traditional last day to pick wild blackberries, because that was the day that Satan landed in a blackberry bush, cursed the prickly plant and spit on its fruit (*Revelation 12:7-9*). The soldiers in the American Civil War made a tea of the leaves to treat dysentery (temporary truces were arranged so that both sides could 'go blackberrying').

Just as our delicate little Pacific Chorus frog is undergoing ethnic cleansing by the American Bullfrog invasion, and our native Red Squirrel is being slowly pushed out by the Eastern Grey Squirrel, our Dewberry is slowly being shouldered out by its Armenian cousin.

The only upside, of course, occurs every Summer before September 29th, after we emerge from one of two thickets beside our first pond, scratched and bleeding, with black hands, purple faces and a bucket full of sweet promise. Thank you, Mr. Burbank, one infidel to another.

Summer Snow 20 June

"Let me be by myself in the evening breeze,
Listen to the murmer of the cottonwood trees,
Send me off forever but I ask you please,
Don't fence me in."

Robert Fletcher and Cole Porter, *Don't Fence Me In*

Robyn and I have two Adirondack chairs under the shade trees, at the edge of the vegetable garden along the berry run. We often sit there with Shiva for picnic lunch breaks from the many yard chores that occupy our long languid Summer days. Yesterday it snowed. Well, that's what we thought initially, especially with the Ice Age atmospherics we've enjoyed so far this year. And then we realized that, floating all over and around us, were puffy white parasols of cottonwood seeds.

When we first moved to Westwood Lake twenty years ago, we were surrounded by forest. It's all gone now, thanks to the Unholy Trinity of speculator greed, developer deviousness, and bureaucratic collusion. In the halcyon days of our young, enthusiastic arrival, however, we were enfolded in a neighbourhood of quiet woods and Arcadian pleasures. Two people, in one old house, on three paddocks, with six donkeys. We couldn't sleep for the first few weeks because of the braying, but when the donkeys moved on, for awhile, we couldn't sleep for the lack of it. After two decades, our periphery is paved, but our old pastures are now woodlands. We owe this to the summer snow.

The seeds of the Black Cottonwood (*Populus balsamifera Trichocarpa*) are released from their cosmic high catkins, and carried on fluffy parachutes, to land on riparian forest floor temporarily devoid of other vegetation. In our case, the paddock soil, that had recently been disturbed for the digging of our ponds, was ideal. Their chance of survival was slim, as the high water table usually falls faster than their germination. The trees that sprouted in our back yard, however, were relentless. Within three years, we had a cottonwood canopy of heart-shaped leaves, silver shivering in the wind like their willow aspen relatives further south. Their rate of growth was *Jack-in-the-Beanstalk* terrifying. The roots began to wind and bulge along the ground like the veins on the arms of a steroid-saturated bodybuilder, drinking the ponds, blocking the paths, tripping our feet. Black Cottonwoods can grow 150 feet straight up, with trunks as large as six feet in diameter. In the old days they were called *'widowmakers,'* because of their proclivity to drop large branches on pioneer husbands foraging for firewood. The trees live for up to two hundred years. Some are still alive that were youngsters when buffalo roamed the plains. I initially loathed them, as a species alien to the Eden we were trying to recreate, an organism too big, too fast, too crude, and too clumsy, for our grand bucolic plan. Robyn and I spoke of chainsaws and tractors. Eventually, we did nothing. Eventually, the bark of the cottonwoods grew heavy black longitudinal grooved ridges, so hard that a chainsaw would have produced only sparks.

There is a specimen of Black Cottonwood preserved in the *Lewis and Clark Herbarium* at the *Academy of Natural Science,* in Philadelphia. It was collected in June of 1806, somewhere on the Bitterroot River in Montana. The man that gathered it was a German Botanist, named Frederick Pursh. He died of alcoholism, several decades later, in a Quebec City winter. Pursh was with Lewis and Clark when they carved cottonwoods into wheels and axles, to portage the Missouri River at Great Falls. Wagon train settlers later knew they were no longer in the Midwest, when the highest point on the horizon was the Black Cottonwood. This was the promise of streamwater, shade, and wood, instead of bison dung, for fuel. Cottonwoods were used by native tribes for dugout canoes, sweat lodge construction, bedding, mats, medicine and toiletries. The Thompson people made soap from the inner bark. Ashes were used as a cleaner, for hair and buckskin. The buds gave a yellow dye, and an infusion for sore throats and whooping cough, later adapted as the *Balm of Gilead* by Christianizing conquerors. The Omahas' *Ceremony of the Sacred Pole* was a celebration of the cottonwood. Kachina doll messengers from the spirit world were made from cottonwood roots. The inner *cambium* layer was food for the Dakotas in early spring. The Okanagans used the cottonwood to make special cradles, for flattening their childrens' heads. These same children used its unripe seeds for peashooter ammunition. Further down the food chain, hollow cottonwoods were homes for squirrels, racoons, and bees that collected resin from the buds, to use as caulking material in their hives.

The Black Cottonwood is the first tree to have its full genetic code sequenced. Although it has less DNA, it has twice the number of genes as humans, a total of 485 million base pairs, with 93 genes devoted solely to the production of cellulose, now a poteniitial biofuel source, despite having the lowest burning BTU rating per cord of any wood in nature.

In late Spring the cottonwood emits a characteristic honey floral odor from its *cinnamic* and *benzoic acids*. On the wind, it smells like boiled potatoes. In the wind, it looks like snow.

"Perhaps you have noticed that even in the slightest breeze you can hear the voice of the cottonwood tree; this we understand is its prayer to the Great Spirit, for not only men, but all things and all beings pray to Him continually in different ways."

Black Elk

Coon Supper 06 July

"The only thing we've seen so far are just raccoons running all over"

James Dean

And to think I blamed Shiva. I used to love to hand dig my Yukon Gold potatoes out from under their mulched beds, gently delivering the saffron-skinned Incan beauties into a big straw basket of anticipation. We marked every Summer solstice with this buttery indulgence but, in recent years, we have harvested only tuberous carnage. Something was getting through the security netting, and eating our prized spuds. It began an arms race, and we were losing badly.

This year the planning and planting was even more careful. I had the Mother of All potato mound defensive perimeters. Guantanamo Bay. Semper Fi. Today, in the naked, still dawn, it looked, instead, like the aftermath of the Battle of the Somme. Falling spirits. No potatoes again this year. Then I spotted Shiva dancing around one of the fir trees, head cocked up, as her paws pounded the circle. Robyn had always maintained that the dog was innocent, and here was Shiva, driven to redemption, bringing in the real perpetrator of the crime. I looked up. There. The striped-tail, beady-eyed, masked marauder, treed like the bandit he was.

Christopher Columbus provided the first written record of the raccoon (*Procyon lotor*), but the English name derives from the Algonquin word *'aracunem'*. It was Pocahontas who taught the captive Virginia colonist John Smith about 'he who rubs, scrubs, and scratches with his hands.' This *dousing behavior* is also undoubtably responsible for the German name *'waschbar'* and the Italian *'orsetto lavatorre'*. If you give these little washbears a sugar cube, they will wash it away to nothing. Nobody knows why raccoons do this, but it has been described as a kind of *vacuum activity*, a mimic latent instinct, foraging at shores.

They exhibit other instinctive behavior as well. Shine a flashlight on them at night, and there is precisely no reaction; make a sound, and they are gone. Pursue a raccoon, and it will break its scent trail (and they have some odour), by backtracking through watercourses, running fence tops, and scurrying along tree branches.

Beyond instinct, they are smart. On the mammalian IQ scale, raccoons rank just below monkeys. In 1908, H. B. Davis found that racoons could open 11 out of 13 complex locks in under 10 tries; they can remember how to perform tasks they first learned three years earlier; and, they have a *number sense-* they can distinguish between boxes containing two or four grapes, and those containing just three.

Beyond smart, their senses are finely adapted. Raccoon fingers possess ten thousand more nerve endings than we have in our hands, likely the reason that they occupy two thirds of their brain's sensory cortex. Their olfactory glands have a specialized *heat sensor*, that can pinpoint the distance to a particular scent. They can hear earthworms moving underground. Their *Zorro*-like mask, which fades with age, reduces glare, and enhances their night vision, already amplified by the same *tapetum lucidum* membrane that bears possess. This is responsible for the *eyeshine* we see at night, when they don't move for flashlights.

Raccoons and bears had a common ancestor, until their mitochondrial DNA diverged about 40 million years ago. About ten years ago, five intrepid dysenteric friends and I were setting up late afternoon camp in a Western Himalayan forest, when a big clown-like orange bear, complete with mask and striped tail, strutted through the clearing. It was a red panda, a raccoon relation that had survived the Ice Age in a Chinese mountain refuge, long before finding us in our Nepali one. We were mesmerized. There are less than 2500 left. Red Pandas eat only bamboo, unlike their Westwood Lake cousins, who are the most omnivorous animals on the planet.

The loss of our Yukon Gold potatoes was far less painful than another we suffered, just over a decade ago. I had given Robyn two Muscovy ducks as a birthday present, and a culinary conspiracy. She promptly named them, transmuted them into pets, and completely shattered my Pinot Noir plotting. She built them a little duck resort, complete with a canopied enclosure, swimming pool, and chicken wire security fence. They grew happy and fat. It was the fat part that eventually killed them. In the middle of a busy afternoon office, There was a tearful blubbering on line one. Robyn had found a bill and two duck feet in their water dish. The second one had waddled, shell-shocked, down to the lake, and was never seen again.

Maybe this type of behaviour is the reason we haven't been very nice to raccoons. Despite the $100 million sales of critter carcass chaos, created by Fess Parker and Disney with the 1954 television series, *Davy Crockett, Indian Fighter*, it was native Americans, in what is now Kentucky and Tennessee, that originally wore coonskin caps (Europeans settling in these states did pick up the headgear tradition, but Davy Crockett and Daniel Boone actually wore felt hats). The Sioux had a *Raccoon Moon* in February.

Plantation slaves ate opossums, but preferred racccoon meat, a phenomenon that morphed from musical '*coon songs*' into the Jim Crow racist reference to blacks, themselves, as 'Coons.' In 1931, the *Joy of Cooking* published a raccoon recipe, recommending that the anal scent glands and fat be removed, to tone down the gaminess.

At just about the same time, near Gillett, Arkansas, five local hunters were creating the correct conditions for the nascence of a famous Southern tradition. Harlan Wolfe, his brother R. C. Wolfe, Burle C. Muse, Fred Elrod, and Preston Mattmiller, habitually chopped down the raccoon-containing trees on Billy Don Truax's land. They ate reasonably well. By 1935, using guns instead of axes, coon hunting was so good and refrigeration still so inconceivable, that families came together for BBQ raccoon fellowship suppers. In 1947, at the junction of the train tracks, the *Farmers' and Businessmen's Club* began holding fundraisers for high school athletics. *Barney's Restaurant* in Dewitt would brine 1000 pounds of racoon meat overnight, smoke it all the next day, and serve it with sweet potatoes to the town citizenry and their politicians. In 1956 the venue was moved to the local high school gym. Barney's bowed out in 1960, but the ritual is still as strong as ever. If you want to be elected in Arkansas, you'd better show up and demonstrate your love for Coon Supper. This little gourmet genocide pales in comparison, however, to the two to four million raccoon pelts that the rest of North America 'harvests' every year.

Mother Nature pitches in, as well. Living to 'a coon's age,' up to 16 years in the wild and 21 in captivity, doesn't match the 2 to 3 year average lifespan of most raccoons. There is a fifty per cent first year mortality, most of these kits dying of starvation their following winter. Thereafter, thirty per cent per year are killed off, with distemper, hunting and traffic accounting for ninety per cent of these deaths. Raccoons carry rabies; animal control officers carry guns.

And yet, raccoons have a history of resilience, adaptability and, aided by the Nazis, a beachhead in Europe. On April 12, 1934, just north of Hesse outside Kassel, forest superintendent Wilhelm Freiherr Sitich von Berlepsch released two pairs of raccoons, at the request of poultry farmer Rolph Haag 'to enrich the local fauna.' Two weeks later he applied for, and was granted, permission from Reichsmarschall Hermann Goering, to do what had already been done. In 1945, another 25 bandits escaped from an East Wolfshagen fur factory, after an allied air strike. In 1966, American soldiers released their mascots near Laon, in France.

Raccoons can now be found all the way to Chechnya. The British tabloid Sun newspaper headlined that it was just a matter of time until the 'Nazi raccoons' cross the Channel. An 80- year-old woman in Kassel has 50 racoons in her attic. She also has no potatoes and no ducks. Almost 70% of these Kassel coons carry a worm called *Baylisascaris procyonis*. Because it can infect humans and there is no treatment, it has been considered to have 'bioterrorist potential'.

The Abenaki tribe considered them 'tricksters.' Texas boys give sharply-bent raccoon penis bones to their girlfriends as love charms. Coon copulation has been known to last for over an hour. Life in my garden just doesn't seem fair.

I'm sorry all my potatoes became a Coon Supper this year. But I fear my biggest disappointment is yet to come. The corn is starting to look fabulous.

Floating Fir Mentations   12 July

"Sleep lingers all our lifetime about our eyes, as night hovers all day in the boughs of the fir-tree"

Ralph Waldo Emerson

It may be a hot summer day, but we are so cool hovering beneath the two big fir trees above the lake path. Robyn and I bought this hammock in San Jose, when Costa Rica was still poor. Today, as we float on this woven cotton raft built for two, I'm amazed at how white it still is. At the beginning of every Summer, we have to take a hammer and chisel to the bark of the two Douglas Firs, to expose the cork-buried iron pins that we hook our hammock to. Our worldly troubles are suspended with us. Shiva is asleep below. The lake is a painting in oil.

We can overhear the Doppler conversations, ambling along the boardwalk, but they can't see us, hanging just beyond the Sword Fern and salal hedging.
"Do you think their house is West Coast?" asks a woman of her walking companion.

"Oh, definitely West Coast," came the astute response. Well not exactly.

"It's more like Shinto Temple Bucky Fuller Frank Lloyd Wright Arts and Crafts West Coast," I offer through the bushes. Silence. Some conversations are more bellicose, some more lurid. Sometimes I lower my voice for effect. Some don't hear me because of the impermeable protection of their iPods, cell phones, and Spandex.

A Western Tiger Swallowtail flits overhead. The Aztecs called her *Xochiquetzal*, goddess of love, flowers, vegetation, and fire. A boat goes by.

"Look at this guy in the hammock," he says. "Nice."

It's nice. I look up to the sunlight streaming through the muscular branches of these two trees, converging on heaven. Four stories tall, quiet sentinels to this Summer's day. I love these coastal Douglas Firs (*Pseudotsuga menziesii*). I feel small and safe, hiking under their forest canopies. They have been around for fifty million years. Because they can't reproduce under their own shadows, they had to wait for the open space, provided by the last Ice Age, to supplant taller coastal Redwoods as the dominant tree on Vancouver Island. Clearcuts initially continued to help their cause. Douglas Firs are still the second tallest trees in the world. Ours are over ten feet around. The biggest was said to be 77 feet around, 415 feet or forty stories high, and 27 feet in diameter. Its bark was 16 inches thick. George Cary found it in the Lynn Valley, on Northern Vancouver Island, in 1902. Then he cut it down. The groan must have pierced his soul. The tallest tree in the United Kingdom today is in Inverness, also a Douglas Fir. It's called *Durgall mor*, only 210 feet, half the height of the Cary Fir. They can all live for more than 1300 years, if you leave them alone.

On March 29, 1778, Captain Cook hove to in Friendly Cove in Nootka Sound, on the West Coast of the Island. He used Douglas Fir spars to remast his ships. Archibald Menzies was the Scottish physician and botanist who first collected specimens in 1791, but it was David Douglas who has provided its common name. Son of a stonemason, he first cultivated the tree in 1826. He died under mysterious circumstances in Hawaii, at the age of 35. He was found in a pit trap under one of the bullocks that Captain Vancouver had left behind. He had ten gash marks on his head, that certainly didn't come from hooves or horns. He was packed in salt (inside and out) and shipped to Honolulu for examination. Turns out Douglas had shown his money purse and the gold in it to a certain Englishman, Edward 'Ned' Gurney, a bullock hunter and escaped convict. Ned had an axe. Douglas was buried in an unmarked common grave. Ned disappeared.

Doug Fir is on the Doug flag of the *Cascadian Independence Movement*, that Ecotopian secessionist dream of hiving off the good stuff of the Pacific Northwest and British Columbia, to create a fish and wine land of peace and plenty. A country based on the geographic range of the Douglas Fir would be a fine nation, and better founded than some others I know. Pacific truffles grow under Douglas Fir. The wood is beautiful, and structurally strong. Howard Hughes' *Spruce Goose*, with its 319-foot wing span, is constructed of Douglas Fir, not spruce. Fir roots were traditionally used in Californian native basketry- there was a myth that the three-ended bracts that peek out from all over their cones are actually the back legs and tail of mice granted refuge from raging forest fires.

Douglas Fir forests support a fascinating ecology. Its needles are the sole source of sustenance for the red tree vole and it constitutes most of the spring diet of the Blue Grouse. Our little Red Squirrel must collect the cones from at least twelve mature fir trees to survive the winter. A single mating pair of Spotted Owls needs a thousand acres of Douglas Fir habitat. They are doomed.

All of the telephone poles and railway ties that cover North America were once the old growth forests of Douglas Fir. The fir trees left are disappearing faster every day, most recently from private lands. South they go, on floating ferrous funerary boats the exact length of the Cary Fir, some named after *Haida Monarchs* and *Braves*, each capable of carrying 12 thousand telephone poles over the horizon. They are black, these boats. Their receding belching smoke will be the only remnant of the Cascadian dream.

But today, we are so cool hovering between the two fir trees above the lake path, floating on this woven cotton raft built for two.

Salaloquy 20 July

"Man's life is like a drop of dew on a leaf"

Socrates

Robyn and I made a Japanese Garden. We had two ponds full of shubunkins, on either side of our big old teak front doors, until the neighbourhood herons and kingfishers found out. They missed the one last survivor who, weighed down by the violent loss of the rest of his clan, sank to the bottom, where he still quietly resides.

One of the little treasures of the garden was the patch of azaleas, in front of the survivor's pond. For one dramatic week every spring, they dazzled us with vermillion flower fireworks. Only their embers flame briefly, these last few years. Slowly, but inexorably, the azaleas themselves began to fall prey, to a green, leathery-leafed native interloper that flexes and bends, rather than shatters, under the weight of the seasonal Winter snowfalls. Where there was once Satsuki, we now have Salal (*Gaulthria shallon*).

The Chinook called this member of the heather family *kikwu-salu* and we, in our fashion, made the name more white-eyes tongue-friendly. In 1826, David Douglas introduced '*Shallon*' to Britain, as ornamental cover on shooting estates, where pheasants were hunted. Twenty years earlier, near Fort Clatsop, Oregon, Lewis and Clark described it for Thomas Jefferson: '*The fruit is a deep perple berry about the size of a buck shot...10 or 12 issue from a common peduncle or footstalk which forms the termination of the twig of the present year's growth...the Elk fed much on its leaves.*' The Elk, as it turns out, were only enjoying an *amuse bouche*, compared to the current voracious consumption I will eventually tell you about.

Salal is found from California all the way north to Baranof Island, in Alaska. It grows small along dry roadside edges and clearings, but it thrives in deep shade under tall trees, growing up to 6 feet high in some untouched canopied refuges. It has deep wide root systems which, after a forest fire or a logging crew rumbles through, so completely outflank hemlock and western red cedar for root nutrients, that the *Canada Forest Service* has declared salal a "menace to regenerating conifer stands in Coastal British Columbia". One of their research scientists has even proposed the introduction of *Valdensinia heterodoxa*, a fungus with octopus-like tentacles that explodes spores all over the underside of shallon leaves, as an 'environmentally friendly method of control.' The main problem is that this little fungal assassin flourishes only in cool conditions, excellent for killing the lush salal under the canopy, useless for controlling its growth in regenerating forest. In the scientific community I operate in, this is termed a 'glitch.'

Salal berries are actually fleshy sepals. They taste like dry, musky, mentholated blueberries, that haven't bathed for a few days. They are best after two autumn frosts. Kwakiutl women wore special cedar bark to harvest them. The Coastal Natives ate them fresh, sometimes mixed with huckleberries, or Oregon grape. Dried cakes were stored in baskets or wooden boxes. Individual berries were dipped in *eulachon oil,* a First Nations fish sauce that produced the extensive trading '*grease trails*' of the Pacific Northwest. The Haida mixed salal berries with salmon eggs to create a sweet casserole. European settlers made jams, preserves, pies and wine with it, but its culinary evolution has likely reached a pinnacle at the *Sooke Harbour House,* where Sinclair Philip's grouse glaze has taken up residence. The leaves had also been used to flavor fish soup.

The leaves are beautiful. Known also as '*Lemon leaf*,' they can stay green almost forever. The florists who use them in arrangements have created a world demand, a covetous culture, and a trail of tears. There are 13,000 salal pickers in British Columbia, mostly here on Vancouver Island. A hectare of salal can fetch $2500. The Government estimates that B.C. earns $40 million dollars a year, but Kenny Crompton, of Kirby Floral storage in Burnaby, thinks it is more like $500 million. Near the end of the picking season on the Island now, there is increasingly not enough. Despite the deep, wide root systems, the greed is deeper. You could land a small jet plane in some of the open air markets in the Netherlands, where salal goes to die. In BC it is just a *NTFP (Non-timber Forest Product)*; further south, they call it a *SFP (Special Forest Product)*. The difference is staggering.

Salal picking in the U.S. experienced its first boom during the Depression years. A *Brush Picker's Association* was established in Washington State in 1952. It went bankrupt two years later, as a result of the anti-union efforts of the buyers. Cambodian refugees constituted the majority of the pickers twenty years ago, but now Hispanics, known as *Pineros*, are the unraveling thread of Mayan manhood, from Guatemala on north. They are slip-sliding away on the new grease trails, exploited and expendable. They pick 150 to 200 bunches of 25 stems each, per, day for 70 cents each, sixty dollars a day. If they get paid. After a 5-10 per cent charge for picking on timber company land, and the fee to be driven to the picking site. A van driver was arrested, in the Olympic National Forest, for having 17 pickers in the back, who had paid $20 apiece to be sardines. Another, in 2004, was caught with a van so full of salal and pickers (including a 13-year-old boy), they had to be physically pried out of the confined space. In the past two years, seven pickers were killed in van crashes. If the driver drops a picker off at a place where he doesn't have a permit, he has a choice: pick illegally, or starve. Living and working conditions are out of view. Pickers are abandoned in remote work camps, for weeks at a time. Home is a blue tarp and a roll of toilet paper or, if luckier, sleeping for a season packed 10 to a trailer. They pick in wet, pounding rain and snow, the illegals working at night undetected, burying their bunches, covertly digging them up at dawn. They live with no insurance, the fear of deportation, and the threat of violence. Circumstances have created a vocabulary of desperation. '*Slowrolling*' is a van decelerating, looking for a place where illegal pickers can bail out and scatter into the woods. '*Rat patrols*' watch for rustlers in vans with darkened windows, seats pulled out to make room for brush, license plates caked with mud. Son Chau, a picker in Matlock, Mason County, was robbed by bandits of 20,000 stems at pistol point. Another was shot by a picker in Grays Harbour County in 1997, because he was picking in a coveted patch. Shelton deputy sheriff, Ted Drogmund, recorded 100 arrests last year for fistfights, slashed tires, and broken windows. The ethos is simple- take what you can, don't get caught, carry a gun. Alfredo Menjevar, from El Salvador, was 21 years old when he confronted

Leonolo Martinez, for poaching the salal he had just picked in Aberdeen, Washington. He was shot full in the face through an open van window. Martinez had even reached across his wife to pull the trigger. Melissa Manwell was Alfredo's girlfriend at the time. She was sixteen, and pregnant with his baby, when he died. Melissa started a scrapbook after the shooting. On one page, pressed between plastic, is a single salal leaf, still green.

A Wounded Deer- Leaps Highest 27 July

"I was a stricken deer that left the herd
Long since-with many an arrow deep infixed
My panting side was charged when I withdrew
To seek a tranquil death in distant shade"

William Cowper 1728

I remember the horror. Shiva and I were climbing a new, alternative route to the far ridges, when we came upon it. Just beside the trail was the decapitated head of a young buck, new velvet on promising antlers, tongue protruding, eyes opaque. At first I didn't trust my own eyes. Then, the connection rejoined, my heart sank under my knees, and I began to ache. What sort of mind could think of doing this? Who lives among us? Weep for the souls of the deer and the man.

The Columbian coastal Blacktail Deer (*Odocoileus hemionus columbianus*) began his journey 13 million years ago, above the Arctic Circle, as a rabbit-sized mammal, with fangs, five-toed feet, and no antlers. By the time it had migrated down to our latitude, four million years ago, it looked a bit more like a deer. Three million years later, we had the blacktail.

They were exceedingly important to Native Americans. Hides provided clothing, bedding and shelter. Sinews were used for bowstrings and fishlines. Antlers and bone became arrowheads, needles, scrapers and ornaments. The heads were decoys above chests and bellies painted white.

William Clark, of Lewis and Clark fame, wrote on September 17, 1804, that '*Colter killed...a curious kind of deer.*' It was a Blacktail.

Then, the killing began in earnest. The biggest predator now is the automobile. Cars and hunting kill about 400,000 Blacktail Deer every year in North America. But the main cause is still Winter starvation, accounting for 40 to 75 percent of first year fawn deaths. Even the adults can't move through snow higher than 30 cm. deep. Parasitic infections, which are the second most common cause of death, kill the deer only when it is starving. One of the parasites is a brain worm.

White people with English gardens cheer for the brain worms, the guns and the automobiles. I, too, understand the frustration of seeing all one's efforts to bring beauty eaten, while one sleeps. I still remember sitting bolt upright with a bad feeling, around four a.m. one early morning, after we had planted our first Pinot Noir. Grabbing only underwear, I ran downstairs and out the big old teak front doors, calling for *Kali*, our first dog. A brindle blur came careening around the corner, and we set off at full charge towards the vineyard. Both of us were barking. Ahead in the distance, growing larger with every stride, were two five point Blacktail stags, calmly chewing their cuds in Bambi's Café. We closed the gap quickly, but I suddenly realized that Kali didn't really understand the game plan. Filled with the adrenalin of an early morning hunt, she ran excitedly right past the two deer, and right on down the road. The bucks stopped here, and she didn't. They simply looked up, and went back to chomping grapevines. It was only with extreme reluctance, and the encouragement of a fusillade of vineyard stones, that they trotted and jumped off down the driveway. The fence erection followed them within a week.

Blacktails feed early in the morning, at dusk, and on moonlit nights. During one particularily bright full harvest moon, I was drawn to the garden by strange, big noises. At first, I didn't see anything, but then gradually, felt a presence to my right. As my eyes adjusted to the milky illumination, I realized that there was a very large antlered deer standing dead still, just three feet away. The moonlight reflected through his eyes or I might have missed him even then. It was otherworldly. It still gives me goosebumps. His experience was likely not dissimilar.

But it is sunlight, not moonlight, that stimulates antler growth. After the equinox, it is daylight shortening that stimulates the rut in November. It is the male's scent glands that stimulate the female. Blacktails have 3 sets of scent glands producing 3 sets of chemicals. The ones on the outside of the lower legs, the metatarsals, produce an *alarm scent*; those located between the toes, the interdigitals, leave a *scent trail* to follow. The most fascinating, the tarsals on the inside of the hock, produce a circular ester called a *lactone*, of the same family as the poisonous oil some termites secrete. This specific lactone, however, is *Z-6-dodecen-4-olide,* and it is the chemical responsible for *mutual recognition* among Blacktails. It is identical to the compound in butter that gives it its 'milky note.' Great stuff this molecular signalling. I've come this way, I'm one of you, be careful.

Blacktails shed their antlers over the winter. If mating is successful, two to four spotted fawns are born 200 days later, each weighing just 6 pounds. If they survive, they will see their mother only at mealtimes, relying on coloration, lack of scent, and silence, for protection. Robyn managed several photos of a frozen, fragile fawn, one day last Summer. If he's lucky, he'll live up to 16 years in the wild. If he's average, he'll live more like 3 to 5 years. This one will spend his whole life eating on the run, thankful he has four stomachs to digest your garden later.

There are those who would kill these Buddhist beasts for the temerity of eating their roses. Weep for the soul of the deer and the man.

One morning last week, deep in my own inner thoughts, driving down Arbot on my way to work, I was halted by rust-coloured movement at the right side of the road. It was a young antlered Blacktail, asking permission to cross. Three of his tribe were behind him, waiting. I've come this way, I'm one of you, be careful.

Tranquility Base 03 August

"As the eagle was killed by the arrow winged with his own feather, so the hand of the world is wounded by its own skill"

Helen Keller

There is a special log in the middle of the Lake. Shiva and I often swim out to it, on hot, still Summer days. Sometimes we arrive to a heron flapping, or a turtle slipping off, irritated at having to cede its sun-blessed tranquility to the splashing invaders. We sit in silence on the log, until Shiva decides it's time to leave. I follow reluctantly, watching the mirrored reflections of the fir trees in the rhythm of my breast strokes.

This Spring, the special log had special visitors. Robyn and I awoke one morning to high-pitched chirping from two Northern bald eagles *(Hallaeetus leukocephalus alascanus*). They were courting, and they were holding court. Over the next few days we were witness to mating roller coaster sweeps, chases, and high altitude cartwheel freefalls with locked talons, separating breathlessly just before hitting water. At one point it seemed they might take up residence on the special log. Then, on another morning, they were gone.

Westwood Lake isn't big enough for Bald Eagles anymore, if it ever was. They prefer Old Growth trees at least 75 feet high, around lakes greater than 3.8 square miles, all more than two kilometres away from the nearest human. They need tranquility to breed, and will abandon nests when humans disrupt their solitude. Our lake is a nonstarter, especially in recent years. There was a breeding pair at the far end when we first arrived twenty years ago, but progress, in the form of ridgeline midnight motocross riders, a galvanized gated ghetto, and other noisy forms of carbon and chrome in general, have driven them away.

Bald eagles are not bald, of course. They were originally called 'balled,' meaning 'shining white', or 'balde' ('white-faced'), or even 'piebald' ('splotched with black and white'). Who knows? The point is, they are covered with feathers, 7000 of them, weighing twice as much as their half-pound skeletons. The whole weight of the bird is, at most, fourteen pounds, but be ye not fooled- this is a killing machine. From far aloft on daylight thermals, it can see subsurface fish shadows, a mile away. Its vision, eight times better than ours, has two centres of focus, one off to the side and one dead centre. When a screaming eagle comes out of the sky, its dive velocity can reach a hundred miles an hour. Its taloned hind toe is designed for piercing the vital organs of prey, as its front claws scoop up to half its body weight out of the water at lightning speed. The last thing that went through the mind of the poodle in an Alaskan RV park was a pair of bright yellow irises and an eight foot wingspan. Bald Eagles sometimes hunt cooperatively, one flushing the prey, the other raptor making the kill. Even with these predatory advantages, however, only one out of eighteen attacks will prove successful. Sometimes they steal fish from other predators, like osprey, a phenomenon known as kleptoparasitism. I've had large eagles take rockfish I've thrown into midair, while we've both been fishing. If a fish is too heavy, the eagle will use its wings as paddles; if he takes too long or gets too greedy, he will die of hypothermia.

The Egyptian hieroglyphic of an eagle was a symbol for the free-soaring spirit of Man. When Linneus first described Falco Leukoencephalus in his Systema Natura in 1760, half a million Bald Eagles soared in North America. There was one eagle for every mile of shoreline on Chesapeake Bay. Sacred among Native North American tribes, eagle feathers were worn as badges of rank and courage. They were considered spiritual messenger connections to the Creator, and a curse if they were allowed to touch the ground. Regalia, especially headdresses, were made from prized feathers. The Kwakiutl welcomed important guests with scattered eagle down. Plains Indians used eagle feathers at the top of the centre pole. During the Sun Dance, the Medicine Man would transmit power with the touch of his eagle feather fan to the pole, and then to the patient. The fan was then held upward toward the sky, so the eagle would carry the prayers for the sick to the Creator. Eagle bone whistles chirped the messages skyward.

On 20 June, 1782, the Bald Eagle became the official bird of the United States of America. Ben Franklin thought this a mistake: 'I wish that the bald eagle had not been chosen as the representative of our country, he is a bird of bad moral character, he does not get his living honestly, you may have seen him perched on some dead tree, where, too lazy to fish for himself, he watches the labor of the fishing-hawk, and when that diligent bird has at length taken a fish, and is bearing it to its nest for the support of his mate and young ones, the bald eagle pursues him and takes it from him... Besides he is a rank coward; the little kingbird, not bigger than a sparrow attacks him boldly and drives him out of the district. He is therefore by no means a proper emblem for the brave and honest...of America.... For a truth, the turkey is in comparison a much more respectable bird, and withal a true original native of America....a bird of courage, and would not hesitate to attack a grenadier of the British guards, who should presume to invade his farmyard with a red coat on.' He needn't have worried. By the mid-1800s, John James Audubon commented on how scarce bald eagles had become: 'A century hence they will not be here as I see them, Nature will have been robbed of many brilliant charms.' He was right. Between 1917 and 1953 the State of Alaska paid hunters $150,000 to kill 100,000 eagles that were regarded as a threat to salmon populations. Habitat loss, power line electrocutions, inflight collisions, oil, lead and mercury took their toll. Further suffering came with illegal shooting, for black market sales of feathers and talons, or for no reason at all. Oologists, a group of incurable kleptocollectors, took thousands of eggs from the nests of wild eagles, and kept them in carefully labelled storage cases.

Despite the arrival of the Bald Eagle Protection Act in 1940, the worst devastation was still to come. Dichloro-dipheny-trichloethane (DDT) was first used as an insecticide the year before. Then the Eagles really started to die. They died because their parents crushed their thin eggshells. Because they contained inadequate calcium. Because the breakdown products of DDT magnify up through the food chain and interfere with calcium absorption. It was Rachel Carson's book, *Silent Spring*, that raised the consciousness. It was a Bank Manager from Manitoba who made the connection. Charles Broley retired to Florida and would 'swing, spiderlike, on a web of fragile ropes, 100' above the earth, until he could secure a death grip on a jungle of sticks and heave himself into a nest of protesting- and sometimes threatening- bald eagles.' He had banded 1200 of them before he died from fighting a brushfire, near his home back in Canada. By 1970, only 412 nesting pairs of bald eagles were left in the continental U.S. DDT was formally banned in 1972, but much damage had been done. On July 4, 1976, exactly 200 years after the American Declaration of Independence, the Bald Eagle was listed as an endangered species by the Fish and Wildlife Service.

And now? There are tentative signs of recovery. In the lower 48 states last year there were just over 7000 mating pairs of Bald Eagles, in addition to the 70,000 birds in Alaska, and a count of 20,000 here in B.C. Just don't break open the champagne quite yet. On June 28th of last year, a land developer in Minnesota sued the Interior Department, and won. Edmond Contowski succeeded in delisting the Bald Eagle from the Endangered Species List. "Eagles don't pay taxes, I pay taxes," said Ed. So now, the 330 feet restriction on building near eagle nests is gone, possibly together with the next generation.

Eagles often build nests within a hundred miles of where they hatched. These eyries can weigh up to two tons, and building material is added every year by returning mating pairs. It takes six weeks for a pair to build their first nest, 2 feet deep and 5 feet wide. The female, up to 25% larger than the male, lays two dull white goose-sized eggs, which hatch ugly little 90-gram eaglets after 35 days of non-stop incubation. It takes two days for the chicks to break out of their calcium confines, and less than 2 months to grow to 5 kilograms. The dominant eaglet may kill his sibling, without consequence. After 6-7 weeks, the chicks are able to feed themselves and begin to show considerable aggression towards their parents. They remain in the nest for around 70 days. Only 40% survive their first flight; 50% of these survive to adulthood. Before they acquire their white heads 4 years and 7 molts later, there is almost a rite of passage, a period of exploration, when the young eagle wanders far and wide. A white-headed eagle is here to stay. They can live up to 30 years. The oldest has been recorded at 50 years. Every November, eagles come together at a Fall Congregation. The largest of these occurs in Squamish, where up to two thousand birds glide in on their thermals, all chirping like seagulls with the hiccoughs.

Then there was Beauty, found in a landfill in 2005, outside Anchorage, Alaska, slowly starving. Poachers had shot off Beauty's beak, and she, with her tongue and sinuses exposed, couldn't grasp, or drink, or preen her feathers. Beauty has been fitted with a temporary nylon composite beak, until her permanent beak arrives. Donated, by the Boeing corporation. Makers of the Lunar Roving Vehicle and, as importantly, the first stage of the Saturn V rocket that took Apollo 11 to the moon. You know the rest. The words that still send shivers down our collective spine. The mantra I always chant to Shiva when we reach the special log, after our long swim.

"Tranquility base here. The Eagle has landed."

"He clasps the crag with crooked hands;
Close to the sun in lonely lands,
Ring'd with the azure world, he stands.
The wrinkled sea beneath him crawls;
He watches from his mountain walls,
And like a thunderbolt he falls."

Alfred Lord Tennyson, The Eagle

Berber Tapestry 08 August

"The bush that has most briers and bitter fruit,
Wait till the frost has turned its green leaves red,
Its sweetened berries will thy palate suit,
And thou may'st find e'en there a homely bread"

Ralph Waldo Emerson, The Barberry Bush

Robyn and I have special neighbours. An Order of Benedictine Nuns resides over our eastern wall. One night, several years ago, they arrived with a flagon of homemade Oregon-grape wine. I know a fair amount about wine made from grapes (goodness knows I've made every possible mistake, in and out of my own Pinot Noir vineyard), but I knew very little about the source of this libation. The Danes have the same word, *gift*, for 'married' and 'poison.' There is a little bit of both in the story of this gift, the givers and the groove in my wine cellar, where it lay before we opened its Moorish muskiness.

Oregon-grape, interwoven in a tapestry of salal and sword ferns, carpets the shady undergrowth of our Westwood Lake shoreline. Merriweather Lewis first described a '*mountain holly*' on April 11, 1806, at Celilo Falls, Oregon. Lewis left on his epic adventure, Thomas Jefferson sent him to Philadelphia for a crash course in botany, from Dr. Benjamin Barton.

While there, Barton introduced him to Bernard M'Mahon, another friend of the president. Trained in gardening in his native Ireland, and America's first national nurseryman, M'Mahon was the author of a horticultural classic, *The American Gardener's Calendar.* Around the table in M'Mahon's kitchen, he and Lewis discussed how to gather and safely store seeds. When the expedition returned to the United States, the seeds were turned over to M'Mahon, who became curator of the collected specimens. He succeeded in getting many to germinate, including the Oregon-grape holly, which he offered to the public, through the pages of his catalog. Within two years of his death, botanist Thomas Nuttall had named the shrub '*mahonia,*' in his remembrance. David Douglas, before he was murdered and packed in ice on his last trip to Honolulu, had also identified it as a fine ornamental shrub. On July 18, 1892, Oregon-grape became the Oregon state flower.

There are three subspecies of Oregon-grape. The largest, *Mahonia aquifolium,* is sometimes called Tall Oregon-grape, and can reach up to twelve feet in height. Robyn and I planted one down at our gate to the lake. Most of what we have around Westwood is Creeping Oregon-grape, *Mahonia repens.* 'Cascade' or Dwarf Oregon-grape, *Mahonia nervosa,* hybridizes, as do the other two, with the other two, blurring all these taxonomic distinctions. What is not blurred are the colours that weave the mahonia tale, along the Oregon trail, and the electromagnetic spectrum. I can shorten the wavelength for you, as the tapestry lengthens.

Yellow. The inner bark and roots (scratch them if you don't believe me) are the colour of a zucchini flower. The compound *18, 5,6-dihydro-9,10-dimethoxybenzo(g)-1, 3-benzodioxolo (5,6-a) quinolizinium* is the source of their vibrant hue. Its common name, when I get there, will clarify. Native Americans tinted their fabrics without knowing the chemical formula; the same dye, from related plants, is still used today to colour wool in Northern India. Also known as ground potatoes, Oregon-grape was a vital food source for Plains Indians. The starchy, tuberous root was boiled and mashed, or dried and pounded into meal. Polished carefully, objects made from the rootwood possess warm tones, timeless and memorable. Early Spanish Americans created beautiful crucifixes, still produced as special gifts (marriage, not poison). The yellow dye has other properties. Its fluorescence is used in histology for staining heparin in mast cells. It decreases resistance to antibiotics, speeds recovery from giardia, candida, viral diarrhea, and cholera, and is showing promise in diabetes, hyperlipemia, coronary artery disease and ischemic stroke. Finally, it and its cousins, *berbamine* and *oxyacanthine*, appear to inhibit abnormal cell growth. The fact that this yellow compound is also found in Goldenseal and the '*Huang sisters*' (Huang Lian, Huang Qin and Huang Bai) allows us to trace its phylogeny, from the now exterminated forests of the Mediterranean, to both China and our own back yard. The flowers are the same yellow, with a honey-like fragrance. They can be eaten raw, tempura-battered, or boiled as a lemonade substitute.

Green. The Oregon-grape's holly-like leaves taste like sorrel. As evergreen as they are, they turn maroon bronze, gold, crimson and purple in winter. Against the snow on the ridges, they are a magical Christmas for the eyes. The plant has a tendency to produce a topknot of leaves at the ends of bare branches, like a stationary family of lime green quail.

Blue. The berries begin green and ghoulish, transforming first into powder blue, elfin footballs and, finally, into concord blue spheroids with a white dusting. They taste a little like black currants, but slightly medicinal and pucker sour. They are best mixed with salal berries and, together, make a fine jelly, especially with game meats. The Navajo and other tribes added its purplish-blue colour to wool with alum mordant.

Black. First, the ***Gift***: Oregon-grape may be a member of the Genus Mahonia, but Mahonias, like the European Barberry (*Barberis vulgaris*) are members of the Family *Berberidaciae* from the Middle English *barbere.* This, in turn, is derived from the Latin *barbaris*, the Greek *barbaroi* 'stammerers' and, ultimately, from Sanskrit as *barbaras* 'stammering.' The name was passed to Arabic as *al-Barbar*, originally any people whom the Moors encountered, who were unable to speak Arabic. In contemporary English, we still refer to those of supposed uncultured origin as 'barbarians'. Soon after Thomas Jefferson's first inauguration, in the winter of 1800, the Pasha of Tripoli declared war on the United States, because he was receiving smaller ransom payments for the American sailors and ships he captured than were his fellow terrorists at Algiers. Jefferson responded by committing a small naval force to the Mediterranean Sea, empowered by a surge of patriotic support at home. In February, 1804, twenty-five-year-old Lieutenant Stephen Decatur sailed into Tripoli harbour, and burned the U.S. frigate *Philadelphia*, to void its captors' demands for tribute, and incidentally avenge his own brother's death with the blood of a few pirates. British Admiral Lord Nelson referred to it as '*the most bold and daring act of the age*.' His famous reply to a congratulatory toast inspired his nation for most of the 19th century: '*Our country! In her intercourse with foreign nations may she always be in the right; but our country, right or wrong!*' The Marine's hymn, the oldest official song in the U.S. military is still sung '*to the shores of Tripoli*'.

Second, the ***Givers***: Our neighbours, the Benedictine nuns of the *House of Bread* and the *Bethlehem Retreat Centre*, had migrated from the Queen of Angels Monastery in Mt. Angel, Oregon (where else?), which had been founded by nuns from the Abbey of Engleberg, Switzerland in 1882. Their order, in turn, had been founded in 1082 by Conrad, Count of Seldenburen, the first abbot being Blessed Adelhelm, a monk of the Abbey of St. Blasien in the Black Forest. The German monks actually owed their evangelization to the English Benedictines, specifically to St. Augustine and his monks, who established the first English Benedictine monastery at Canterbury, soon after their arrival in 597. The Benedictines were called *'Black Monks'*. St. Augustine was originally from Hippo, in North Africa.

Third, the ***Groove*** in my wine cellar: sits beside two woven carpets, bought for 352 dirhams and 230 dirhams, amidst the mint tea, tents, spices, donkey saddles, heat, flies, sorcery, olives and apricots, and the sad crowing of a Moroccan rooster in a minor key, during my sojourn through the Atlas mountains in May of 1982. The carpets are Berber. St. Augustine was a Berber. Thomas Jefferson's Barbary pirates were Berber. The yellow compound is called berberine. Oregon-grape is a Berberidaciae because that's where it's ancestors came from. It is a gift, both marriage and poison. There's a little Moor in all of us.

Postscript: There is another plant called Cnicus benedictus L. (Blessed Thistle). It was used as a remedy for the Black Death that came to Europe through the black Berbers of North Africa, especially by Thomas Brasbridge, who in 1578 published hids Poore Man's Jewell. Sixty-eight years earlier, a monk named Don Bernardo Vercelli incorporated it for this and other purposes into a liqueur you can still buy at 'Terminal' Park. *Benedictine.*

Requiem for a Brass Rat 17 August

"Beaver: 'Gee, there's something wrong with just about everything, isn't there Dad?'
Ward: 'Just about, Beav.' "

Leave it to Beaver, 1957

We miss Bucky. Some nights, he would startle Robyn and me, as we floated under the Milky Way in our hot tub. Like a gunshot, his tail cracked the firmament. Bucky was on patrol. He was ultimately dispatched by the City of Nanaimo, possibly by another kind of gunshot, just a few years ago. He was removed, for building without a permit on Westwood Lake. Bylaws are bylaws. And Bucky was taking the lake to a new level. Littorally. When it comes to the *Official Community Plan,* unless you have bucks instead of just being one, you just can't beat City Hall.

Bucky lived in a lodge on the shore across from us. On a cold winter's day you could see the moist air, rising from the vent hole in the top of his dome, like smoke from a chimney. He was warm and snug, inside the two stories of his Alder villa. (The alders were gnawed from our front yard one night, leaving an Asian tiger trap ribbon of pointed sticks along the path next morning.) Bucky's first floor was just a few inches above water level, and covered with a layer of shredded wood and vegetation. This was ideal for drying off after coming out of the lake. It was also the formal dining room. The second floor was the family bedroom and nursery. The lodge interior was almost five feet high, and the walls had been plastered with mud before the first snowfall. There was one opening for entering and exiting, and another for transporting food. No one went to the bathroom inside the lodge. It was a modest West Coast waterfront home. Shiva and I used to walk on the roof.

Bucky's house construction didn't get him killed, however- it was his other engineering project at the far western end of Westwood Lake which did that. It was the dam. When Bucky first constructed it, the City brought in several workers and a Bobcat. Water flowed again that day but, by next morning, all was quiet. Back came the Bobcat. Back came Bucky, full of brass. Bobcat. Bucky. The balance of power finally tipped over completely one night. And more than water flowed out of Westwood, when Bucky disappeared forever.

The beaver (*Castor canadensis*) is the second largest rodent in the world, after the capybaras Robyn and I visited in Venezuela two years ago. The Castor part comes from the Latin, *castratum*, because the beaver appears at first glance to have no sexual organs (they are tucked up internally, along with their digestive and urinary glands, in a common cloaca, like a chicken). The *canadensis* part is a given. Sir William Alexander was granted title to Nova Scotia, and included the beaver in its emblem, in 1621. In 1678, the Governor of New France, Louis de Buade de Frontenac, proposed the beaver be included in the armorial bearings of Quebec City. The very same year, the Hudson's Bay Company put four beavers on its coat of arms, because they were totally indebted to Bucky's brethren. They later struck a coin equal to the value of one male beaver pelt- it was known as a '*buck*'. A *buck beaver* was the name given to the foreman of the men ('*beavers*') engaged in roadmaking near lumber camps. The first Canadian postage stamp, the '*3 penny beaver*', was struck by Sir Sanford Fleming in 1851. The beaver appeared on the masthead of *Le Canadien*, a newspaper published in Lower Canada. It was one of the emblems of the *Société Saint-Jean-Baptiste*. It is still found on the crest of the Canadian Pacific Railway Company. The most famous bush plane in history is the de Havilland Beaver, first flown in 1947. An 'act to provide for the recognition of the beaver as a symbol of the sovereignty of Canada' received royal assent on March 24, 1975.

If the beaver is the story of Canada, it is a saga forged of iron, mercury and brass...Bucky's teeth were orange because their calcium had been replaced by iron. They never stopped growing while he was alive, and perhaps a little longer. His ancestors were felling trees and building dams 10 million years ago, before the woolly mammoths. These Miocene beavers were 7 feet long. Their fossilized underground spiral burrows can still be found as twisted stone '*devil's corkscrews*'. There is an Ice Age giant beaver skeleton on display in Chicago's field museum, the size of a black bear. He weighed in at 200 kg, about seven times heavier than Bucky was. There are western tribal tales of orange beaver teeth so large that they were used to hollow out canoes. The descendents of these beavers can still fell trees over 3 feet wide. The trees are sustenance as well as building material. In addition to a palate for water lily tubers, clover, and apples, a beaver's main sources of food are the leaves and green bark from alders, poplars, willows, and birch; an acre of alder will support one beaver for one year. Intestinal microorganisms break down thirty per cent of the cellulose from the bark. To extract the most calories from its high-fiber diet, the beaver eats everything twice when food supplies are low, an adaptation known as '*coecotrophy*'. Double-digested beaver stool looks like pure sawdust.

Just above the sawdust is the first reason Bucky's ancestors were hunted to near extinction. A pair of scent glands, near the base of the tail, secrete a compound known as *castoreum*. Beavers use the two split nails on their hind feet to spread the musky oil over their bodies and then comb their fur with their front paws. They also rub castoreum on dome-shaped mounds a foot high and 3 feet across to mark their territory. *Castor mounds* often leave a reddish stain on the bank, and the odours are powerful enough for a human to detect easily. And ultimately exploit. As medicine, bait, and perfume. Its medicinal use derives from the high concentration of salicylic acid it contains from the beavers' ingestion of willow bark. Bucky was a walking aspirin tablet. Yupik Eskimos used dried beaver testicles to relieve pain-take two and call me in the morning. Beaver testicles from Bucky's European relative, *Castor fiber*, were exported from the Levant from the tenth to the nineteenth century. Claudius Aelianus comically described beavers chewing off their testicles to save themselves from hunters. The Romans found that fumes produced by burning castoreum could induce an abortion. Paracelsus thought it could be used in the treatment of epilepsy. Medieval beekeepers used it to increase honey production, and it was a popular medicine in the Middle Ages, said to cure ailments ranging from headaches to impotence. Castoreum was described in the *1911 British Pharmaceutical Codex* for use in dysmenorrhea and hysterical conditions, for raising blood pressure and increasing cardiac output. North American trappers mixed castoreum with cloves, nutmeg, cinnamon, alcohol, and anything else that came to mind. Each trapper guarded his recipe and swore it was the best. A small bottle of castoreum sold for ten to twelve dollars in St. Louis. Long used as a base for perfume, its scent is described as a pungent, waxy, burnt-orange odor, with smoky notes of Irish peat fires and good pipe tobacco and undertones of cardamom and tea. I think it smells more like Russian leather and tobacco. Yes, Virginia, there is an actual beaver in your *Shalimar.*

Just above the sawdust, just above the scent glands, is the second reason that *Castor Canadensis* almost disappeared forever. A beaver's tail serves several functions. It is used as a four-way rudder while swimming, as a third leg while standing upright, as a lever when dragging branches, as winter fat storage and, as that rifleshot warning signal when slapped on the water. Older beavers often ignore the warning slaps of the colony's younger members. They do so at their peril. Because the use that humans had for the beaver tail was protein. They were served at medieval banquets as '*bear's paws*'. In the 17th century, based on a question raised by the Bishop of Quebec, The Roman Catholic Church ruled that the beaver was a fish for purposes of dietary law. Strike two.

Just above the sawdust, just above the scent glands, just above the tail, was where the iron hit the rest of the beaver. In 1590 Leonard Mascall described '*a griping trappe made all of yrne, the lowest barre, and the ring or hoope with two clickets.*" in his British classic *A Book of Fishing with Hook and Line ... Another of Sundrie Engines and Trappes to take Polecats, Buzzards, and Rates.*' The first beaver traps used in North America were based on the Mascall trap, and had a round or oval baseplate. By the 1800s, the design had changed to a flat baseplate, with jaw pillars mounted at either end. The trap made simple work of harvesting beavers: instead of staking the stream and destroying the lodge, the trappers could drown the animals one by one. The traps cost $12 to $16 in the early 1800s, weighed 5 pounds, and were secured by a 5-foot chain with a swivel to prevent kinking. The trapper would wade up the stream to cover his tracks, and set the trap near the bank under 3 or 4 inches of water. To secure the trap, the chain was stretched to its limit and anchored to the streambed with a strong stake. A castoreum-coated twig was fixed above the trap, waving a few inches above the surface of the water. Any beaver that happened along would swim over to sniff the castoreum, place its foot on the trigger, and spring the trap's semi-circular jaws. Diving down to conceal itself underwater, the beaver would find its movement restricted by the chain. If the trap caught only its paw, the beaver could gnaw its foot off and would try to gnaw through the chain- most often, it would be unsuccessful and drown. Even if a beaver succeeded in wrestling the stake out of the streambed, the combined weight of the trap, chain, and stake would eventually exhaust and drown the animal. As effective as this method was, it was limited by the total weight and cost of each trap. In 1823, Sewell Newhouse, a blacksmith at the impoverished religious communal dormitories in Oneida, NY, changed this equation forever, when he began to mass produce the small, light *#4 Newhouse beaver trap.* This allowed trappers to carry six traps. Sewell had instantly created a new American icon. He had brought into existence the *Mountain Man.* American fur companies no longer had to rely on various Indian tribes for beaver pelts. Today the Oneida company makes mostly silverware but they still make the #4 Newhouse. Clearly, there was no planned obsolescence for the trap, the trapper or the trapped.

Before the Europeans arrived, there were over two hundred million beavers living almost everywhere there was water, from the Arctic tundra to the deserts of northern Mexico. They were scarce only in the swamps of Florida and Louisiana, where their dams and lodges were no match for hungry alligators. Everywhere else, along thousands of streams, lived colony after colony, as many as three hundred dams per square mile, each with its own ring of wetlands. There were almost that many killed during the frenzied period of trapping, that ended suddenly in the year 1840. Trapping was big business. One expedition in 1823-24 consisted of 55 men, 25 women and 64 children. They had 75 guns, 212 beaver traps and 332 horses, plus ammunition, clothing and trading goods. About twenty were actual trappers. The expedition traveled more than 1,300 miles to reach trapping grounds. The trappers accounted for 5,000 beavers. Trapping was a harsh and dangerous life, but the rewards were irresistible; a good trapper could make more than $15 a day, compared with a half-dollar a day working on a farm.

The age of iron begat the age of mercury. The dead beaver became the economic engine of North America for one main third reason- hats. Felt hats. Socially essential, fashionable, felt hats. A large adult beaver skin yielded enough fur for 18 hats. By the late 1500's, the beaver was extinct in Western Europe, and was close to extinction in Scandinavia and Russia. Cod fishermen off the Newfoundland Banks had developed a regular and profitable side trade with eastern seaboard natives, during their weeks-long fish-drying period. As word of this lucrative endeavor spread, King Henry IV of France, before his own assassination in 1610, encouraged his colonists to move in and lay claim, quickly establishing a comprehensive network centred on the extensive St. Lawrence waterways. Both English and French fur traders were soon selling beaver pelts in Europe, at twenty times their original purchase price. A year before Henry died, explorer Samuel de Champlain used his harquebus to shoot three braves in a gang of dozens of Mohawk warriors, determined to break into the beaver business. The trade had been monopolized by tribes of the Huron confederacy, and the Mohawks were members of the larger Iroquois nation competing to exchange pelts for muskets, blankets, iron tools and coloured glass beads. By 1650, the Iroquois had eradicated most of the fur-bearing animals in their own homeland. They swept through the Ohio Valley like wildfire, exterminating the Indians living there who were already weakened by European diseases. These 'Beaver Wars' changed the course of North American human and natural history for all time. Further south, Dutch settlers shipped 1500 beaver skins to Europe in 1624, the year New York was first settled.

By 1630, English settlers along the New England coast had taken over the beaver trade. Furs became the cash crop they could sell to England, in exchange for the manufactured goods necessary to sustain everyday life in the neophyte colony. Between 1652 and 1658, John Pynchon shipped to England '9,000 beaver skins weighing about 14,000 pounds' from his trading post in Springfield. 'Trade goods valued at one livre when they left Paris,' Mr. Brook wrote, 'bought beaver skins that were worth 200 livres when they arrived back there.' The demand for beaver hats was so intense, that the second-hand hat trade boomed- though it was closely regulated 'out of a reasonable fear of lice-borne diseases'. Britain exported several hundred thousand pounds worth of beaver hats per year, to other European nations. By the late 1600's, the French were importing all their felt beaver hats from England. In 1700, 69,500 beaver hats were exported from England, and almost the same number of felt hats. Over seventy years, the British exported 21 million beaver and felt hats.

There were two kinds of beaver skins used to make hats. The first was called *Greasy Beaver* or *Coat*

Beaver, because it came from the used, smelly winter coats worn by Natives. Friction over time wore the coarser guard hairs off the pelts. They were prized until the late 17th century, because they were easier to process, and were thought to make a more luxuriant hat, despite the uneven quality that came from the field. *Parchment beaver* pelts were those trapped for immediate trade. Initially only the Russians knew how to comb the wool from parchment beaver, and those pelts had to be sent to Russia for processing. This added more to the cost of the hats produced. Once the English and French felt makers learned the Russian technique, parchment beaver replaced the increasingly elusive Coat Beavers.

To prepare the fur for felting, the guard hairs would be pulled out with the Hatter's thumb and a large knife or tweezers, leaving only the beaver wool on the skin. A solution of *nitrate of mercury* was then brushed on the pelt, producing a yellow-red color on the fur tips during this *carroting* part of the process. The mercury caused miniature scales to raise and roughen each individual fibre, which increased the wool's matting ability. The pelt was dried and the wool shaved or *carded* from it, with a semi-circular knife. Once the wool was removed from the pelt, it was called *fluff.* The finest hat *batt* contained one part parchment and two parts greasy beaver fluff.

Heat and moisture were used to begin the shaping of the hat. This caused the mercury to be released as a vapor. After long-term exposure to these fumes, the amount of mercury in the Hatter's body would reach dangerous levels, attacking the nervous system. Many Hatters eventually died of mercury poisoning, with uncontrolled muscle twitching, a lurching gait, and difficulties talking and thinking...right through the looking glass, they became 'Mad as a Hatter'. A stiffening agent like *gum Arabic* was applied, the hat was steamed and ironed and, finally, a silk lining was added, sewn into the *Continental* cocked hat of 1776, the *Navy* cocked hat of 1806, the *Army* of 1837, the 18th century *Clerical*, the 1812 *Wellington*, the *Paris beau* of 1815, the popular 1820 *d'Orsay*, and the *Regent* of 1825. 'The Restoration gallant wore his high-crowned beaver with an air, as did his lady; and he was even prepared to buy a beaver second-hand, to borrow an unbecoming hat so as to save his beaver from the rain, or to purloin his friend's beaver and leave a cheap hat in exchange.'

The man who profited the most from the trade not only sold dead beavers, but made compounded subsequent fortunes smuggling opium and carving up Manhattan. John Jacob Astor was born in 1763 in Walldorf, Germany, and arrived in the United States in March, 1784, just after the end of the Revolutionary War. He was the Astor and the Waldorf of the Waldorf Astoria Hotel. He traded furs with Indians, and then started a fur goods shop in New York City in the late 1780s. By 1800 he was worth almost a quarter of a million dollars, and had become one of the leading figures in the beaver pelt trade. When the US Congress disrupted his import-export business with the *Embargo Act of 1807*, Astor received special permission from Thomas Jefferson to establish the *American Fur Company*. Subsidiaries were formed: the *Pacific Fur Company* and the *Southwest Fur Company* (in which Canadians had a part), eventually controlling fur trading around the Great Lakes and along the Columbia River. He financed the overland Astor Expedition in 1810-12, to reach an outpost of what is now Astoria, Oregon. It was the first United States community on the Pacific coast. Members of the expedition were to discover South Pass, through which hundreds of thousands of settlers on the Oregon, California and Mormon trails would pass through the Rocky Mountains. By 1834, Astor recognized that all fur-bearing animals were becoming scarce, and he retired. In 1800, following the example of the *Empress of China*, the first American trading vessel to China, Astor traded furs, teas and sandalwood with Canton in China, and greatly benefited from it. In 1816, Astor joined the opium smuggling trade. His American Fur Company purchased ten tons of Turkish opium, then shipped it to Canton on his *Macedonian.* In 1804, Astor purchased from Aaron Burr what remained of a ninety-nine year lease on property in Manhattan. At the time, Burr was serving as vice president under Thomas Jefferson, and desperately needed the purchase price of $62,500. The lease was to run until May 1, 1806. Astor began subdividing the land into nearly 250 lots, which he subleased. In the 1830s, John Jacob Astor foresaw that the next big boom would be the buildup of New York, which would soon emerge as one of the world's greatest cities. Astor purchased more and more land, out beyond Manhattan city limits. His conditions were that the tenants could do whatever they wished with the lots for twenty-one years, after which they must renew the lease, or Astor would take back the lot. At the time of his death in 1848, Astor was the wealthiest person in the United States, leaving an estate estimated to be worth at least 20 million dollars, worth $115 billion in 2008 U.S. dollars, making him the fourth wealthiest person in American history. He ordered that his business papers and ledgers be incinerated. We can still only wonder what he was trying to hide.

From 1818 to 1821, the North West Company sent three fur trapping brigades to the Upper Snake River country under Donald Mackenzie, a former Astorian. The Snake River brigades outfitted each trapper with six beaver traps. Between the years 1853 and 1877, the Hudson's Bay Company harvested over 3 million beaver for sale in England. The beaver was on the brink of extinction by the mid-19th century. What finally saved the species was the increasing popularity of silk (instead of felt) hats, starting around

1840. The current beaver population has come back 10 to 15 million strong, after its near annihilation. There is even one named *Jose* back in the Bronx River, gnawing in the shadow of John Jacob Astor. Beavers have been introduced in places where they never lived before. There is a Valle de los Castores on Tierra del Fuego, containing the descendents of 26 pairs brought from Canada in 1940. By latest accounts, they have jumped the fence and, in the absence of any predators, are moving, like Africanized bees, up through the forests of Patagonia.

In the wild, beavers will live about ten years, although in captivity some have lived as long as thirty. On land, a beaver can waddle about ten kilometres in an hour, but Bucky was born for life in the water, capable of traveling half a mile, or fifteen minutes, under the surface, before he needs to surface for air. They are close relatives of squirrels, if you consider a sixty-five pound squirrel a squirrel (the heaviest on record, found in Wisconsin, was 110 pounds). They are *crepuscular* rather than nocturnal, active at dawn and dusk. Although beavers are considered social animals and form monogamous bonds, they work independently and have little actual contact with each other. Mating takes place in January or February, and 1 to 9 (usually 4) kits are born in late April to June, after a gestation of 105 days. A colony consists of a cluster of lodges, each occupied by a family. The family consists of a male and female and their last two litters, a total of approximately 18 animals. One family of beavers may need half a mile of river habitat. Kits leave after 3 years to form their own families and usually stay within ten miles of their parents. This short odyssey is when they are the most vulnerable to predators in their entire lives. Before European contact turned them into a commodity, natives thought of the beaver as the '*sacred center*' of the land. They '*helped the Great Spirit build the land, make the seas, and fill both with animals and people: Long, long ago when the Great Waters surged in a blind and shoreless world, the gigantic beaver swam and dove and spoke with the Great Spirit. The two of them brought up all the mud they could carry, digging out the caves and canyons and shaping the mud into hills and dales, making mountains where cataracts plunged and sang.'* Some tribes believed that thunder was caused by the Great Beaver slapping his tail. In some Native American dialects, the word for 'beaver-like' also means 'affable'. They were commonly kept as pets around Indian encampments.

Beavers are a keystone species. They build and maintain wetlands that soak up upstream floodwaters, prevent erosion, raise the water table, and create an ecosystem that purifies the water and breaks down toxins and pesticides. They create rich habitats for other mammals, fish, turtles, frogs, birds and ducks, with a biodiversity no less that of tropical rain forests. Almost half of the endangered species in North America rely upon these wetlands. Beaver dams are a nursery for salmon. Dams more than 4,000 feet long and 18 feet high have been recorded and nineteenth-century reports describe dams encrusted with lime and half petrified, attesting to hundreds of years of continuous repair. Nova Scotia native elders knew of an old beaver dam so vast that it flooded the Annapolis Valley; a family of beavers can build a 35-foot long dam in a week. A single beaver can fall trees 150 feet tall and 5 feet wide. By gnawing a groove around the trunk in an hourglass shape, Bucky took only twenty minutes to cut down a six-inch wide alder. He was as sensitive to the danger of a falling tree as a human lumberjack. As the tree began to fall, Bucky ran. His jaws were so powerful, he could cut a half-inch sapling in one bite. When kept indoors, beavers will cut down the legs of tables and chairs and build little dams between pieces of furniture.

Their industriousness is mythological. On January 17, 1914, President MacLaurin formally appointed the Beaver as the mascot of my alma mater, the Massachusetts Institute of Technology, at the annual dinner of the Technology Club of New York: '*We first thought of the kangaroo which, like Tech, goes forward in leaps and bounds. Then we considered the elephant. He is wise, patient, strong, hard working, like all who graduate from Tech, has a good hide. But neither of these were American animals. We turned to Mr. Hornady's book on the animals of North America and instantly chose the beaver. The beaver not only typifies the Tech (student), but his habits are peculiarly our own. The beaver is noted for his engineering, mechanical skills, and industry. His habits are nocturnal. He does his best work in the dark.*' The class ring at M.I.T. is called a '*brass rat.*' I lost mine somewhere in Boston in February of 1980. If anyone finds it, it is inscribed with my name, Class of '75. It has tremendous sentimental value, because for four long years there, I did my best work in the dark, busy as a beaver.

Unlike my roommates at M.I.T., the beaver's ratio of brain size to body weight is the lowest found among mammals. Beavers don't have much gray matter, and they don't see well. Much of their building technique appears to be learned during their long childhood, but other behavior is definitely instinctive to beavers, such as patching a dam at the sound of running water. The sound of running water drives them crazy. The beaver's pond is necessary for their food and housing. If the dam breaks, they will rush around frantically to repair it. If they do not hurry, they could lose all of the water in their pond. This would expose the underwater lodge entrances to predators.

The beavers faded, *trap by trap,* and *hat by hat.* Across the country, they disappeared by the tens of millions. As they were exterminated, their old dams slowly collapsed, and the streams flowed again to the sea, rapidly sweeping away silted soil, swimming in suspended animation. Muddied water blocked sunlight from the algae, killing the food chain, resulting in fewer plankton, then minnows, then insects, then birds and mammals. There were fewer places for ducks to breed. Otters and muskrats, raccoons and mink found less to eat, and were flooded, and frozen out. Rabbits, red foxes, deer and moose lost fecundity. A tenth of the total land area of the continent was once beaver-built wetland. With it's disappearance went the primordial wildlife richness of the country leaving us... Mississauga.

Here's the real brass. On July 12, 2008, the Nanaimo Daily News reported that the City of Nanaimo had formally applied to the province to use water from Westwood Lake for salmon enhancement. It appears that the Department of Fisheries and Oceans wants to raise the level of the lake. *'It will be less than four feet of beach that will disappear and that's at the beginning of the season and will soon catch up through the season as it evaporates. If too much beach is used, more sand could be added later.'* It seems the bureaucrats want to build a dam. Gee, there's something wrong with just about everything, isn't there Dad? Just about, Beav. Just about.

> *"One has but to observe a community of beavers at work in a stream to understand the loss in his sagacity, balance, co-operation, competence, and purpose which Man has suffered since he rose up on his hind legs. He began to chatter and he developed Reason, Thought, and Imagination, qualities which would get the smartest group of rabbits or orioles in the world into inextricable trouble overnight."*
>
> James Thurber

Dance on the Striped Lightning 03 September

"Always carry a flagon of whiskey in case of snakebite and furthermore always carry a small snake."

W.C. Fields

Shiva sits mesmerized in front of the garden compost bin. For hours at a time. With head cocked one way, then another. She is awaiting the emergence of a ribbon, rippling like water over a rock. Shiva loves to dance on the striped lightning.

The very first garden is supposed to have had snakes, or at least one. Ours has 'heaps' as Robyn would say, in her Kiwi vernacular (but of course she comes from a country that doesn't have any). Here in Lotusland a garden just isn't a healthy garden, without a resident population of striped lightning.

There are four subspecies of serpent around Westwood Lake (if you don't count the developers). The most common is still the Common Garter Snake (*Thamnophis sirtalis*), followed by the Western Garter Snake (*Thamnophis elegans*), the Northwestern Garter Snake (*Thamnophis ordinoides*), and the Pacific Coast Garter Snake (*Thamnophis atratus*). Clearly, taxonomy is not an extreme sport.

When I was a budding young scientist growing up in Northwestern Ontario, I collected garter snakes, among other things. I kept them in a homebuilt plywood and screen mesh terrarium, in my basement 'lab', next to my mother's laundry room. I religiously fed them frogs, in the name of science. I remember being fascinated by how they would shed their integument like an opaque stocking, reclusive, irritable, and temporarily blinded by the milky fluid they secreted between their old and new skins. On one chilly autumn day, thirteen of them escaped from a corner gap in their enclosure. In retrospect, there was only one place for a baker's dozen of thermally-challenged reptiles to go after a jailbreak. They made for a heat source. My mother used to pile sheets that had just come out of the dryer on a piece of carpet, next to the vent connecting the two rooms. You can see the rest coming. After the screaming stopped, she recounted to me her sheer amusement as, picking up the bundle of toasty warm sheets, she was greeted by an impromptu puppet show of thirteen heads, with protruding forked tongues. As punishment, my serpents were banished from the basement. It could have been worse. I was only able to find twelve of them. I held my breath for a long time, wishing the thirteenth Godspeed.

When they're not in Lila's laundry, garter snakes like to get their heat directly from the sun, or retained in the 20 mm thick rocks they prefer as retreat sites. They emerge midmorning to sunbathe, and then spend a short part of their day foraging. They will attack anything that they are capable of overpowering: earthworms, insects, spiders, amphibians, birds, fish, rodents, and slugs. Cold-blooded slug specialists have an energetic advantage over non-slug-eating snakes. When hunting, garter snakes use vision, ground vibration 'hearing', and taste and smell, combined in the *Jacobson's organ* located in the roof of their mouths. Hence, the molecule-seeking tongue protrusion.

Contrary to prevailing theory, garter snakes are venomous. They make a chemical called a three-fingered toxin (*3FTx*), that is spread into wounds with a chewing action. They are harmless to you and me because of the very low amounts of venom produced, the fact that it is relatively mild, and that they lack a truly effective means of delivery. Their enlarged rear 'fangs' do not have a groove running down the length of the teeth that would allow the neurotoxin to actually be injected. Prey is swallowed alive, sometimes pushed against a rock to anchor it, while the snake works its jaws up and around it.

Some of the animals that garter snakes eat, also eat the garter snakes back. Frogs and shrews eat baby garters, but the big predator list includes herons, raccoons, turtles, hawks, crows, crayfish and, especially, domestic and feral cats. Shiva isn't one of them. She's only dancing, not dining. As well as possessing no small speed and agility, garter snakes will discharge a malodorous secretion from their anal glands, and urinate on their attacker to get away. There is also a parasitic nematode called *Dracunculus ophidensis,* which lives part of its life cycle in amphibian larvae. When snakes eat hosting frogs, the parasite migrates into the serpent's tail and proceeds to progressively shorten the infected snake, and its future, from the back end. Tadpole's revenge. The biggest overall threats to garter snakes, however, are the usual evil trio of pesticides, water pollution, and habitat loss. It is likely for this reason that the most endangered garter snake in the world is, like the Raven's Manzanita in the Presidio, the San Francisco subspecies.

As the days shorten and temperatures drop in the autumn, garter snakes will travel almost four kilometers, to congregate in their large communal *hiber-*

nacula. Winter temperatures within the hibernaculum never drop below 3-4 degrees centigrade, because every dormant snake in this living spaghetti had stocked up on body fat by feeding aggressively during the late summer. After they emerge and recharge in springtime, they will stop eating just before mating, to rid their stomach from any food that might otherwise rot there. A touch of romance. This *brumation* period lasts about two weeks, and then their fun begins. Hundreds of snakes form mating balls, occasionally larger than a basketball in size. The strangest part of the festival is that not only the girl-snakes catch the garters. There are some males that are female impersonators. These 'she-males' are born with both male and female *skin lipid pheromones,* that they use to their advantage in two ways. Firstly, there is now evidence that she-male garters are slower and more vulnerable to predation in the cold spring awakening. By having both pheromones, they can get to the warm body-guarded centre of the mating ball more easily. Secondly, while some males are courting the wrong sex, other she-males can mate with the remaining females first. The old bait and switch Tootsie roll. No dinner and a movie, the weirdness isn't quite over yet. If the female garter snake hasn't truly fallen for any of her current slithering suitors, she can simply use sperm she might have saved from the previous autumn. Up to three months later the mother gives birth to about 25 live babies, up to 9 inches long, and immediately on their own. Most baby snakes die in their first year. Although they can live as long as ten years in captivity, most first year survivors will only last one more.

Over my lifetime, I've had many snake encounters- the Tanzanian green mamba, flying through a pharmacy chased by a crazed mob with sticks and machetes; the puff adder I slid an envelope under, thinking it was a rock beside me, in Malawi; whatever that was, on the pillow in my room, in the now-ruined Gwaii River Hotel (bless your true Zimbabwean heart, Harold); the anaconda under our truck in Venezuela; the double serpent *caduceus*, that has sustained my art, as a physician. But it's the common garter snake that ties it all together, sliding me from my earliest Canadian Shield enchantment, to this September sunlit scene with Shiva- still trying to tap dance on the striped lightning.

Barefoot Jay 14 September

"What, is the jay more precious than the lark because his feathers are more beautiful?"

William Shakespeare

They usually take over the conversation this time of year. The noise is grating, and impertinent. John James Audubon had them pegged in the early 1800s: *'In autumn, their loud and trumpeting clangour was heard at all hours of the day, calling out djay, djay, and sometimes chattering and uttering a variety of other notes scarcely recognisable as distinct from the calls of our common Blue Jay. They are, however, far more bold, irritable, and familiar. Watchful as dogs, a stranger no sooner shews himself in their vicinity than they neglect all other employment to come round, follow, peep at and scold him, sometimes with such pertinacity and irritability as to provoke the sportsman intent on other game to level his gun against them in mere retaliation. At other times, stimulated by mere curiosity, they will be observed to follow you in perfect silence, until something arouses their ready ire, when the djay, djay, is poured upon you without intermission, till you are beyond their view. So intent are they on vociferating, that it is not uncommon to hear them busily scolding even while engaged with a large acorn in the mouth."*

This one had one of my hazelnuts in his mouth. It was 6 a.m., and he was determined to be my wake-up call. *"Shaaa-aak, Shaaa-aak, Shaaa-aak!',* like metal gears stripping in reverse, or the sound coming out of an almost empty aerosol shaving crème can. His crested head tilted to inquire why my participation wasn't more enthusiastic. Suddenly, he drove his sharp beak into the ground, and flicked a large clod of leaves and dirt sideways. He did it a dozen more times before throwing me a loud nasal '*Waaa-aah,*' and a look of contemptuous warning.

The Steller's Jay (*Cyanocitta stelleri*) was named after Georg Wilhelm Steller (1709-1746), a German physician, naturalist and explorer, who worked in Alaska, when it still belonged to the Russians. He sailed with Vitus Bering on his *Second Kamchatka Expedition*, mapping the Arctic Ocean's Siberian Coast and searching for the Eastern Passage. In 1741, three years after leaving Peter the Great in St. Petersberg, and having his young German wife abandon him in Moscow, Steller, Bering, and their 75 crewmembers arrived at Kayak Island, Alaska. Here is where Steller first described the jay that would later bear his name. The expedition was shipwrecked on the return journey. Half of the crew died from scurvy, as did Bering. Steller himself died of a fever, halfway back to St. Petersberg, leaving a legacy of medical excellence, scientific enthusiasm, self-sufficiency, passion for the natural world, and a jay.

Stellers are a king-sized, self-assured, cobalt cacophony. The top half of their bodies are black charcoal; their stern is a vibrant midnight blue. Black racing stripes cross their wings and tail. They are a highly social species, usually living in flocks of ten or more. Robyn and I often see them flying across our vineyard and orchard, single file. They exhibit several kinds of antagonistic behavior. The first consists of aggressive fighting while flying. Birds will fly upward, and attempt to grasp each other with their feet, while pecking each other with their bills. Stellers use crest displays, and an act called *aggressive sidling,* to determine social status, a pecking order, if you will. Wing spreading expresses submission. Finally, Steller's Jays also employ *mobbing* in large numbers, to vocally harass and fly at predators, as a primary form of defense. Their vocalizations are more than abrasive crowings. They make their own soft, warbling chitchat, can imitate other songbirds and, most impressively, can mimic the cry of the Red-tailed hawk (or even the Eagle), both to chase away other birds from its feeding area, and to fool the hawk into thinking that the area of feeding on Steller's Jay is already covered. Audubon noted that it was called *ass-ass* by the Chinooks, who 'regard it with a superstitious feeling, believing that should a person hear it enunciating certain notes, which resemble the syllables *jaa-jaa,* he will shortly die, whereas its other notes, *kuc, kuc, kuc, kuc,* rapidly repeated, portend good.'

Steller's Jay pairs are monogamous. Before mating, they strut alongside each other, in a display of *sexual sidling.* At their nest site, Stellers' are uncharacteristically shy, and silent. The nest itself is a weighty bowl of leaves, moss, needles, and twigs, held together with mud. There are often bits of paper adorning the outside. The female Jay lays anywhere from 2-6 bluish-green eggs, with dark brown spots. She incubates them for just over two weeks, relying on the male to feed her. Steller's Jay used to be the sole crested jay species west of the Rockies, but Blue Jays are moving westward and, through occasional interbreeding, producing hybrids. Unlike most other fauna I have written about, Stellers' are actually thriving with increasing forestry and development. So far.

Steller's Jays eat a wide variety of plants and animals. The menu includes berries, seeds, fruits, arthropods, and small vertebrates. They will steal bird eggs and hatchlings from the nests of small birds, and have even been known to attack adult birds. They are totally at home at your picnic, your bird feeders, and your campground, where their omnivorous nature shines. They are food hoarders, and just like our red squirrels, they don't know when to stop. Their favorite food for hoarding? Nuts. Their favorite nuts in my backyard on Westwood Lake? Hazelnuts. But there is a bizarre symbiosis that has developed between the hazelnuts, the Steller's Jay, and the Red Squirrels, none of it working to our advantage. It begins with the Jays, who hang out in the hazelnut orchard as the nuts begin to darken. Before I consider them mature enough to harvest, the Stellers' have wrenched half of them off the trees, for fun. The other half have befallen one of two fates. They may have been dropped from a dizzy height, on the rocks mulching the rows of pinot noir adjacent to the hazelnut trees, in the hope that they will break open. I get to keep the ones that haven't. Or, more likely, they have been express-flown, all the way down the farmstead, to bomb the flagstone terrace curving round our front deck. This is where is gets interesting because, lying in wait for the Steller's Jay bombadiers, are the Red Squirrel resistance. They quickly make off with the nuts, as they hit the flagstones, and before the Jays can land to claim their prize. On the birdfeeder today was a Red Squirrel, jabbering at me incessantly. At first I thought he wanted me to refill the feeder, but with a second glance, I realized that he was simply taunting me with one of my own hazelnuts, holding out his two front paws, like Oliver Twist. Bastard.

The real weirdness is that all of this competitive nutcracking benefits the hazelnuts most. Every spring Robyn and I find dozens of new hazelnut trees growing in the containers on our front deck, courtesy of the Steller's Jay and the squirrels, despite the fact that both are very good at stealing from each other. Both have the same attitude. Zane Grey wrote about that in 1926 in *Under the Tonto Rim*: *'Here Lucy had opportunity to observe a small reddish-brown squirrel that was the sauciest little animal she had ever beheld. It occupied a branch above her and barked in no uncertain notes its displeasure and curiosity. Presently its chatter attracted a beautiful crested blue jay that flew close and uttered high-pitched notes, wild and fierce in their intensity. I hope the people here are not as antagonistic as this squirrel and bird,' observed Lucy.'"* Only the developers, Lucy.

The final Jay vignette is about my middle brother, Jay. He was a little like the Steller's Jay, but not much. Jay was a hoarder and his basement in Calgary was a wonder to behold. His wife, Helen, has stories about overripe bananas, and other good deals, that became sagas of storage. Jay was a king-sized social animal, self-assured, gregarious, and a bit impertinent. I remember a dogfight that he and his friend had, with forty model airplanes I had meticulously assembled over many years. He lost a tooth, but not his Belushi-style irreverent humour. He refused to wear shoes which, for someone in an industry which required him to call on very conservative clients, was a potential obstacle to success. Barefoot Jay made sure the potential was never realized. He captivated everyone who had the good fortune to get to know him. He was widely loved and admired. Then one day Jay woke up, and peed blood. He was forty-three, and had Helen, three young children, and anaplastic bladder cancer. He was dead in three months. Before he died, the whole family came out to visit Robyn and me. We hiked up the ridges, and Jay walked barefoot most of the way. When we hit the rocks, I pulled him aside and handed him a pair of shoes I had hidden in the daypack. He took them, and smiled. When we reached the top, he whipped out a cell phone and called Alberta, to describe the view. The next summer everyone but Jay, lit sweetgrass on the same spot to pay homage to his passing, and his barefoot soul.

I guess I could net the hazelnuts like I have the grapevines. I could stop the Jays from stealing all my hard work. I could, but I don't think I will. Instead, I plan on yielding.

> *"Then came the screech of blue jays. Soon they too discovered me. The male birds were superb, dignified, beautiful. The color was light blue all over with dark blue head and tufted crest. By and by they ceased to scold me, and I was left to listen to the wind, and to the tiny patter of dropping seeds and needles from the spruces."*
>
> Zane Grey, *Tonto Basin*

Harlequin   17 September

"Where, oh, where, shall he begin, Who would paint thee, Harlequin ?
With thy waxen burnished leaf, With thy branches' red relief,
With thy polytinted fruit, In thy spring or autumn suit,
Where begin, and oh, where end, Thou whose charms all art transcend?"

Bret Harte 1870, *Madrono*

You don't really see her until she sways into your left peripheral vision, on the first ridge. From out of the craggy fissures, a burled trunk stretches four burnt sienna coffee-striped arms, and reaches for sunlight. Floral fractals of grey green lichen are paste-patched on the underside of her violent curves. Her shape traces the cracks of a whip. She is textured smooth wood, waxy leaves, and crunchy bark; her colours are glorious and seasonal. Red and green, pastel in between, my *Arte Nouveau* French drama queen. The sentient soul of these Westwood Wuthering Heights, she is my favourite tree in the whole wide world.

Arbutus menziesii has different names, depending on where you live. In British Columbia, we know it by its proper Latin, 'Arbutus.' The Scottish naval surgeon who named it, Archibald Menzies, collected specimens in 1792. In the U.S., the Siskiyou Mountains of southern Oregon form the boundary for its other eponyms. North of them, it is called *Madrona*, south of there, *Madrone*. It was Father Crespi, of the Portola Expedition, who first mentioned the Arbutus in 1769. In his diary, he referred to it as *'Madrono,'* after a related European bush, that he knew as the Strawberry Tree. The Vancouver Island Salish revered Arbutus as the Wisdom Tree, because it bends around other trees, assuming dramatic horizontal ballet postures to find the sun. They used arbutus bark to treat tuberculosis, colds, as a contraceptive, and to add a pink colour to cooking camas bulbs.

Arbutus is Canada's only broadleaved evergreen. It can live for half a millennium- the oldest living specimens were seedlings when Albrecht Durer was still drawing nude self-portraits of himself. They are slow-rowing, but can reach a hundred feet in height, and ten in diameter. Somehow, they survive the harshest exposed Pacific Maritime climate- from wet, snowy winter gales, to the summer parched aridity of as little as 37 mm of rain per year. Burls form anywhere from the ground up, to store water for release when needed. Arbutus will even allow one of their bonsai branches or a portion of the main trunk to die off slowly, so that the rest of the tree can survive through times of extreme drought. The charcoal black branches and tree cavities that result serve as nesting sites for woodpeckers and crows. Arbutus are tolerant to extremes of temperature and shade, and are often the first trees to reemerge after a fire, or the carnage that passes for forestry in these parts. Found up to 1500 metres above sea level, arbutus can grow in the poorest soil, and in very little of it at that. Shaped by the wind, their toughness is surpassed only by the beauty of their fat gnarled cliff-hugging presence, on the southwest rocky bluffs of Westwood Ridges.

The wood is a stunning result of this austerity-diamond hard, brittle, and fine-grained in many patterns. Mexican *caballeros* fashioned their spurs from Arbutus because of its durability, and its spectrum of pink to black colours. It is used in fine cabinet-making, but not for anything large, as there is no straight timber. Arbutus wood burns hot and long, and makes excellent charcoal.

The bark is the spice of the species. It was used by the natives to tan leather, and as a soothing tea for sore Salish stomachs. As a young tree in the Spring, Arbutus is covered with a bright deep copper-orange salacious-sleek paper, which gradually deepens to a thicker reddish- brown parchment, in successive springtimes. During the summer, arbutus moults like a snake with a bad sunburn. Scaly slivers and strips curl and peel off to expose younger satin smooth wood, that varies in colour from yellow to silver ghost green to pistachio. Cool to the touch, impossible not to touch. It glistens in the rain, the water running trains of boxcar droplets, down the undulations. As winter deepens, its colour reddens to cinnamon, and the cycle begins anew.

Arbutus leaves hang on year round, green jade against the snow and the muted blue-green needles of their conifer companions. The spiralled oval finely-serrated blades contain a natural deer repellent, a liquid reduced sugar secreted at the tip of the leaf bud. This attracts flies and ants, which the deer find an unpalatable symbiosis.

Between March and May, the arbutus flowers into long pearls of creamy white, yellow or pink bell blossoms. Bees are attracted to their strong honey smell, and deer return to a favoured springtime food.

By autumn the flowers have produced prodigious amounts of rough textured blood-orange berries, containing scores of tiny seeds, and mouth-puckering tannins. Band-tailed pigeons and mourning doves find them irresistible, and mule deer, bears, raccoons and rodents only slightly less so. The natives ate them, but more often made them into cider. The berries are heavy, and don't travel far by gravity. But the leaf cover they fall into, and the prickles they develop as they dry out, outmanoeuvre their total consumption, and allow some dispersal by hitchhiking out of town on larger animals.

Despite the ability of arbutus to survive its many adversities, we are now witnessing the terror of their impending decline. The same pressures that threaten other natural Westwood wonders, are killing off the Harlequins. The first hazard, paradoxical as it may seem, is fire control. Arbutus rely on intermittent naturally occurring fires, to reduce the conifer canopy. Mature trees can regenerate more quickly than Douglas fir, and produce larger numbers of sprouting seeds. The second menace is greed. Property developers eradicate habitat, out of ignorance or deliberate malice, by changing the grade and drainage near the root crown. The bluffs that are its bedrock water sources, that other trees can't utilize, are also prime view real estate. The final horseman is a fungus, *Phytophthora ramorum*, the pathogen responsible for *Sudden Oak Death.* Together, with the nineteen other fungi that cause disease in arbutus, what chance does the poor Harlequin have?

There is talk of a new 'resort' development on the other side of the Ridges, just under my favorite tree in the whole wide world. There are rapacious real estate proponents of a gondola to the top of Mount Benson. I hope it is all just rumour, but I am, in my Westwood wisdom, increasingly aware that avarice will donald trump arbutus every time. *Being alone in the wilderness, it had looked within itself and, by heavens I tell you, it had gone mad.*

In Conrad's *Heart of Darkness*, the Harlequin gets it right.

> *"Through my glasses I saw the slope of a hill interspersed with rare trees and perfectly free from under-growth... He looked like a harlequin. His clothes had been made of some stuff that was brown holland probably, but it was covered with... scarlet edging at the bottom...and the sunshine made him look extremely gay and wonderfully neat withal, because you could see how beautifully all this patching had been done... His face was like the autumn sky, overcast one moment and bright the next."*
>
> Joseph Conrad, *Heart of Darkness*

Lazy Green Man 29 September

"I come from haunts of coot and hern, I make a sudden sally
And sparkle out among the fern, To bicker down a valley"

Alfred Lord Tennyson

There's a reason that Shiva and I choose the path we take, returning from the ridges. After the giddy vertigo and pumping heartbeats of the top trails, we suddenly find ourselves rafting down through a green ocean glade of giant ferns. Life slows. The toothy viridescence seems to be smiling at the sky, as it engulfs us. We stop. The gravity, draining us back into the woods at the bottom is softened by streams of sunlight, undulating on emerald fronds. We emerge from doing to being. Serene. Zen.

The Western Sword Fern (*Polystichum munitum*) is the plush carpet under the canopy, the spinach in our primordial soup. Polystichum comes from the Greek words *polys*—many, and *stichos*—a row, which refers to the way the *sori* spot on the underleaf are arranged. Munitum means 'armed with teeth'. The Indians sometimes referred to it as *chi'quon taunt*, which translates as 'lazy green man'. Sword Ferns may be lazy, but they are also well-mannered. They coexist with salal and Oregon-grape, the other two members of the undergrowth Holy Trinity. Their needs are modest. They may prefer a well-drained acidic soil of humus and pebbles, but they will grow in a wide range of earth, microclimate and lighting conditions. When truly favoured, in moist forests of low to moderate altitude, they will grow four feet tall, and eight wide. They act as host plants for butterflies. Deer, elk, black bears and mountain beavers forage on the fronds. As older fronds die, they provide a perfect habitat for amphibians, around their inverted conical base.

The fern family made its debut in the late Silurian period, about 400 million years ago. Lifting themselves out of the water and onto land required major changes in physical form and physiological function. They developed an outer skin to prevent losing water. Internal vascular systems evolved, to circulate nutrients. Pores developed, to allow the exchange of carbon dioxide and oxygen. Without the buoyancy of water, they needed to develop greater antigravity structural support. The Golden Age of Ferns occurred around 360 million years ago, during the Carboniferous period, when the world's coal deposits formed, from compressed layers of lazy green men. Conifers and other seed plants began to replace and displace ferns as the dominant form of vegetation 230 million years ago, in the Mesozoic era.

Natives used nearly every part of the Sword Fern. With no other food available in early Spring, First Nations peoples dug up the rhizomes, peeled and roasted them over a fire (or steamed them in a baking pit), and served them with dried salmon eggs. The Quinaults boiled the roots and used the water as a remedy for dandruff, and to treat diarrhea. Because of their non-stick property, the fronds were used on berry-drying racks, to separate food in storage boxes and baskets, as a protective layer in pit ovens, and for flooring and bedding, sometimes piled as mattresses. The young curled fronds were chewed to soothe sore throats, and Lummi women nibbled on them to hasten childbirth. Spores were scraped off the leaves as a treatment for burns. Children played a game with the fronds, the object of which was to see who could pull off the largest number of fern leaves, while holding their breath, saying '*pila*' with each leaf pulled.

I used to mutter something similar, when I was pulling Sword Ferns out of new clearcut, in an attempt to save them, and reintroduce the species to the regenerating forest in our backyard. Four quick compass point digs with my serrated edge shovel, and a Sword Fern would pop out of the moss like a paint can lid. On rare weekends in late Winter, the hatchback of my old white 1988 Honda Civic was occasionally filled to the roof with lazy green men. Robyn would chide me for 'bringing home half the forest' and, I admit it- the Honda's carpet gradually became a sort of groundcover in its own right. But the result, over many years of digging, is beautiful. There's something about living amid an incoming sea of swordferns that brings peace and harmony to the landscape. They are slowly transforming our West coast home into a Shinto temple.

Sword Ferns are a Cascadian icon, but there are also isolated populations in the interior of northern British Columbia, the Black Hills of South Dakota, and on Guadalupe Island off Baja California. For some delicious reason, they are impossible to grow satisfactorily in the eastern part of the continent, except for one accidental prissy mutation. In 1894, grower Robert Craig sent an order of 200 Sword Ferns for houseplants to M.C. Becker, a distributor in Cambridge, Massachusetts. Becker singled out one specific plant as more elegant and possessing longer fronds. Initially he thought it was a new variety. Approximately 50,000 of them were propagated and sold as *Nephrolepis davalliodes*. Ultimately, the

Royal Botanic Gardens in England decided that it was a mutant child of the Sword Fern. They renamed it *N. exaltata 'Bostoniensis,'* or the Boston Fern. What grows naturally, in the full view of our western windows, has, out of New England necessity, become a commercial greenhouse mass-produced mutant for Easterners to enjoy. Such is our comparative aesthetic. Such is the stuff of poetry.

As Sword Ferns mature, more and more dark green lance-shaped fronds grow from the rhizome at the centre. Eventually there may be up to a hundred fronds on a plant, each reaching six feet long and lasting several years. In early spring, new curled growth appear as *fiddlenecks*, and slowly begin to unravel. The young frond spirals have several names and meanings. In the Maritimes, they are known as *fiddleheads*, a seasonal culinary delicacy, best from Ostrich or Cinammon ferns. They must be cooked first to denature the *shikimic acid* they contain, a compound named after the Japanese flower, *Shikimi*, and the active ingredient in the influenza antiviral drug *oseltamavir* or Tamiflu (although shikimic acid is usually isolated from Chinese Star Anise). Not all ferns can be fiddlehead food, however, and that includes our Western Sword Fern. Bracken fiddleheads cause stomach cancer. Other fern fiddleheads contain the enzyme *thaminase*, which can lead to Beriberi. Young frond spirals are also called *crosiers*, like the Catholic shepherd crooks of abbots and bishops. The most powerful naming of the new unfurling fern frond, however, came from the New Zealand Maori. A vital symbol in their carving and tattoos, to them, the *Koro* symbolizes creation, growth, strength and peace (it is also the current symbol for peace in Japan). The logo of Air New Zealand is a stylized koro of the national emblem, the *Ponga* or Silver Tree Fern (*Cyathea dealbata*). Making a track through the bush at night, Maori warriors would lay silver fern fronds white side up, tips pointing in the direction of travel. The track could be seen at night by the glow of the white frond, contrasted against the dark undergrowth. This enabled surprise attacks on enemies, at first light.

My own most poignant experience with the silver fern occurred in 1985, when I arrived in New Zealand, after almost five years travelling around the world. Robyn met me at the airport and, after a few days with friends, we decided to go trekking in the Coromandel. After hitchhiking most of the day to the trailhead, we hiked for hours, before realizing that we were not going to make it to our Waiawa hut destination. Undeterred, we set up our tent on a stony riverbank peninsula, complete with campfire, a swath of glistening Southern Cross starlight, hooting *Morepork* owls, and the sound of running water. It was elfin otherworldly and, as I looked up through the twenty-foot umbrella canopy of tree fern fronds, I was enraptured.

Eventually we will have a proper Victorian fernery, just behind the living room sofa.

The lazy green men that have always lightened Shiva and me on our hikes over the ridges, will continue to elevate our souls, long after our bodies can no longer make the climb.

Forager Fanatical dei Funghi 03 October

"There are old mushroom pickers
and bold mushroom pickers,
but there are no old bold mushroom pickers"

Old Bold adage

"I always look forward to our annual foraging holiday with Uncle Wink... a restful marathon of hunting and gathering". This was my sixteen-year-old niece from Toronto speaking, as we pulled away from the Comox airport. Out of the mouths of babes. She was always demure, but clearly, in just over twelve months, she had found self-confidence, and her voice. I was delighted. Not only to see her hitting her stride, but to finally get a glimpse of what she actually thought of these yearly pilgrimages to her eccentric West Coast relatives, with their bizarre attachment to the land they live on. One of my colleagues had once told me, "Never trust a man who doesn't kill his own food". I'm not quite so mercenary, but I take the point.

Last year I introduced Leora to the foraging front row- an experience which likely fomented her opening line this summer. I took her mushroom picking on Mount Benson. And watched her catch the bug.

It's a big, fanatical bug. There are few activities that provide an opportunity for peaceful communion with nature, exercise, a slow deliberate application of the senses, the thrill of discovery in secret places, and a delicious death-defying culinary conclusion. It should be an Olympic sport.

Like any worthwhile activity, mushroom picking forays have ritual. They begin with the right mushroom knife. Mine is Italian, made of rosewood, with a wild boar bristle brush for cleaning, stainless curved pruning blade, ruler with map scales and built-in compass (I tend to get lost when I look at the ground for too long), tweezers, and *molto importante*, cachet baby, cachet. I have lost this knife a dozen times over the years, but I always find it again, retracing my steps for several kilometres, even several days later. It is vital to the experience. I can tell with my eyes closed what kind of mushroom I am harvesting, just by how the weight of the blade slices through the stem at ground level. Like it has nerve endings. The knife goes into a special Velcro pouch, on the front of the left shoulder strap of a specially modified daypack. I can also tell if the pouch has the mushroom knife in it or not, just by feeling the heft of the pack. There is room for a water bottle, removable semi-permeable collecting bag, and two additional pockets- one for a sandwich and one for a Milkbone. Because the third essential mushrooming tool is Shiva.

It's not that Shiva is any sort of truffle hound. She wouldn't know a chanterelle from a chinook- but she does warn me about bears, cougars, and other people. She can usually help me find my way home if we lose the path. Finally, and the true north reason, she is my companion. Also finally, and unfortunately, she is getting too old for the climbing. Lately, this has been heartbreaking. Not only do Robyn and I have to devise an elaborate distraction while I sneak out the front gate without her, but I also don't get to use the

Milkbone pocket in the daypack anymore. It's just not the same.

The last thing I take foraging is my walking stick, increasingly more important, as my own joints and balance begin to decay. Again, I've had this same stick for years, burnished to a rich auburn colour by so many climbs of time and space. I have fancier walking sticks in the garage, but this simple stave is the one that fits my hand the best, and the one I always go back for, if left behind in furtive fields of funghi.

Where, specifically, do I go to find mushrooms on Mount Benson? Nice try. A correct answer is a contravention of the first rule of foraging. This is a military operation. Don't ask, don't tell. Everyone has their own secretive sweet spots that they return to, year after year. If you come across fresh cut marks on stems that you feel belong to mushrooms you should have had, there is immediate indignation and a sense of violation. In the U.S. Pacific Northwest, this sort of territorial encroachment has resulted in violence, sometimes murder. Once again, I'm not quite so mercenary, but I take the point. This is a serious avocation for some, a more serious livelihood for others. Just log onto the *Buyer and Picker Messages* website, and enter a different world. It's the police bandwidth for those who make their living harvesting mushrooms in our woods. It's a hard life humping the hills from dawn to dusk, and sleeping in the back seat of your old car. Like other foraging tribes in history, they have their own culture and rules. Like other foraging tribes in history, they are slowly dying off, as more and more old and second growth logs go south, on trucks and barges. Forests are more than dead trees. There is a mycelium internet, the health of which is essential to the functioning of the ecosystem. Not that I'd expect this consciousness to hold back the two-stroke imperative that continues to be promoted as progress by anyone who stands to make a dollar off falling trees. The degeneration is inexorable and inexcusable. And far too big and noisy to remember what we're collectively foraging for.

This time of year, we're mostly looking for the Pacific Golden Chanterelle (*Cantharellus formosus*), the food funnel that concentrates autumn ferment into chewy mouthfuls of black-peppered nut-buttered apricot earthiness. I swear they're smiling, as I first catch sight of them among the needles and the leaves. The heavier the daypack, the lighter my step. In 1748, Linnaeus first described what he called *Agaricus chantarellus*, in his *Flora Oeconomica*, as 'suitable for cooking'. They match well with an equally understated 'beverage', like, say, Grand Cru Burgundy. Their deep yellow comes from the same *carotenoid* pigments found in carrots. Of the 39 volatile compounds identified in their flavour profile, three are most prominent: *Octenols* provide the characteristic smell of mushrooms, in general; *Caproic acid* yields an odour reminiscent of goats (also the chemical responsible for the unpleasant smell of the Gingko tree); finally, *acetic acid* is a top note. The sum of the parts is far more than a vinegar goat mushroom, however. If this were the level of sophistication of Chanterelle flavour chemistry, no mass production would be happening in any lab, anytime soon. Fact is, we haven't even successfully cultivated them. The only place to find a Pacific Golden Chanterelle is where they grow naturally. In old growth and second growth forests, the ones that are left. This is also the only place to find the other kinds of chanterelles, and other kinds of mushrooms.

I usually return from my forays with a multicolour mushie melange that completely covers the kitchen island countertop (much to Robyn's horror)- large, curly, cauliflower mushrooms for lasagna, hedgehogs, porcinis, the almond-flavoured 'Prince' (*Agaricus augustus*), angel wings, matsutake, and the bizarre blood orange lobster mushrooms (not mushrooms at all, but actually a parasitic *ascomycetes*, that converts other mushrooms into seafood-scented alien lifeforms. One has to be careful that the ascomycete is parasitising an edible *Russulla*, and not a poisonous host.)

Which brings us to the important cautionary we started with. How do I really know that my foraged funghi won't kill us? Mushrooms are like men. The bad most closely counterfeit the good. I have looked after mushroom-poisoned mycology experts in the Intensive Care Unit, and lost them. Not pretty. There are four kinds of mushroom toxicities out there. The first are simple gastrointestinal irritants, usually self-limited, although unpleasant. The second is a little worse- mushrooms like the Inky Cap, containing *coprine*, which blocks the breakdown of alcohol, and requires a two-day washout period. As a diehard oenophile, these mushrooms are off the menu. The third category of toxins are neurotoxins, ranging from *muscarine*, which kills up to twelve per cent of Amanita eaters, to *psilocybin*, the active ingredient in 'magic' mushrooms. Fourth, are the extremely dangerous protoplasmic poisons, *amatoxins*, *gyromitrins*, and the *orellanines*, *cortinarins A* and *B*. With the latter, two weeks go by, and only then do your kidneys and liver fall out. Hard to get a good history of ingestion. Finally, some mushrooms concentrate toxic heavy metals, so picking on the side of the road is a bad idea.

Despite the dark side, humans have had a mostly favourable relationship with funghi for a long time. The *Ice Man of Otzi*, discovered in 1991, on the Schnalstal glacier in the mountains bordering Austria and Italy, carried birch polypore and tinder fungus, 5300 years ago. The Greeks believed that mushrooms came from Zeus' lightning, appearing as they did without explanation after a rain. The Romans had recipes for Chanterelles, and we have been eating them ever since.

What Leora hasn't yet experienced in her marathons of hunting and gathering (but I hope she someday does) is what happened to Uncle Wink, way up behind Westwood Lake, one special autumn day. Along a remote path, I came upon a small moss-blanketed creek, rising off to the right. Shiva and I followed it up, into a tiny sun-streamed clearing. The light played on an orchestral gathering of fat penny loafering King *Boletus edulis*, Paganini porcini, playing *Caprice in A minor* at full volume. I looked down. Just beside my right boot sat a complete cello section of rare *blue chanterelles*, in a cobalt cluster. I hadn't exhaled yet. Looking over to my left about another foot away, was a section of cracked ground, conducted up through which was an *Oregon white truffle*. The choir kicked in. Mother lode.

In his *Great Dictionary of Cuisine*, Alexandre Dumas wrote that '*nothing frightens me more than the appearance of mushrooms on the table, especially in a small provincial town.*' Leora knows different. He should have come to our place.

"Out mushroom hunting--
dangerously close to caught in
late autumn showers."

Basho

Murders and Conspiracies 05 October

" To the raven her own chick is white."

Irish proverb

The sky would turn black over our house. A grayish autumn strobe light would pierce the blanket of crow *caw-cawphony*, winging up towards Mount Benson's peak. The birds extended to the horizon in all directions, flowing like a river Styx cloud, to the communal winter roost, a crows' nest *corroboree*. It was a natural wonder never described locally, as far as I could determine. They came again yesterday, but not in the same numbers that used to eclipse the sun, when Robyn and I first moved to the Lake. Somehow, at some time, there seems to have been a mass murder of our murder of crows.

The Corvus denizens of Westwood and elsewhere (both crows and their raven brethren) have many legends and as much mythology as they do, for one simple reason. Their brains are larger than any other bird species. They are the smartest birds on the planet. Long before Aesop penned the fable of *The Crow and the Pitcher*, crows (*Corvus brachyrhynchos*) have been viewed by humans as endowed with unique intelligence. Henry Wadsworth Longfellow noted that *'method is more important than strength, when you wish to control your enemies. By dropping golden beads near a snake, a crow once managed to have a passer-by kill the snake for the beads.'* Crows will drop seeds into heavy traffic, and wait for a car to crush them open. Common ravens (*Corvus corax*) call coyotes and wolves, to open the carcasses of dead animals. Dominant juvenile ravens call other young ravens to a food find, so that the prepubescent punks will outnumber the resident adults, allowing them to feed without being chased away. They remember the locations of each other's food caches, and steal from them. Ravens fly extra long distances to find better hiding places, because this thievery is so common. They have been observed pretending to make a cache without actually depositing the food, to confuse hungry spies.

Crows have the ability to count. If three people enter a bird observation hut, and two then leave, they know that the hut is still not empty. Crows in Australia have learned how to eat toxic cane toads, by flipping them on their backs and violently stabbing the throat where the skin is thinner, allowing access to the non-toxic innards. Israeli Wild Hooded Crows have learned to use bread crumbs for bait-fishing. In Scandinavia, Ravens have been caught using ice fishing gear to pull in fish, while the owner was away from the ice hole. Ravens play catch with sticks. They dive-bomb mating eagles and pull their tails, when predator talons are otherwise occupied with a fresh kill, because they know they can get away with it.

Why are these birds so intelligent, if they don't even have a cerebral cortex? We used to consider their actions to be robotic, until neurologist Stanley Cobb, in the 1960's, found that birds have a part in the forebrain, the *hyperstraiatum,* that allows them to perform synonymous functions. More recent studies of the New Caledonian Crow have shown an ability to make a larger variety of tools than previously known, including a hooked implement made by plucking and stripping a barbed twig, and a 'stepped cut tool', with serrated edges.

So if crows and ravens are both this intelligent, what, other than size, distinguishes them from each other? First, of course, is their appearance. Ravens are bigger, the largest species of songbird and largest all-black bird in the world. They have a larger and heavier beak, and a wedge-shaped tail, rather than a crow's square tail. They have shaggy-spiked throat feathers called *hackles*, used in social communication. The second differentiating feature is their behaviour. Crows have large family groups, and gather at communal roosts of thousands, at dusk (and in Winter). Some roosts have been forming in the same general area for well over a hundred years, and some contain up to two million birds. Crows adopt a passive strategy when attempting to take food from close family members, but become aggressive when trying to steal a morsel from an unrelated crow. However, they will also still come to the aid of any crow in distress, and are able to coordinate complex ambush attacks. Presumably, this is where the group term, '*Murder*', originates. Ravens, on the other hand, don't flock. They are solitary birds, although they can sometimes be seen in pairs. Rare congregated groups of ravens are referred to as '*Conspiracies*' or '*Unkindnesses*'. Ravens tend to remain in wild undisturbed areas, and have retreated as a result of human development. The crow population had exploded until recently, mostly because of our invention of road kill and dumpster dining.

The greatest difference between raven and crow behaviour may be in their patterns of flight. Ravens soar as high as raptors do, but also make frequent acrobatic rolls, and do somersaults in the air. They have been observed flying upside down for as far as a kilometer. Crows not only typically flap their wings during flight, but also literally fly into a collective frenzy when their space is encroached upon by raptors. They will dive *en masse* into the treetops, where a hawk, or especially an owl, is discovered, a term formally known as '*mobbing*'. Raven temperment, despite less concern about needing to remain vigilant for predators, is not that dissimilar. When confronted simultaneously, in an experiment by observers in dangerous-appearing and neutral masks, ravens were more likely to scold and persecute wearers of the threatening faces.

Thirdly, crow and raven vocalizations match their personalities. While the usual crow call is a harsh '*caw*' and the raven has a more musical '*gronk gronk,*' there are wonderful nuances. One can hear crow '*caws*' echoed back and forth between birds, a series of '*caws*' in quanta, counting out numbers, a long '*caw*' followed by a series of short '*caws*' when taking off from a perch, and a deep-throated '*caw-aw-aw*' to indicate hunger, or to mark territory. Softer, almost purring, sounds are heard as a come-hither call of affection. Domesticated crows can imitate words, and human laughter. The Raven, too, has more than thirty varied vocalizations. In Tolkien's *Hobbit,* the raven hereditary chief, *Roac,* could speak 'the language of men'. The occasional intense musicality of overhead calls in my garden is not unlike that of New Zealand *tuis*- but the moving Doppler effect, and simultaneous stereophonic swoosh of pinions catching air, reveal it as a raven.

Fourth, historic human mythologies distinguish the crow from the raven. In European legends, crows tend to be viewed as a symbolic spiritual transition to death, whereas ravens are more often associated with the negative and actual physical act of dying. When crows gave bad news to the Greek goddess Athena, she flew into a rage, and cursed their feathers to be black. Because of this dark plumage, shrill calls, and tendency to eat carrion, the crow grew wings as a morbid harbinger. They were commonly thought to circle above scenes of death, especially battles. The ancient Chinese believed that the primordial world had ten suns, caused by ten crows. Because of their unsustainable, catastrophic effects on nature and agriculture, the gods sent in their greatest archer, *Houyi*, to shoot down nine crows and spare only one. In Tibetan lore, crows heralded the birth of the First, Seventh, Eighth, Twelfth and Fourteenth Lamas, the latter being the current Dalai Lama, Tenzin Gyatson.

The raven has been more traditionally revered as a spiritual figure or god, than a simple portent of death, especially in the New World. The Northwest Tlingit, Haida, Tsimshian, BellaBella, and Kwakiutl all viewed the raven as the creator of the world, and bringer of daylight. To the first two tribes, the raven was both a Creator god and Trickster. He tends to become less deity and more rascal as he moves East. The raven is important in the creation myths of the Arctic Inuit. Killing a raven is an ultimate taboo, that can result in nothing but harm to the assailant. An archeological excavation on the St. Lawrence River, found bones of 45 different species of birds. Importantly missing were any raven bones, suggesting that this Eskimo culture had revered the raven for over 1100 years.

In the Chaldean *Epic of Gilgamesh*, Utnapishtim released a dove to find land, but the dove merely circled and returned. Then he sent out a raven, which didn't return. The same raven disobeyed Noah by failing to return to the ark, after being sent on the same search. According to Livy, the Roman general Marcus Valerius Corvus had a raven settle on his helmet during combat with a gigantic Gaul, which distracted the enemy's attention by flying in his face. Norsemen believed that the ravens *Hugin* and *Munin* sat on the god Odin's shoulders, saw and heard all, and, as his messengers, reported to him the events of the day. A raven banner standard was carried by such Viking figures as the Norse Jarls of Orkney, King Canute the Great of England, and King Harald Hardrada of Norway. In Sweden, ravens were considered the ghosts of murdered people and, in Germany, the souls of the damned. In Danish folklore, a raven that ate a king's heart gained human knowledge, could perform great malicious acts, lead people astray, and possessed superhuman powers. In an old English poem, *Judith*, the raven is seen at times of battle with the wolves, waiting for fresh kills: '*...the wolf in the forest, and the dark raven, the slaughter-greedy bird. Both knew what the warriors intended to provide for them a feast of doomed warriors; and behind them flew the eagle eager for prey, and the dewy-feathered one, the dark-coated one; he sang a battle song, the horny-beaked one.*' King Arthur was said not to have died, but to have been transformed by magic into a raven. In *Beowulf*, the black raven is '*eager for the doomed ones, as he shall say much to the eagle of what success he had at feeding, when he, with the wolf, plundered the corpses.*' Because of such associations, the word *Ravenstone* became a term for places of execution.

In medieval times, ravens represented virility. In *Macbeth* the raven '*croaks the evil entrance*' and in *Othello* the raven flies '*o'er the infected house*', both screaming evil. A legend later developed that England would not fall to any foreign invader, so long as there were ravens at the Tower of London. They still clip one wing periodically, to ensure that none can ever leave. *Hotel Caw-lifornia*. The raven is the National Bird of Bhutan, on the Coat of Arms of the former Viking colony of the Isle of Man, the Official Bird of the Yukon Territory, and the emblem and namesake of the American football team of Edgar Allan Poe's hometown, Baltimore.

The *Baltimore Sun* apparently doesn't think much of the inspiration for Poe's poem, referring to ravens as '*Dirty. Brooding. Noisy. Road-kill pecking.*' The description is unfair, and misses the raven's dedication to fun. Ravens are the most playful and mischievous of bird species. While they can be very destructive (e.g. pecking holes in airplane wings, peeling radar absorbent material off buildings at the China Lake, Naval Weapons Centre), they have also been observed sliding down snowbanks, purely for the thrill of it. They engage in games with other species, playing *catch-me-if-you-can* with wolves and dogs. They love to steal and cache shiny objects, such as pebbles, pieces of metal and, especially, and with no small measure of poetic justice, golf balls. Perhaps they do this to impress other ravens. More likely they are simply deeply curious about all new things, especially bright, round objects that look like bird eggs. *And his eyes have all the seeming of a demon's that is dreaming.*

The final difference between ravens and crows is their geography. The original Old World raven, described by Linnaeus in the 18th century, crossed the Bering land bridge into North America several million years ago. Recent mitochondrial DNA studies indicate that, about two million years ago, the common Raven diverged into two distinct *clades*: a *California clade*, found only in the southwestern United States, and a *Holarctic clade*, found across the rest of the northern hemisphere. Just north of us, in Qualicum, there are ravens carrying a mutant gene which makes their coats white, similar to the white bears of the BC Central Coast. From melancholic midnight melanism to *Spirit Ravens*. The Kwakiutl would have carved a special totem.

Crows are faring worse. The crows of island groups such as New Zealand, Hawaii and Greenland, are long gone. Despite the dynamic dumpster demographic, in the U.S. it is legal to hunt crows in all fifty states, from August until the end of March, and anytime if they are causing a 'nuisance or health hazard', whatever that means. And the current source of ongoing murder of our murder of crows? It turns out that crows are very susceptible to the West Nile virus. They die within a few days, almost no survivors. When the sky above our house stops turning black, we'll both be blue.

"And the Raven, never flitting, still is sitting, still is sitting
On the pallid bust of Pallas just above my chamber door;
And his eyes have all the seeming of a demon's that is dreaming,
And the lamplight o'er him streaming throws his shadow on the floor;
And my soul from out that shadow that lies floating on the floor
Shall be lifted - nevermore!"

Edgar Allan Poe, *The Raven*

Falling Water 07 November

"Let the stormy clouds chase everyone from the place
Come on with the rain, I've a smile on my face
Just singin', singin' in the rain."

Nacio Herb Brown, *Singin' in the Rain*

Robyn starts her seasonally-affected disapproval about this time of year, but I love it all the same. Westwood Winters can be dark and cold. Spring has charm, but there is often enough farm work to convert me to condominimalism. Summer is glorious, but the walkway along the front of our house becomes a human conveyer belt of sun worship, inebriated hormonal indulgence, and aerobic competition. At all hours there seems to be a frenetic swarm, celebrating life and fearing death. And then, suddenly, the rain washes it away.

The old serenity returns. Life slows. Skies are grey but the feeling is cozy. I've just finished an omelette breakfast, with too many chanterelles I collected with Shiva yesterday on the ridges, and now I'm going to throw a log on the fire, and enjoy the rain.

In other less soggy parts of the world, it is easier to tell when rain is coming. The drier the climate, the more predictable the precipitation. When the wind is from the east, when dust and a pale moon are rising, and clouds and chimney smoke descend, when a ring appears around the sun or moon, when there is thunder or a red sky or dry grass in the morning and no dew at night, and when clouds appear as rocks and towers, it will rain. When sound travels farther, when chairs squeak, drawers catch and doors and salt get sticky, it will rain. Watch the animals. When the crow flies low, when cats wash behind their ears, when flies bite more, when spiders leave their webs, when ants move their eggs and climb, when sea gulls sit on the shore, it will rain. If your own joints and broken bones ache, it will rain. The pressure drop just before a rainstorm and the rise in humidity can enhance your sense of smell. If flowers are more fragrant...

There is also the unique pleasant smell of rain itself. *Petrichor.* In 1964 two Australian researchers, Bear and Thomas, published in the Journal, *Nature*, a description of a complex oil, composed of more than fifty different chemicals, released by certain plants during dry periods, and taken into clay soils. When it rains, the oil is released, together with another compound, the combination of which constitutes petrichor. The compound the oils are released with is the smell of Mother Nature's armpits. It is a *terpene, octahydro-4,8a-dimethyl-4a(2H)-naphthalenol*, but you can call it *geosmin.* Your nose can detect tiny concentrations of geosmin, as little as 5 parts per trillion. Geosmin is the smell of beets. It has the aroma of freshly dug earth and musty turnips. Geosmin is the mud smell of bottom-feeding freshwater fish. Under acidic conditions, geosmin breaks down into odorless substances; the reason you add lemon or vinegar to your catfish and carp recipes is to reduce their muddy flavor.

Where does geosmin come from? It is released by dying and dead microbes, mostly actinobacteria and blue-green algae. The mother of all geosmin-producing actinobacteria is *Streptomyces coelicolor*, a spore-producing filament-branching plant-munching bug, that has had its complete genome sequenced at the Sanger Institute in Cambridgeshire, England, right alongside the Human Genome Project. The enzyme responsible for converting *farnesyl diphosphate* to geosmin has just been identified as *germacradienol/germacrene D synthase*, important for the following reason: geosmin smells good in the garden, but not in the glass. Many communities depend on surface water. When the occasional sudden death of large numbers of these microorganisms releases geosmin into the local water supply, it can leave a very bad taste. With the discovery of geosmin's bi-functional enzyme, there may be a way to prevent this.

If bad-tasting water isn't bad enough, geosmin can also affect wine. In fact, the French may be absolutely right. There is likely real honest *terroir* in every glass. Geosmin has been measured in recent vintages from Bordeaux and Burgundy. It comes from *Streptomyces, Botrytis* and *Penicillium* on the grape skins, not directly from the deified dirt itself. Geosmin may also be a factor in cork taint. Goodness knows what would happen to the French winemaker's psyche if we purged the terror of *terroir*.

So, why and how does it rain? Simply put, it rains because of ice crystals. In a cold cloud, water evaporates to reach its *vapor pressure equilibrium*. The ice condenses this vapor and grows into a larger ice crystal. Larger crystals collide with other larger crystals forming yet larger crystals. Eventually, they grow heavy enough to fall. In meteorology we call this the *Bergeron Findeisen Process*. At Westwood Lake, we call this rain. Raindrops are not shaped like this , they are shaped like this . They fall at speeds of up to 22 miles per hour. In more heavily-populated areas near the coast, there is a 22% higher chance of rain on Saturdays than on Mondays. This is the effect of five working days of air pollution, creating additional substrate for ice crystals to form on, over the weekend. This is the same principle of cloud seeding discovered by Vincent Shafer over Schenectady, New York, in 1946. The initial use of *dry ice* (frozen CO2) to induce more rapid cooling within clouds, eventually gave way to the employment of silver iodide. Once the meddling had begun, it was just a matter of time before Rain Dancers morphed into Rain Makers.

Most recently, the Chinese have been curiously observed, firing missiles and cannons into the sky. The *Beijing Weather Modification Office* tried to create sunny skies for the Olympic games, to rinse away the pollution, and wash away decades of communist environmental sin. Mao originally began seeding clouds to ensure a good harvest, but he was not satisfied with just more rain; In the spirit of Marxist Man's rightful total supremacy over Nature, Mao also demanded eradication of the *Four great pests*: rats, mosquitoes, flies and sparrows. When you have a billion people playing *Simon Sez*, you don't want to play for the sparrow team. Today there is no birdsong in China, and not just because most were eaten. Mao wanted rain and he got all the flooding he could have wanted. And locusts. And drought. And starvation. Now he also has *acid rain* (and, thanks to prevailing winds, so do we). A *Great Leap Forward* from a little Rain Dance.

There are certainly other cultural differences (assuming that one could have used the term 'cultural' to describe the *Cultural Revolution*) in the way we look at rain around the world. In Botswana, the national currency, *pula*, is named after the Setswana word for rain. Worshipped in desert societies, feared in monsoon lowland countries, rain brings us melancholy from our inherited temperate European attitudes.

Rain rain go away,
Come again another day.
Little Johnny wants to play;
Rain, rain, go to Spain,
Never show your face again.

This nursery rhyme was written about the wreck of the Spanish Armada in 1588. (Napoleon also lost the battle of Waterloo because of rain- when it comes to natural allies against foreign enemies, rain is to the English what snow is to the Russians.)

The English, appropriately enough, have a panoply of words to describe falling water (as do the Quechua in Peru). Rain-bearing clouds ahead are *imbriferous*; mud and rain-splashed pedestrians or vehicles are *bedrabbled;* rain-soaked possessions are i*mpluvious*; a whimsical rain adjective is *hyetal*; and rain-dripping clothes sound like *platch*. The Scots, understandably, speak of *blirts*, *driffles*, and *bracks*, to describe their different types of rain. The wettest place on Earth is Cherrapunji, on the southern slopes of the Eastern Himalayas, in Shillong, India, with the highest recorded rainfall in a single year of 87 feet in 1861. In contrast to the rain never stopping, a phenomenon, known as *virga,* occurs when the rain never reaches the surface, in hot dry terrestrial deserts, or on other worlds. On Venus, *sulfuric acid* virga evaporates 40 miles from the surface. Methane rain falls on Titan, Saturn's channeled moon. Liquid neon and helium rain occur in the upper atmospheres of gas giants. Back here on Earth, it can literally rain animals, usually fish, frogs or birds sucked airborn from a remote waterspout. I'm not so sure about raining cats and dogs, but I am absolutely enthralled by a Red Rain which fell in Kerala, India, from July to September, in 2001, that appeared to contain a hitherto unrecognized red microorganism. I wonder what that petrichor smelled like.

Whether you love the rain or not, you will acknowledge that it brings its own poetry. I came across this one the other day:

Raining today. There is a water puppet show of dancing concentric rings on the flashing outside my den window. Our dogs bark in the downpour. The last crimson leaves of the Japanese maple are hanging on for dear life.
Yesterday, I turned forty-six.
Robyn was on a predawn ferry to a ballet workshop in Vancouver and I have this autumn falling water all to myself. I'm not really sure what I'm supposed to do with it.
It doesn't lend itself to sculpting. It seems instead a lichen patina drizzling down fir bark furrows. Turning forty six. Like turning leaves. In English we make too small a distinction between turning as a rotational direction, and turning as a metamorphosis. We can never turn far enough to see the old horizons.
The rain has intensified, white noise from a quicksilver landscape. The lake is the color of skim milk. Zen monks know the mood. Breath of our souls.
I am fortunate. She is an extra chamber in my heart. I live in fine geography in a prosperous era. I have a noble profession. I do good anyway. When I go, I know I will be gone. There could be grace in that.
But for now what means fortunate at forty-six, the frying pan downpour outside, and the howling of the dogs? Just me and the rings of orange-capped boletes melting on the lawn under the hammock trees. Like a watercolor.
Raining today.

I wrote that over a decade ago. And then I lost it. Someone found it in Robyn's old ballet studio downtown. I'm older now. Still fortunate, although I'm down to one dog. Robyn is still the extra chamber in my heart. The geography is a little more crowded, but still fine. The era is less prosperous, but my profession is still noble, still doing good anyway. And the rain? Still love that too. As my drug and alcohol-addled ex-Marine Vietnam Vet Amazon guide, Richard, said to me one particularily soggy afternoon, soaked to the skin, and five river tributaries down and away from hope, *Wink, that's why they call it the rainforest.*

Frank Lloyd Wright built a place in Western Pennsylvania, in 1936. *Fallingwater.* I'd like to see it, before the watercolours run dry.

Damn. Sun just came out.

Alder Ego 10 November

"The Alder, whose fat shadow nourisheth,
Each plant set neere to him, long flourisheth."

William Browne, *Britannia's Pastorals*

I've only used a chainsaw a few times in my life. Frankly, it causes shivers as well as splinters. The teeth continue to gnaw away at our community canopy; its throaty voice ruptures our silent serenity. I know it is only a tool, but it always seems to end up in the wrong hands. The last time it was in my hands, a decade ago, I used it to serve what I thought were two simultaneous purposes- first, I needed some logs for a new shiitake mushroom project I was excited about and, secondly, I thought I was getting rid of an invasion of trashwood weed trees, that seemed to have exploded out of the ground around our ponds, overnight.

It turns out that I had underestimated these Red Alders (*Alnus rubra*) I dismembered. While not the most beautiful trees in our Westwood sanctuary, they are not without their own character and charm. A member of the small order *Betulaceae*, they are distinguished, like their Birch tree cousins, by fruit-bearing catkins. In early spring, I sometimes have trouble distinguishing these droopy cylindrical inflorescences from the hazelnut catkins in the next paddock over.

The term Alder originated from the Proto-Indo-European root *el-*, meaning 'red' or 'brown,' also the source for the English words *elk* and *elm*. When alder bark is scraped or bruised, it oozes that bright rusty red colour for which it is named. Laplanders dye their leather garments by chewing Alder bark with their saliva, both becoming red in the process. Alder bark was used for tanning in Ayshire in the 1600s. The various layers of the red alder bark yield different colours, from yellow through orange, red, burnt sienna, to brown. These were used to colour baskets, hides, moccasins, and hair by Native Americans. In northwestern California, the Whilkut tribe made brown baskets from Red alder roots. A russet dye was used by other groups to disguise fishing nets, so they wouldn't be so visible underwater. Quills were coloured Yellow by soaking them with alder catkins.

The cities of Ravenna and Venice were founded on poles of alder, including the original Rialto Bridge, across the Grand Canal. In Holland, they are still used for pilings, for the staves of herring barrels, and for wooden shoes. The wood is pliable because it grows so fast (a meter per year for 20 years), as even Virgil noted in his *Eclogues*, translated by John Dryden: *'As Alders in the spring the boles extend, And heave so fiercely that their bark they rend.'* This softness makes it particularly suitable for carving and turning. Wheelbarrows and stone-carts were constructed of alderwood, because it resisted splitting under loads. For the same reason, Alaskan Indians hollowed out alder trunks to make their canoes. The original industrial timber barons initially considered the alder a 'trash tree.' Beginning in the early 1970s, the *Bureaus of Land Management* of Oregon and Washington State began spraying vast tracts of coastal alder forest with herbicides. They were dropping Agent Orange, long after the U.S. Army had banned the defoliant from use in Vietnam in 1971. The real harvests were lawsuits from residents, because of birth defects, miscarriages and other adverse health effects. The spraying stopped, appropriately enough, in 1984. Since then, there has been an enhanced awareness of alder's potential value, not only as a source of fine lumber, but also as a growth accelerator of other timber species. The current annual cut of more than 300 million board feet is used to make furniture, flooring, panelling, cabinets and, most importantly, Fender *Stratocaster* guitar bodies. Alder charcoal is high grade stuff. It is used for all grades of gunpowder, including heavy ordnance. An alder charcoal and sap mixture was used by the Cree as a softener for bending boards for toboggans, and for sealing canoes.

Alder is food. Smoked salmon is not a truly West Coast epicurean experience, without the oilyness of alder smoke. Alder sap smells like bananas, and boils down to a glorious pancake syrup. Coastal Salish ate the inner bark of alder, storing it in dried cakes for winter use. Alder catkins are edible and high in protein, but bitter, and mostly eaten in survival situations. They are, however, the first sources of spring pollen for honeybees, and a food plant for butterflies. Beavers like their alder straight, with water, or on the rocks.

Alder is medicine. Alder bark contains *salicin*, an anti-inflammatory that is broken down to aspirin in the body. Natives used it to treat insect bites, poison oak and other skin conditions, tuberculosis, and lymphatic disorders. Red alder also contains *betulin* and *lupeol*, compounds that may have potential in treating HIV and certain cancers.

Red alder is our most prodigious hardwood. It is found west of the Rockies between California and Alaska, except for a few lonely stands in Idaho (and Hawaii where it was introduced, although I'm not sure what they were thinking). The tallest red alder stood 105 feet tall in Clatsop County, Oregon. They can live for a century, but most start to decline after fifty years. Trunk diameters of 18 inches have been reported. They tend to form shrubs in open exposed areas. Epiphytic lichen covers alder tree bark, like an oil-painted mosaic of greyish pink bobbin lace. Some lichen looks like pencil script (*Graphis scripta*) and others resemble barnacles (*Thelotrema lepadinum*). Decreasing amounts of lichen are a marker for worsening air quality; similarly leaves turn purple in the presence of increasing ozone levels.

Before we had clearcuts and skid trails and developers, alder was limited to growing alongside streams and the lowland wet. Dryden referred to it as '*swimming alder,*' and noted that '*Light alder stems the Po's impetuous tide.*' Now we have a pox of excavated landscapes that can host millions of alder seedlings per hectare in the first year after the soil is disturbed. One of the few things that Robyn and I disagree about, is the need for thinning alder trees. She thinks they should be left to their own devices. I maintain they grow faster and bigger if they're culled. Even with evidence, I always lose.

One of the most important features of Red Alder is its symbiotic relationship with the nitrogen-fixing Actinobacteria, *Frankiella alni.* Root nodules can be as big as a human fist. Every year an acre stand of alder will fix up to 500 pounds of nitrogen. We know that Douglas fir girth increases 2.5 times faster when grown with alder, because of the increased available nitrogen. We just discovered the story of the bears. It seems that when young bears come into a mixed forest of Douglas fir and alder, they go a little crazy. The bears use their claws to partially or totally ring the firs and then use their canines to remove the new sapwood. This slowly kills a proportion of the Douglas fir, but the remaining trees seem to compensate gradually for the loss. No one knows why, but it doesn't happen in pure stands of fir. There must be alders. I haven't told Robyn yet.

About five years after I drilled and plugged my chain-sawed alders, I got a crop of Shiitake mushrooms. They were tasty enough, but- for all the effort, and knowing what I've discovered about colours, catkins, nitrogen, bears, salmon, lace and the Grand Canal in Venice, I've decided to leave them in the ground (although I might just thin a few when no one's looking).

Backyard Binky   22 November

"For a good life: Work like a dog. Eat like a horse. Think like a fox. And play like a rabbit."

George Allen

It's a rare November weekend morning that is as sunny as this one. Robyn is downstairs making coffee, and I'm looking out the ensuite window at a fat juicy one. Sometimes in the Summer, the sunrise finds the orchard festooned with them. Today, however, there is just a lone buck, quietly chewing up the last of this year's salad garden. Suddenly, he shoots into the air, twisting his head and body in opposite directions, before firing sideways into one of the cedar plank raised beds. Stunned cold. Luckily, he regains consciousness quickly enough to evade the charge, zigzag jumping a wide circle into the safety of the blackberry bramble, before Shiva has a chance to turn him into breakfast.

That was a *binky*, a happy rabbit dance. Fortunately, the rabbit had four lucky rabbits' feet and Shiva had none, or the result might have ended less happily for the dancer.

Rabbits, like much of our flora and fauna, are not native to Vancouver Island. The Eastern Cottontail (*Sylvilagus floridanus*) that threw his binky today, was a descendent of those introduced in the late 1920's to western Washington for hunting. These white-tailed *lagamorphs* (they are not rodents) didn't take very long to migrate across to the lower Fraser Valley, but it wasn't until 1964 that they were introduced to the Island, in Sooke. Hopping north along the eastern coast, they finally arrived at Westwood Lake, about the same time that Robyn and I did. The only other species of rabbit found on Vancouver Island is the introduced European Rabbit (*Oryctolagus cuniculus*). Every day on my way to the hospital, at the bottom of Westwood Lake Road, there are herds of these big black bunnies, chewing obliviously along the roadside. Occasionally, one gets too oblivious, and ends up *debinkified.* I do confess that there have been occasions, driving home in the middle of a night on call, when I've had to swerve. Sometimes, the rabbit even gets away. More often (and tragically), the following evening I am compelled to fetch a young Italian red, up from the depths of the cellar, in honour of his passing. This skill set has not been without some degree of unfair social stigmatization. Certain friends have insisted on seeing supermarket receipts, before agreeing to come for dinner.

That rabbits survive at all is impressive, considering some of their design flaws. They have a large *blind spot* right in front of their face- this is a feeble defensive advantage in the game of binky, and even less so in a world of carnivores. Rabbits generally use the same trails every day (their home range is between three to six acres), where all of a bunny's needs can be met. Even when running from danger, a Cottontail rabbit will usually stay on its trail. When encountered, predators can literally scare a rabbit to death. Rabbits suffer *heat stroke,* because the only place a rabbit sweats is through the pads on its feet. A four pound rabbit will drink as much water as a twenty pound dog. Rabbits need to eat hay to prevent fur balls obstructing their stomachs and, at the same time, are incapable of vomiting. Unlike hares, which are born with hair and able to see (*precocial*), rabbits are *altricial*, having young that are born hairless and blind. Several years ago my father-in-law, Ron, and I were digging in the garden when *Precious*, our adopted feral Maine coon cat, made three distinct appearances within an hour, each time with a poor little blind bundle, waiting to come into full view of our potential appreciation, before the crunching began. "Now you're just showing off," said a disgusted Ron, after the third *Kit-Kat* snack attack. About 85% of rabbits are killed every year by predators, and only 25% live more than one year.

So what species survival mechanisms do rabbits have, that counterbalance these various disadvantages? Running, hiding and breeding. The running part is crucial, if you are born a cute blob of pudgy protein. Rabbits can run up to 35 miles an hour, with jumps as long as 15 feet, and as high as 36 inches. Shiva knows, all too well, how hard it is to hang onto the scent of a crisscrossing Cottontail at full torque. Rabbits also move about on the tips of their toes (*digitigrade* locomotion), which assists with a lightning burst out of the starting gate. Unfortunately for the Cottontail, Shiva shares this advantage. Other than coloration and quiet, rabbits have other special advantages when laying low. Despite their forward blind spot, their large eyes allow them to see behind, without rotating their heads. Their long sensitive ears can turn in any direction, and also help with temperature regulation. Rabbits are *crepuscular*, most active around dawn or dusk. When frightened or caught by a predator, a rabbit will either produce a loud foot thump, or produce a horrible, eerie, high-pitched banshee scream to warn the warren. Once you've heard one, it will haunt you forever. Because rabbits need to eat and run, and what they eat is almost indigestible *cellulose*, they have evolved a unique solution to both challenges, by possessing 28 continuously growing teeth and passing two distinct types of feces: hard droppings which you will find, and soft black viscous pellets, which you will not. These are called *Cecotropes* or 'night feces' and, because they come from the cecum, are high in protein, vitamins and minerals. Rabbits re-ingest them at night at their leisure, chewing them 120 times a minute (unfortunate that, with over 17,000 taste buds, this all occurs in the absence of a young Italian red). Rabbits, like some humans, are social, loving, and interactive. Each rabbit has his own strong individual identity, and all have very good memories. Finally, even if you can run and you can hide, it may still not be enough to absolutely guarantee the perpetuation of your genes. The third counterbalance to extinction is, well, that they breed like rabbits. Does produce their first litter of 4-9 kits when they are 3 months old, after a gestation period of about 28 days. As soon as she has covered her new young in one nest, she will immediately mate again, producing 20-40 babies in a year. The kits are fed for about 5 minutes a day, at night. At 10 days of age they open their eyes and immediately begin to sample the grass, just outside the den entrance. After a month, the young rabbits are weaned, and are completely on their own. Nobody hibernates over the winter. Domestic rabbits are incapable of breeding with the wild ones.

How many rabbits would you have after a given period of time? How vital is the math? Utterly. The solution for the rabbit breeding calculation problem laid the foundation for all modern mathematics. It gave us our decimal number system. It gave us the number zero. It gave us the mathematics of nature (tree branches, the family tree of honeybees, the pattern of florets in a sunflower head, artichokes and pineapples), art and music (the first movement of Béla Bartók's *Music for Strings, Percussion, and Celesta*), our financial markets (also giving us the number zero recently), and many other treasures. It was solved by the son of a thirteenth century Italian merchant, who served as a customs officer in North Africa. His name was Leonardo da Pisa, but he is better known as Fibonacci. He published his masterwork, the *Liber Abaci*, in 1202. In Chapter 12, Fibonacci posed, and solved, a problem involving the growth of a hypothetical population of rabbits, based on idealized assumptions. In 1225, Emperor Frederick II had organized a tournament, at which the following question was posed:

'Beginning with a single pair of rabbits, if every month each productive pair bears a new pair, which becomes productive when they are 1 month old, how many rabbits will there be after n months?'

The solution, generation by generation, was a sequence of numbers now known as the *Fibonacci numbers*. The answer is $xn_{+1} = xn + xn_{-1}$. After one year, a single pair has produced 377 rabbits. If there are no predators, as Thomas Austin found out when he brought 24 pairs to Barwon Park, Australia in 1859, Fibonacci quickly becomes the most significant historical figure in your life. By 1890, the population of rabbits was a plague. The Government of Western Australia's solution was to construct an 1833 kilometre-long anti-rabbit fence from Starvation Boat Harbour in the south all the way to Cape Keraudren. It was finished in 1907. So was the solution. By the time it was done, the rabbits had left it far behind. In 1918 a Brazilian scientist, Beaureparie Aragao, suggested that Australia import the rabbit-killing *myxoma virus*. In the 1950s, after considerable testing, the CSIRO introduced myxomatosis into the Murray River Valley, but the intial success lasted only a few years. Subsequent attempts at eradication have included the introduction of European and Spanish Rabbit fleas, *caliciviruses* (mutations of which are used on rabbit-breeding farms in Spain), and attempts at immune-mediated contraception. Good bloody luck, mate.

Fertility is just one of the many ways we symbolize rabbits in folklore and mythology. But it is the most important and often associated with innocent playful sexuality or rebirth, from the *Playboy* bunny to the Easter bunny, and everything in between. A pantheon of four hundred rabbit gods in Aztec mythology represented fertility, parties, and drunkenness. The Chinese associate a rabbit's foot with fertility, prosperity, hope, abundance and good weather. African-American folk magic, called *hoodoo*, is the reason why so many Americans carry a rabbit's foot as an amulet on their keychains. This is thought to bring good luck, likely untrue as the rabbit would confirm. After fertility, the rabbit is the symbol of the trickster. In Central Africa, *Kalulu* the rabbit is known to always get the better bargains. American African slaves, mixing their rabbit tales with those of local Native American tribes (who thought the rabbit danced on a tightrope between the good and evil), created *Br'er rabbit* who, although getting himself into all sorts of mischief, was always saved by his clever tongue. The Cajuns also had a trickster rabbit, *Compare Lapin*, undoubtedly inspired by Br'er Rabbit. The most famous anthropomorphised cwafty wascal wabbit was, of course, Bugs Bunny, a major source of Warner Brothers' prosperity. There are many other types of rabbit myths, legends and children's tales (e.g. Peter Cottontail) of course, but the themes of fecundity and flimflam seem to predominate.

Rabbit fertility is far from being a totally negative phenomenon, by any means. In the 1920s, it was discovered that pregnant women's urine contained the hormone *HCG*, and that this could change the appearance of rabbit ovaries. The only way to find out at that time was to sacrifice the rabbit to inspect them, and that gave rise to the erroneous expression, 'the rabbit died'.

One man's pest is another man's productivity, and rabbits are deliberately bred for food and companionship. The food part is called *cuniculture*. When I'm not bringing home the fruits of my careless driving technique, Robyn and I are more than happy to have one of Deborah's domesticated lapins, to accompany that young Italian red for dinner. One can't make a regular diet of rabbits, however, because they are missing some essential amino assets. Those who eat nothing but bunnies develop a condition known as *rabbit starvation*. We didn't truly appreciate this in 1975 at NASA Ames Research Centre where, as the Life Support Consultant for a space colony to be built at *Lagrange Point 5*, we had to pick a source of rapidly producible protein for 10,000 inhabitants. We picked bunnies.

The companionship part is a booming business. The *American Rabbit Breeders Association* has over 30,000 members cuddling 45 recognized breeds of rabbits (I shudder to run the Fibonacci numbers on where this is going).

There are other aspects of Bunny behavior that are a bit unusual. Rabbits will box each other in territorial disputes (no *rabbit punches*, however; these refer to the manner in which the rabbits themselves were dispatched with a brainstem blow to the back of the head, illegal in human boxing). In courtship, rabbits urinate on each other, and then groom, before mating. Females will pull out their own fur to line their nests. The best bizarre behavior, though, is still the binky. And I know it's not limited to rabbits.

Shiva will do a spontaneous backyard binky, consisting of a sudden burst of careening around the garden boxes and orchard trees, and ending in a contorted ass-over-teakettle rollover. Robyn and I have had our own backyard binkies. My father, the Summer before he died, came out to visit. He moved slowly, as if through water, with his Parkinson's, and his age. He ended up in the Chardonnay vineyard, my Chilean sombrero on his head, a glass in his hand, and the wry wascal smile that was his trademark, when he was about to be innocently naughty. The sun was streaming through the vines in the late afternoon. Then, without warning, Kelvin did a rabbit dance. It was the best binky I ever saw.

The Queen of Westwood 29 November

"And I will prepare destroyers against thee, every one with his weapons: and they shall cut down thy choice cedars, and cast them into the fire."

Jeremiah 22:7

She is sleek, this cedarstrip craft, paddled through the early morning mists, among the ghostly spires from which she was fashioned. The brass on the bow is engraved with her name. Another silent stroke guides the Queen of Westwood through smoked glass. Every year, Robyn and I carry her out of the wine cellar as a rite of spring, and every autumn she seems to resist her return to hibernation. Like most empresses, she tends to be a tad unbalanced and tipsy, especially at full speed. On one occasion, we made the mistake of leaving Shiva behind on the shore. About halfway across the lake, we turned to the unmistakable sound of slapping on water. People paddles failed to stay ahead of dogpaddles. The last thing we saw were two paws over the left gunnel. Angular momentum took us halfway to the waterline, and overcompensation did the rest. Everybody paddled home wet, and warm with the laughter that fell out of the canoe.

The water we fell into wasn't always there. Its history began with the birth of Joseph Westwood in 1792, in Old Swinford, Worcester, in England. In the same year, a French physician, Pierre Ordinaire, invented *absinthe,* the bitter wormwood-based *green fairy* or, as the English described it, the '*green curse of France.*' Joseph was a career soldier, and fought in the battle that defeated Napoleon at Waterloo in 1815. The same year he married Jane Pearson. Three years later, they had the first of five sons, William Joseph Westwood, the man after whom the lake is named. Joseph retired from the army in 1850, and emigrated to Canada ten years later. He worked as a blacksmith in Nanaimo, and died in February of 1888.

Son William, meanwhile, had found his own way to St. Louis, Missouri, where he lived for several years. In 1852, he crossed the west in a Prairie Schooner heading to California. He was detained by the Mormons in Salt Lake City, who refused to allow him to move on because, as strange as this seems, he was a musician. William was persuaded to play and sing in their *Tabernacle,* until he ultimately found a way to escape with a company of soldiers, also heading to California. In 1860, William moved to Victoria, where he purchased and managed the *Lion Brewery.* Two years later, he moved again, this time to Nanaimo. He bought six hundred and fifty acres in Mountain District (now East Wellington), all the way from Jingle Pot Road to Departure Bay.

When William purchased the land, the lake that now bears his name was just a marsh. William started a dairy farm, the first dairyman to supply milk to the residents of Nanaimo. Eleven years after William's death in 1883, the *Wingate Coal Company* bought his land. The coal, which we can still find on the trail around the lake, was used to power the electric plant, built in 1888, by the *Nanaimo Electric Light,*

Power and Heating Company. In 1904, the company built a hydroelectric plant and dam on the Millstone River and, in 1908, the *No. 2 Dam* was completed on Darough Creek at Westwood Lake, to hold water during the winter, and release it over the summer months.

The many remaining redcedar snags we paddle through, are the pyramids of our local history; the water we fell into is our Aswan. Under the water there is an old goat farm, originally owned by two brothers. There is also a grim local legend about how one of the brothers was chopping wood, while the other was in town, and accidently hacked off one of his legs. Because the truck was also in town, the injured man waited in pain and frustration until, going quite mad, he hacked off the leg of one of the goats and used it to replace his own. When his brother finally returned, the only thing he found was a human leg. To this day, if you're swimming in the lake and feel something touch your leg, it's the *Goat Man of Westwood*, looking for his lost appendage. I am not writing a ghost story about the water, however. This is an account of the ghostly spires, and the reason they still stand in the lake.

Western redcedar (*Thuja plicata*) is the provincial tree of British Columbia. There is no space between the red and the cedar because it is not a real cedar. The Americans have provided, (as is their wont), the more accurate name of *Giant Arborvitae*, the proverbial 'tree of life'. The ethnobotanist Wade Davis has described redcedar as home to '*a constellation of life unique on earth*', and in danger of being logged to extinction. The largest known specimen on the planet is the Quinault Lake redcedar, in the Valley of the Rainforest Giants, 40 km. north of Aberdeen, Washington. It is 144 feet high, 20 feet in diameter, hollow, and over 2000 years old. The biggest redcedar used to stand 243 feet high in Cathedral Grove just down the road, until it was set on fire and destroyed by vandals, in 1972.

Some West Coast tribes refer to themselves as the '*People of the Redcedar*' because, for them, the tree really did sustain their lives. There is archaeological evidence that immense canoes were used over 4,000 years ago to harpoon whales on the high seas. (In 1901, one of these 38-foot-long Nootkan craft was bought by adventurer Captain John Voss for $80 from a native woman, with the help of a '*drap of ol Rye*'. Voss, who was wanted by the Americans for alleged smuggling of drugs and illegal Chinese labour, rigged her, christened her *Tilikum* ('friend,' in Chinook), and sailed her on a three-year fascinating voyage from British Columbia to London).

The First Nations' harvesting and use of redcedar was defined by gender and season. In springtime, as the sap rose, women of all ages ventured into the forest to strip bark. This had to be done with care, or the tree would die. Bark was taken only from redcedars that had not previously been stripped, and always less than half the circumference of the tree. Cuts were made above the buttresses, and stripped upwards with the aid of rope-hung platforms, suspended up to 65 feet into the upper branches. Surviving redcedars with evidence of this former activity that predate 1846, are considered archeological sites, and protected under the *B.C. Heritage Conservation Act*. The women folded the harvested bark and carried it home in backpacks, where it could be safely stored without concern about decomposition.

How did they use the bark, branches, and rootlets they collected? For everything for which we now use petroleum: baskets, bags, weavings, ropes, string, bindings, blankets, bedding, towels, skirts, mats, ponchos, capes, belts, necklaces, rain hats and ceremonial headdresses, children's balls, canoe bailers, sails, nets, fishing line, and the tree-climbing equipment they needed to harvest more. The inner bark was dried and ground, for thickening soups and in other food preparation. The pitch from the trunk was chewing gum.

The men would take over and harvest the rest of the tree in the drier summer and autumn. This was permeated with ritual, as the redcedar's spirit required propitiation, if it were not to drop it's branches on the fallers. The unfaithful and modern day professional Native loggers still say a little prayer before firing up their chainsaws. There was no steel and no infernal combustion for the First Nations harvesters, of course. All they had were stone tools, fire, and time. Lots of time. After removing the bark at the base of the tree above the buttresses, adzes and mauls were used to make a wide triangular cut in the trunk. Wet clay and moss were packed above and below the cut as a fire retardant. Kindling and tinder were packed into the cut and ignited, and then the stone tools were brought in again, when the fire died. Cutting and burning would alternate for many days with a continuing rotation of attendants, until the tree was finally penetrated, and fell in the chosen direction. Depending on its intended use, the redcedar was stripped and towed in the round, for totem poles or building materials, or rough-carved for canoes before dragging. Rough planks could be split from live trees, which continued to grow because of their inherent resistance to decay.

How did they use the wood they collected? For everything for which we now use wood: building posts and beams, boards for walls, roofing, chests, bowls, platters, children's cradles, cooking tongs, looms, drying racks, canoes and paddles, from toys to coffins and a few things we don't use it for: carved poles, posts, figures, and masks, fishing floats and spears, salmon traps, fire drills, arrows and quivers, paint brushes, rattles and whistles, speakers' staffs, and the magnificent bentwood boxes, with all four sides constructed by notching and steaming a single redcedar plank. *'Like the bountiful salmon of the sea, the ubiquitous tree gave of it self to sustain and enrich their lives.'* It really was their tree of life.

Since the mid 1800's, we haven't used redcedar for anywhere near as many applications. We just use much, much more of it. About 6 million cubic metres per year, or about 900 million board feet, worth about $1 billion annually (and 85% exported to the U.S.- as is their wont). Since we only have around 750 million cubic metres of redcedar left (nearly three-quarters of it in old growth forest more than 250 years old), and since stand dominance in Coastal Alaska and BC is declining due to poor natural regeneration, and an inherently slower natural growth rate, Wade Davis may be right about logging it to extinction. How do we use the wood we collect? Mostly? For roofing shakes and shingles (and the occasional guitar soundboard).

The only weapon a mature Western Redcedar has, to retaliate against a determined industrial logging juggernaut, is *plicatic acid.* This low molecular weight compound is the cause of the most common form of occupational asthma in the Pacific Northwest, affecting about 10% of the exposed population. It doesn't give them a bloody nose, just a runny one. (Amazingly though, another extract of cedar leaf oil is used in *Vicks Vap-O-Rub,* that salve that your mother used to dab under your nose at night, to help clear your sinuses and loosen your chest.)

The other chemistry of *Thuja plicata* is equally enthralling. Redcedar is legendary for its durability and resistance to disintegration. This is due to a unique family of chemicals contained in the heartwood. Thujic acid repels moths, termites and other insects.

Three *thujaplicin* compounds have unusual seven-member rings called *tropolones*. The *alpha thujaplicin* (*hinokitol*), and the *beta* form, have antibacterial properties. The beta form has anti-fungal properties (the *gamma* form is effective against some stomach cancers). Redcedar closets and chests exist because these chemicals also protect their cloth contents from being eaten. The wood can remain sound for over a hundred years. The Ghostly Spires of Westwood, in fact, are celebrating their centenary this year. There are two other redcedar molecules that are even more marvelous. The first is *thujone* which, aside from having deterrent weevil-eating properties, is the psychoactive ingredient in wormwood. It is the inspirational green fairy in absinthe. By the 1860s, when William Westwood began milking his first cows, absinthe was becoming so popular in French bars and bistros that 5 o'clock anywhere was called *l'heure verte* (the 'green hour'). It was the mother's milk of Van Gogh, Manet, Toulouse-Lautrec, Verlaine, de Maupassant, Modigliani, Picasso, Hemingway, and Oscar Wilde, who described the absinthe sensation as like having tulips on his legs. Thujone is a *GABA antagonist*, and no one knows how it synergizes with the alcohol it's dissolved in. British Columbia, unlike other more Presbyterian provinces, has no restrictions on the thujone concentration that absinthe can contain.

My favorite redcedar molecule is the crushed apple pear drop pungent menthol smell molecule, *methyl thujate (5,5-dimethyl-1,3,6-cycloheptatriene-1-methylcarboxylate)*. It is the backbone of the redcedar leaf oil used for making perfumes, shoe polish, deodorants, insecticides, soaps, dog collars, and instant fire logs, although nothing, nothing at all, smells as wonderful as a handsaw going through a real fresh redcedar log.

From the Battle of Waterloo, to milk and green fairies, coal and chainsaws, goats and ghostly spires, the Western Redcedar is the true Arborvitae. I love the empress of the lake and her little brass plaque on the bow. But, in my heart, I also know- the real Queen of Westwood is Robyn.

Ice Flowers 28 January

"I used to be Snow White, but I drifted"

Mae West

I've just come in from some sunny Winter pruning in the vineyard. There are still undulating seas of snow, from the blowing December storms that Robyn and I missed by leaving early for New Zealand. Last week, we travelled from barefoot beachcombing, back across the dateline, into the deep freeze. This afternoon, I worked on white islands of crunch and sparkle, between the rows of vines. On my way back through the hazelnut orchard, I slowed my wheelbarrow, tossing in my secateurs, *Cowichan* sweater, and toque. Shirts followed. It was one of those rare, solar, zigzag, glistening January days, that make you want to lie down naked in the hoar frost diamonds, and make angels. Snowblind from the reflected glare, and with all sound muffled by the ground cushion of frozen coral, I started a *Tai Chi* set, moving like syrup through the grove of glazed filbert branches. Shiva jumped into the routine, in a wolfish attempt to ward off the witchcraft. When I finally gave in, she went back to rolling in the snow.

Most of my memories as a child, in Northwestern Ontario, occurred in ice and snow. My trudge to school was a hunched-over meeting of parka hood and galoshes. It kept out the wind and cold, and parental instructions. We built snow forts, and stored our snowball ammunition in the family freezer, whenever there was an escalation in hostilities. We shoved snow down each other's clothing, slid down hills on toboggans, and peed our names in the snowbanks, with yellow calligraphic flourishes. We raced our snowmobiles across frozen lakes, and shovelled our driveways so the snowploughs could come by and then, of course, we shovelled again. We made snowmen and cross-country ski trails, and holes in the lake ice, to sauna and catch fish. Very rarely, we had a '*Snow Day*,' when we were allowed not to go to class. Missing school was a profound admission of existential failure. Snow was a medium of expression, and an integral substrate of life. While Robyn was growing up in New Zealand, with the sting of salt spray surfing, and the abrasive sand blown off the dunes at Port Waikato, I was catching the branches, needles, and bullets of snow crystals with my rosy face, on Rabbit Lake.

We thought we knew everything that was important to know about snow. We knew how to walk on it, ski on it, and drive our father's car on it. We learned not to put our tongues on metal signposts. We knew that each snowflake was unique, but we didn't know that Nancy Knight would find two identical snowflakes in Wisconsin, in 1988. We also didn't know that a snowflake, sixteen inches wide, was measured at Fort Keogh, Montana a hundred years earlier. Turns out we didn't know much about snow at all.

The second century Chinese wrote about ice crystal symmetry. A Dominican bishop, Albertus Magnus, studied snow crystals in the late 1200s. In 1611, Johannes Kepler, the guru of planetary motion, printed a small opus, *Strena Seu de Nive Sexangula (*A New Year's Gift of Hexagonal Snow*).*

'These were little plates of ice, very flat, very polished, very transparent, about the thickness of a sheet of rather thick paper...but so perfectly formed in hexagons, and of which the six sides were so straight, and the six angles so equal, that it is impossible for men to make anything so exact.'

In 1635, Rene Descartes also mused about the hexagonality of snowflakes. (We now know that the two hydrogen atoms branching off the oxygen atom do so at an angle of 120 degrees; this is the grand determinant of all the various shapes that snowflakes can take). Thirty years later, Robert Hooke published *Micrographia*, containing sketches of snowflakes viewed under his microscope. But it was Wilson 'Snowflake' Bentley, an American farmer from Jericho, Vermont, who took the study of the snowflake to the next level. Bentley found a way to catch them on black velvet, so they could be photographed before they melted, More than two thousand images were published in *Snow Crystals*, in 1931. It was Bentley who referred to snowflakes as *'tiny miracles of beauty'* and *'ice flowers.'* He was commemorated by an obscure indie pop group, *Tilly and the Wall*, on their 2006 Album, *Bottoms of Barrels:*

> *'Like Wilson Bentley found on black velvet,*
> *A beauty so strange,*
> *Something he didn't expect,*
> *It's a unique find that only some people get.'*

Not long after Mr. Bentley captured his snowflake images, the bean counters arrived. In 1951, the *International Commission on Snow and Ice* brought out an *International Classification System*, which defined seven main snow crystals (needles, plates, stellar crystals, columns, spatial dendrites, capped columns, and irregular forms- plus ice pellets, hail, and graupel. (Oh yeah, and diamond dust). Simple, but too simple. Nuclear physicist Ukichiro Nakaya published his classification of 41 falling snowflake morphologies, in his *Snow Crystals: Natural and Artificial*, in 1954. The most complex system (Magono and Lee, 1966) now has over 80 types of snow crystal documented. There are needles, sheaths, columns, pyramids, cups, bullets, plates, scrolls, branches, dendritic crystals, stellar crystals, stellar crystals with plates, dendritic crystals with branches, hollow bullets, bullets with dendrites, plates with scrolls, plates with spatial dendrites, rimed particles, rimed needle crystals, lump graupels, graupel-like snow with non-rimed extensions, yada yada.

With this many types of snow crystals, you can imagine how many kinds of snow there are. The Inuit have fifty-two names for snow (and Margaret Atwood feels that there should be as many names for love; but there are, just as there are as many names for Margaret Atwood). We actually do have a large number of names for snow- we have *fresh snow, equitemperature snow, melt-freeze corn* or *spring snow, kinetic snow* or *sugar snow* or *depth hoar* (mother-of-all-avalanches snow), *firn, blowing snow, chopped powder, packed powder, packing snow, crud, crust, finger drift, penitentes, pillow drift, slush, snirt, wind slab,* and *grits* (artificial snow). And ice. The world's glaciers are quickly disappearing and, with them, a window on the ancient natural history of the planet. A borehole in Greenland several years ago found the ice at the bottom had formed from snow that fell 200,000 years ago.

Snow is usually white because of the pattern of random light refraction described as the *Wegner-Bergeron-Findeison process*- but there are snows of other colours. On February 2, 2007, a heavy sandstorm in Kazakhstan caused 580 square miles of Siberian Orange Snow. My favorite snow is caused by a red algae, *Chlamydomonas nivalis*. It's called *watermelon snow* and smells like a summer picnic.

If snowflakes and snow have qualitative nuances, it's usually the quantity that most captures our attention. We got more snow this year than in any other year in the previous forty-four. But complain as we do, the snowpack continues to be the most consistent guarantee of our having enough water in our reservoirs. The annual snowmelt from the Columbia River, alone, is about 26 trillion gallons, enough to cover a state the size of Kansas in knee-deep water.

Snow has imprinted every one of my senses. Some of my best memories are still lit by snowlight. Sound travels more smoothly over snow. I know the tactile characteristics of the thirty-two kinds. In my youth, I could probably have told you the day of the year by the smell and the taste. And now I'll tell you something else- love it as we do for a few days, Robyn and I didn't move to Westwood lake for the ice flowers.

Benson 02 February

"Great things are done when men and mountains meet.
This is not done by jostling in the street"

William Blake

It was late afternoon when Shiva and I met them on the ridges. We were climbing, and they were lost. British couple, mid-thirties, corpulent, very posh. "Excuse me, but is this the way to the top of Mount Benson?" asked the man. I said no. "Would you be so kind as to point us in the right direction?" I commented that it was getting rather late in the day for a stroll up to over a thousand metres, and inquired if they had a map. "Oh yes," he replied, pulling a folded tourist brochure out of his pocket. I asked if they had a cellphone. "No, but we have a GPS." I must have been staring. "Great," I said. "So you'll know exactly where you are when you die."

Mount Benson is the anchor rock Westwood Lake backstop, that stops us falling away to Tokyo. It is our *mundaily* toxin cleanser, our chanterelle pantry, and our almanac. No summer garden is planted, until all the snow is gone from the summit. From the Island Highway, a B.C. Ferry, or a puddle-jumper plane from Vancouver, when Mount Benson comes into view, Robyn and I know that we're almost home.

As harsh as my comment to the English couple was, Benson is not a salvatory. It has always been an aerial arena of clashing natural forces, economic and recreational vested interests, and last refuges. Its slopes, like those of most other mountains, have been witness to, and the cause of life and death, and occasional rescues. Snowmobilers have fallen through mountain lake ice, hermits have burned alive and, on October 17, 1951, the three people on the Queen Charlotte Airlines Flight 102 from Kitimat flew right into the mountain face at 1600 feet, when the Canso pilot mistook Nanaimo for Vancouver. Two hikers died of hypothermia in January, 2002. They had no means to start a fire, no map or compass, no flashlight, no extra clothes or a space blanket, and no extra food and water. Their cell phone ceased working for 'unknown reasons'. The lives of those that died elsewhere are often commemorated on the mountain, with bronze plaques, scattered daffodils, or scattered ashes.

The mountain is named after Alfred Robson Benson, physician, photographer, and naturalist, '*well known for his open hospitality and cordial good nature.*' In June of 1849, at the age of 34, he arrived in Esquimault, on the three-masted barque, *Harpooner*, crowded with men bound for the coalfields in Fort Rupert, just northwest of Port Hardy. Benson had signed on as a Hudson's Bay Company Surgeon and Clerk, and initially served in Victoria and Vancouver, Washington. It was in his role as a Clerk that he likely had more historical influence. In his drafting of the 1850 Treaty with the Swengwhung Tribe, Dr. Benson traded seventy-five pounds Sterling, for a vast tract of land which became '*the entire property of the white people for ever.*' The deal was sealed with the signature of '*Snaw-nuck, his X mark and 29 others.'* Five years later he 'retired' to England, but something drew him back and, in August of 1856, Benson once again sailed from London to Vancouver Island, on Captain Trivett's *Princess Royal.* Because of some trouble with the Chinook natives, the ship was armed with eight 9-pounder guns, and smaller firearms for possible defense, if required, in the Juan de Fuca Strait. On the outward journey, the crew and passengers were drilled in *'call to quarters'*. Benson had boasted that he would be the first to be dressed and on deck. One night the call came, but Benson did not appear. Someone had stolen into the Doctor's berth, switched where his coat and pants were hanging, and tied his leg bottoms together. The prank's victim was, apparently, unimpressed.

From 1857 to 1862, Benson was the Hudson's Bay Company's Nanaimo Western Department Surgeon. His warmheartedness and eccentricity were legendary. Charles Wilson described him, in 1958, as *'a great character, never seen without a pipe in his mouth and his rooms are crowded with Indian curiosities, bird skins, geological specimens, books and tobacco in the most inextricable confusion.'* It was common to meet the Doctor with his coat buttoned over by the first button through the second button-hole, or even a more ludicrous hitch than that, or with one leg of his pants inside, and the other outside his sea boots. "*Ah,*" he had said to his colleague, John Helmcken, "*you laugh, but if you were to remain here a few months you would, of necessity, become the same.*" His Irish terrier, *Bizzie*, occasionally bit the legs of his patients and, if the victims retaliated, they were rewarded with more vigour and less anesthesic than they might otherwise have received. And, although medicine was supplied free of charge by the HBC, patients were told to *'bring a bottle'*. He had a promissory note in the amount of $300 from Ulysses S. Grant, in connection with *'some horse deal'*. No one knows if he ever collected on that, but he certainly had a banner year in 1859. He was elected to the provincial legislature, as the representative from Nanaimo (there was only one qualified voter and that one vote, strangely enough, belonged to Dr. Benson). More significantly, the good doctor acted as chairman of a '*literary meeting*', at which the main speaker was a Doctor Wood of Her Majesty's surveying vessel, the *Plumper*. Shortly afterwards, the vessel's Captain Richards christened the large rock in our back yard '*Mount Benson*'. Alfred married in 1861, but his wife died a mere two years later, a year after he was recalled to Fort Victoria. Benson's historical record then starts to fade. He was a partner in the *Harewood Coal Company*, until he failed to raise enough money to exploit his claim. He ultimately died at the age of 89, in Whitby, Yorkshire, England.

And what of his namesake, and how it has fared, since Alfred's death? Mount Benson was logged in the 1930's, and a fire destroyed the regenerating forest twenty-one years later. By the time that Robyn and I moved to Westwood Lake in 1988, however, the mountainsides were revitalized and native flora and fauna were returning. The hiking was world class. Then, once more, came the commodity merchants. Seven years ago, the whine and roar of chainsaws began again, when the expatriate landowners of the mountaintop began to cut down trees, punch in roads, and generally lay waste to natural watercourses, moss and mycelium undergrowth and special places you had to hike up to appreciate. They did it fast and furious, the way most developers do it. But they did it for all to see, and the resultant outrage did them in. One autumn morning, I emerged onto a plain of devastation, a pristine stream bed, lined with huckleberries and salal only a week earlier. There was a sign posted on one of the fir trees that did not have a pink plastic ribbon of selection wrapped around it- '*WANTED for information leading to the arrest and conviction of terrorists breaking gates* *and locks on mt benson road $1000'*, followed by a phone number. I looked at the moonscape. I looked back at the sign. Moonscape. Sign. I came home and wrote the local paper a letter:

'We all likely see and feel something a little different when we look at Mount Benson. Logging companies see cellulose and feel avaricious. Mountain bikers see topography and feel adrenalin. Mushroom pickers see moss and feel the rains coming. Realty companies see the top and feel a buyer any day now. Native people see their heritage and feel hope and disenfranchisement. Communication companies see the spires at the summit and feel microwaves. The Department of Defense, the Canada Lands Corporation, and the Regional District of Nanaimo see 'stakeholders' and feel conflicted. Hikers, bird-watchers, picnickers, and pilots appreciate the Mountain in different ways. Whether driving from the north or south, we see Mount Benson and know we are home.

The problem is there is no one really protecting the Mountain from Weyerhaeser or the Mountain bikers. The latter group have created more root damage, subsoil disturbance, and erosion from carving new trails-of-the-day than they are likely to admit to. Occasionally, a minority also pose a hazard to hikers when they seem to come out of nowhere at warp speed. The logging company, for its part, has been turning second growth forest into a mud bath on the slopes of Benson since at least early summer (and I found out today have also cut off the trail to Ammonite Falls with similar activity).

We need to ask the question: What activities will serve to protect the special qualities of Mount Benson while, at the same time, maximize taxable revenue that will benefit our community most directly? The answer has already been discovered in many other parts of the world. Do not export natural resources in their primary form using the fewest local workers hired by large foreign companies that send profits overseas- as much as we need to support the needs of these workers.

Instead, bring people with money and specialized interests to very profitable local niche ecotourism ventures that will leave the area as unimpacted as possible. It is the same principle that makes a sport-fishing salmon more valuable than one on a commercial fishing boat. British bird-watchers, French hikers, German mushroom foragers, Japanese solitude seekers-they're all out there waiting for the right marketing appeal to their specific consciousness.

I propose that we establish a Mount Benson Ecological Reserve so that mountain bikers may continue to bike, that hikers may continue to hike, picnickers to picnic, solitude seekers to find solitude. These activities all have commercialization potential, if we tread lightly. If you agree, please write the Regional District and this newspaper. If you don't, write them anyway.

We will not get many opportunities to get this right. We certainly don't have it right at the moment. Henry David Thoreau once said that 'a man is rich in proportion to the number of things which he can afford to let alone'. Maybe we can do something together to ensure that one part of our world continues to be special. So that we can continue to see and feel something a little different when we look at Mount Benson'.

Actually, Henry David Thoreau had an awful lot to say about mountains. Here's a sampling:

"I keep a mountain anchored off eastward a little way, which I ascend in my dreams both awake and asleep. Its broad base spreads over a village or two, which does not know it; neither does it know them, nor do I when I ascend it. I can see its general outline as plainly now in my mind as that of Wachusett. I do not invent in the least, but state exactly what I see. I find that I go up it when I am light-footed and earnest. It ever smokes like an altar with its sacrifice. I am not aware that a single villager frequents it or knows of it. I keep this mountain to ride instead of a horse. You must ascend a mountain to learn your relation to matter, and so to your own body, for it is at home there, though you are not."

Henry David Thoreau, *Letter to Harrison Blake,* November 16, 1857

"The tops of mountains are among the unfinished parts of the globe, whither it is a slight insult to the gods to climb and pry into their secrets, and try their effect on our humanity. Only daring and insolent men, perchance, go there. Simple races, as savages, do not climb mountains – their tops are sacred and mysterious tracts never visited by them."

Henry David Thoreau, *Ktaadn, 1848*

For the moment, at least, Alfred Benson's namesake appears to have a future (as long as you don't fly over the other side of the mountain, or hear the whine and roar, or see the damage to the undergrowth now being created by ATVs, BMXs, and other acrid acronyms, now that the mountain is becoming a 'regional park'. Hopefully, it will not become just a sterile canopy.

I'm no mountaineer, but I have climbed mountains in my life. Kilimanjaro, Toubkal, Adam's Peak, dozens more whose names I can't recall. I'm still on fire from this one in our backyard, though. I have a favorite *You Tube* video of another young European couple sitting on the knoll at Westwood Lake. Looking up at Mount Benson. She is painfully contemplative, and he thinks there is something wrong.

"*What are you thinking?*" he says.
Slowly she answers, "*I think this is the most beautiful place I have ever been to in my life.*"
He asks, "*Your life?*"
"*My life*".

I think so too.

"Men go back to the mountains, as they go back to sailing ships at sea, because in the mountains and on the sea they must face up."

Henry David Thoreau

Afterthought:
The ghost of Alfred Benson might agree.

At Night Returning 15 February

"At night returning, every labour sped, He sits him down, the monarch of a shed"

Oliver Goldsmith, *The Traveler*

It was still three years before his death that he made the comment.
"A man needs a shed," he said, after a careful inspection of the orchard, raised beds, and ramshackle collection of rakes, shovels, hoes and other garden implements, barely supporting each other against the garage wall. My father was undoubtedly thinking of the *Canadian Tire* can-opener prefab metal shed that he had in Ontario years ago- a tiny windowless box of protruding sheet metal screws, and flimsy tin doors that always seem to come off their plastic sliders. This is not, however, the way Robyn and I do things.

That autumn we poured a concrete slab beside the garden. On it, we placed a palatial red cedar shelter, *compleat* with plexiglass skylight, and built-in potting bench that ran the length of the northern aspect. It was the *Cadillac* of garden sheds. We filled it with tools and joy, and wondered how we ever did without it before. When my father returned the following summer, he was initially horrified at what he perceived was extravagant overkill. But, as he was leaving for his return flight home, he uttered a final taciturn mumble.

"Like your shed."

The modern Oxford Dictionary (there is no other) defines a '*shed*' as

A slight structure built for shelter or storage, or for use as a workshop, either attached as a lean-to to a permanent building or separate; often with open front or sides. A special purpose is often indicated by a defining word prefixed, such as cart-, goat-, tool-.

The word derives from an old Teutonic root for *division* or *separation*. Maybe. The Old English word *sceadu* meant '*shade, shadow, darkness*'. A similar term, *skadwo*, was a '*shady place offering protection from glare or heat*'. The closest and first recognizable form of our modern word occurred in 1440 with a '*schudde, hovel, swyne kote or howse of sympyl hyllynge* [covering] *to kepe yn beestys*'. In 1481, note was made of a '*yearde in whiche was a shadde where in were six grete dogges*'. Whether *shadde, shad, shud,* or *shedde*, contained within the concept of a shed, was the idea of covered protection from without.

It was also a very old idea. In our cave-dwelling days, we had alcoves and smaller caves, that were used as separate storage areas. Geography determines climate; climate determines culture; culture determines how local materials are used to build covered protection. Underground silos lined with reed basketry were constructed by the ancient Egyptians, to store grain. Mammoth tusks and skins were bricks and mortar for early Europeans. Where the Anasazi used soft volcanic rock, the Inuit had only blocks of ice and snow. The essential difference between a house and a shed is, of course, not in building material but in material building. A shed is a separate shelter to store certain possessions. The notion of 'separate' is paramount. If cattle had been allowed on the living room carpet, Jesus, Mary and Joseph would have had a more commodious delivery room.

But a shed is more than a volumetric halfway between a cupboard and a barn, or a mini-storage rental. A shed has an infinite number of diverse uses, depending on the individual shed-owner. One can store tools and garden supplies and lawn equipment, keep yn beestys, hoard root vegetables or preserves, house a collection, hold trash and recyclables, hang sports equipment, or hone any number of hobbies in a shed. The most important purpose I'll return to.

It was the British who promoted the simple shed to an eclectic artform, as only their penchant for specialized knowlege can. The *Grand Tours* of English aristocrats in the 17th century returned home with a burning need to recreate the landmarks and ancient ruins they saw abroad. Elaborate buildings, with no purpose other than to decorate the gardens of the Wealthy, were constructed on hundreds of Estates. The proliferation of Gothic towers and fluted-columned pseudo-Classical outbuildings evoked an appropriate name for these grandiose sheds- they were called, very simply, '*Follies*'. There are, still in existence, outstanding examples of architectural indulgence: the Palladian Bridge in Buckinghamshire, and Wimpole's Folly in Cambridgeshire, being two of my favorite examples. Fortune affects the shed. Thomas Jefferson, on his estate at Monticello, had elegant sheds of maroon brick and white parapets (at least his had function as well as form). Robyn and I have cement and cedar and plexiglass.

As you approach our Folly, you would be greeted with a bonsai juniper and a Manzanita branch, on a bed of pea gravel, in front of a wide double zed door (actually you would be greeted by Shiva, but let's assume that you had an actual invitation). Above the door is an embossed sign brought over by New Zealand relatives that says '*Winkler's Whare*' (a whare is a 19th century Maori term, one of the meanings of which is '*a simple hut in the bush on newly occupied land*'). The only thing behind the door is sensory overload. Robyn's big orange Husqvarna riding mower crouches on its runway, ready to pounce. Along the southern wall hang all those garden implements that were barely supporting each other back in the old garage days, a bulletin board with pinned planting schedule and grape grafting instruction sheet, and cloth bags from trips to Peru and India, containing clips for the vineyard netting. Across the back are more tools, a license plate from *WINK Radio* in Fort Meyers, Florida, and the 5 hp Honda rototiller that I use to bounce off rocks in the spring. Along the north wall is the potting bench and under it, backpack sprayers, fertilizer, bone meal, lime, peat moss, potting soil, vermiculite, exotic vineyard antifungals, watering cans, gas cans, and a pushmower. Numerous shelves full of magnesium, Bordeaux mix, Roundup, tape gun staples and insecticide, are just off to your right. The rafters overhead are boobytrapped with bamboo poles, iron digging bars, a pole saw, weedeater, reemay, and other gravitational dangers.

That is what is in the shed.

'*Wisdom at times is found in Folly,*' if I quote Horace correctly. Another Horace (Walpole) had remarked that all Nature was a garden potting shed. Because the most important thing about a shed is not what is in it, but what is not. A shed is, above all, a private sanctuary. It fulfills the need for solace, retreat, and reflection, a '*male necessity*', especially in retirement, according to author Gordon Thorburn, in *Men and*

Sheds. One in five of this endangered subspecies uses the shed to escape from his spouse. Over twenty percent of Britons own a shed. The math is impressive. Almost 2.5 million men in Britain are hiding from their wives in their shed. They're called '*sheddies*', have their own magazine, *The Shed* (what else), and their own *National Shed Week* in July. This is not a bad thing. Clarkson of the Sunday Times said that '*Every invention that has ever mattered in the whole of human history has come from a man in a shed in Britain*'. The Aussies and the Kiwis have a similar proportion of sheddies.

There are two things one should never find in a shed: a mirror and a clock. For a shed is a place where a man should be content, to gain no little reflection and lose a little time. Oliver Goldsmith's Traveller *at night returning* had found that happiness depended more on the temper and regulation of his own mind than on what went on outside the shed. Maybe that's why my Father told me that every man needs one.

"If the fool would persist in his folly he would become wise."

William Blake

Love Potion Number Nine 21 February

"And fill all fruit with ripeness to the core;
To swell the gourd, and plump the hazel shells
With a sweet kernel"

John Keats, *To Autumn*

The image is always exquisitely surreal. Hundreds of long mustard-coloured caterpillar catkins, suspended against snow glare and tiny crimson flower buds. Because this nut case flowers in mid-winter. And then goes back to sleep until June.

They are all the children of a sudden solemn oath I swore to myself, while travelling through Central Turkey in July of 1983. It came flying off my taste buds, somewhere between the free cologne and beverages, handed out on every bus in Cappadoccia. My libation of choice in Asia Minor was mouth-puckering *Visne Suyu*, the most sublime cherry juice in the world. On the morning I had the epiphany, bottle in hand, one of my fellow passengers handed me a piece of bread, smeared with a brown paste that smelled of honey and earth. The taste was extraterrestrial. This *Findik Ezmesi*, this Turkish hazelnut butter, hit my hippocampus and I was resolved. Someday, I would plant a hazelnut orchard. Five years later, mapping out a scale drawing of our new Domaine on an old sheet of NASA graph paper, I sketched a half acre rectangle with 42 circles, each one representing a hazelnut tree. By the next summer they were in the ground, and I began to dream of opening jars of Westwood Lake Findik Ezmesi.

The hazelnut is a venerable old tree, but the nomenclature is enough to put you on your back. It belongs to the Birch (*Betulaceae*) family, and is a cousin to the nitrogen-fixing alders in the next paddock over. The term *'hazel'* comes from the Anglo-Saxon word for bonnet, *haesel*; and this, in turn, derives from the greek *korys* (as in Corylus), for hood or *helmut*. The involucre, the leafy husk that covers the ripening nut, is the inspiration for the name. Alternatively, hazel may have come from the early English *haes*, a behest, from the German *heissen*, to give orders, as the hazel wand was the chieftains' symbol of authority, among ancient tribes of the *Limes Germanicus* (hazel wands were still being placed in the coffins of medieval eccelesiastics centuries later). There is an obvious philological lineage from the German *hasselnuss* and the Swedish *hasselnot* to the 'hazelnut' trees in our orchard but, of the 9-20 recognized species in the genus, ours are not native *Corylus Americana* but European *Corylus avellana*, named for the Italian town in Neapolitan Campania. It was originally described as the 'wild nut of Avella' (*Avellana nux sylvestris*) by Linnaeus from Leonhart Fuch's *De historia stirpium commentarii insignes*, in 1543. A Filbert is not the same as a hazelnut. *Corylus maxima* produces larger seeds, and the involucre is longer and covers most of the nut. There is some question as to whether the name derives from this 'full beard', 'feuille (leaf) beard', or whether the filbert is named for the Norman Saint Philibert, whose feast day of August 20 is when the nuts start ripening. The English poet, John Gower, may also have had a hand in the naming. In his late 14th century *Tales of the*

Seven Deadly Sins (Confessio Amantis), Gower wrote of poor *'Phyllis in the same throwe Was shape into a nutte-tree, That alle men it might see; And after Phyllis, Philliberde This tre was cleped in the yerde.'* Pick your take or take your pick. More confusing, there has been so much hybridization using both hazelnuts and filberts, we should likely refer to our trees as *hazelfilbernuts*. They're also called *Cobbs, Cobb nuts, Spanish nuts, Lombardys*, and *Pontiac nuts*.

In 1995, a large shallow pit, containing hundreds of thousands of burned hazelnut shells, was excavated out of a midden on the island of Colonsay, in Scotland. It was a 9000-year-old mesolithic nut- processing factory. A Chinese manuscript, written in 2838 BC, listed hazelnuts as one of the *'five sacred nourishments'*. They were important in the diet of Stone Age Swiss lake dwellers. When Moses smote the rocks to compel water to come forth, he wielded a hazelnut rod (why later magicians' wands were supposed to be made from hazelnut). One of Aesop's Greek fables concerned a boy putting his hand into a pitcher full of filberts, whose lesson it was to be satisfied with less, if you are to have any. The Greek physician, Pedanius Dioscorides, purportedly cured the common cold with a concoction of hazelnuts and black pepper (and baldness with hazelnut shells and suet- for external use only). According to Virgil, grapevines were bound with hazel twigs, and hazel spits were used, in the sacrifice to Bacchus, of any goat caught browsing his vineyards. The Roman name for filberts was *Nux Pontus*, after the Turkish northern coast, although Pliny the Elder believed that they originated in forests near Damascus, in Syria. He documented the Roman fondness for gathering them as food. There is a lovely recipe for hazelnut candy in Apicius' first-century gourmet cookbook. Hazelnut torches were burned as a symbol of fertility during wedding ceremonies. The Romans considered the tree to be under the mercantile domain of Mercury but, in Norwegian mythology, the hazel is the tree of Thor.

There does seem to be a naturally greater profusion of hazelnut lore in ancient cultures with more magic. The one replete with the most magic, the Celts, equated hazelnuts with poetic inspiration and distilled wisdom. The Gaelic word for wisdom was *cnocach*, for hazelnuts, *cno*, for hazel trees, *coll*. The 7th century Gaelic poem *Laoi Shuibhne* (Sweeney's Lay) was a mouthful of more than nuts: '*A chollain, a chraobhchain, A chomhra cno cuill*' ('O hazlet, little branching one, O fragrance of hazel nuts'). There are place names in Argyllshire, in West Scotland, where hazels are common and the Gaelic gives it away- the Isle of Coll and Bar Calltuin being two notable examples. The hazel is the badge of Clan Colquhoun, and the MacCuills and MacCumhaills are '*Sons of the hazel*'. The Romans actually named the whole country '*Caledonia'*, after the Gaelic *Cal-Dun* ('Hill of Hazel').

Celtic hazelnut magical wisdom begins with the sacred number, nine. In the Old Irish tree alphabet the hazel was the ninth tree, and the symbol of the ninth month. The 12th century Celtic Book of Place Names (*Dinnschenchas*) refers to the tree as the '*poet's music-haunted hazel'* (W. B. Yeats would later agree- he thought the hazel was the common Irish tree of life). The *Dinnschenchas* also mentions '*the nine hazels of Crimnall the Sage*' which '*stand by the power of magic spells*'. This alludes to the ancient tale of nine hazel trees growing around a sacred pool, dropping nuts into the water where they were then eaten by salmon. The fish that ate the magical nuts absorbed the wisdom they contained, and the number of bright spots on the salmon's back indicated how many nuts they had eaten. In one variation of this legend, one salmon had consumed all these magical nuts. A Druid master caught the salmon, and instructed his apprentice to cook the fish, but not to eat any of it. In preparing the fish, however, boiling juice from the salmon splattered onto the student's thumb, which he instinctively thrust into his mouth, and thereby imbibed the trees' mystic inspiration. Hazels of wisdom grew at the heads of the seven chief rivers of Ireland, and nine grew over both the *Well of Segais* and *Connla's Well*, the fabled common source of the Shannon and the Boyne. The theme of nine hazelnuts extends to Celtic protective amulets and is still used in neopaganistic rituals. Using black-coloured twine to thread the nuts, to consecrate the charm, involves passing it three times across a fire on the night of *Samhain* (a Gaelic harvest festival from where we acquire Hallowe'en) chanting *'Hazelnuts nine in a ring, By the smoke of the Samhain Fire bring, To those within our humble home, Form over this a protective cone, Guard for a year, I charge thee, And as I will, so mote it be!'* You'll need one in every room (save some of the nuts to bury during the Spring Equinox, to attune yourself with the cycle of birth and death).

Hazelzuts resemble, and have been used as, a symbol for the human heart. The Celts gave hazelnuts to encourage fruitfulness in marriage, and to protect against lightning (the two being not that dissimilar). They also considered the hazel and its nuts to be effective against fairies, demons, and witchcraft. There are tales of hazel wands being used as weapons against black magic, and hazel logs being swapped for bodies. Horses wore hazel breastbands on their harnesses. In Scotland, double hazelnuts were hurled at witches, and cattle were singed with hazel rods at Midsummer fires, to keep fairies away.

In Lowland England, meanwhile, hazel hedges formed traditional property boundaries and agricultural fencing. Children were customarily given a school holiday on September 14 (Holy Cross Day), to go a-nutting. The collected nuts were saved until

Nuterack Night (or 'Nutcracker Night,' or Hallowe'en) on October 31, when they were allowed to be burned and opened, although some waited until the following Sunday's church service, to crack them open noisily during the sermon.

Here in the Americas, our old friend Meriwether Lewis wrote about the natives eating raw and roasted wild hazelnuts, upon his reaching the mouth of the Deschutes River, in October of 1805. The Indians called them *chinquapin*, and often ground them into a flour to make bread. By 1850, the town of Scottsburg had grown out of a Hudson's Bay Company trading post, at the end of the Umpqua River tidewater. Eight years later, a company retiree, Sam Strickland, planted the first cultivated filbert brought from Europe. The first commercial nursery in the U.S. was established in 1737 in Flushing, New York, by Robert Prince. Just after being elected President, George Washington visited by river barge, and was so impressed (particularly by the '*Barcelona*' filbert trees imported from Spain), that he sent armed guards, to surround and protect the Prince nursery during the Revolutionary War. By 1885, the Barcelona had made it to Oregon, courtesy of Felix Gillet. This became important, because hazelnut orchards in the eastern U.S. completely died out because of the fungal disease, Eastern filbert blight (*Anisogramma anomala*). Oregon became the American hazelfilbernut's New Jerusalem, and it was made the official State Nut in 1989. There are plantings of over 28,000 acres, generating revenue over $50 million in 2004, with 13-33% of the annual crop exported abroad.

Yet total hazelnut production in Oregon and Washington state accounts for only 2% of the world market. European cultivars and hybrids are found from the British Isles, south to France, Iberia, Italy, Greece, Cyprus, north to central Scandinavia, east to the Urals, Turkey, the Caucasus, Iran, Australia, New Zealand, and Chile.

They are found from sea level, to altitudes of 3,800 feet in the Alps (although, over the next five years, ten million hazelnut trees are scheduled to be planted across Bhutan. (They'll need more Bhutanese, to pick them.)

Italy produces 15% of the Earth's hazelnuts. The most important is the Piedmontese *Tonda Gentile della Langhe*, the essential ingredient in *Torta di Nocciole*, Dante's and my favorite *dolce*. The mother of all hazelnut production, however, accounting for 625,000 tonnes and 75% of planetary production, is still ancient Pontus, modern Black Sea Turkey, the '*Hazelnut Coast*.' There are two classes of quality, *Levant*, grown everywhere else in Turkey, and *Giresun*, the fattest, finest hazelnuts in the world, and the direct cause of my earth-and-honey extraterrestrial Findek Ezmesi epiphany on that Cappadoccian bus in 1983.

Just how many cultivars of Corylus avellana exist? There's *Tombul* from Turkey, *Negret* from Spain, and *Ennis, Daviana, Casina, Clark, Cosford, England, Halls Giant, Jemtegaard, Kent Cab, Lewis, Tokolyi, Wanliss Pride*, two other *Tondas, Contorta* (also known as *Harry Lauder's Walking Stick*, discovered in an English hedgerow in the mid-1800's, while roamin' in the gloamin') and many more from many places. There's even a *Winkler* cultivar, described as 'most colourful, with big nuts and no suckering' (or so it is written).

Why the need for so many cross-fertilization candidates? Because hazel is wind-pollinated. Why? Because it flowers in the middle of the winter and, last time I checked, there were no insects wearing thermal underwear. And, because male catkins and female flowers mature at different times, so a single tree cannot pollinate itself, Robyn and I have *Davianas, Butlers, Royals* and *Barcelonas*. This may not be as screwball a 'non-adaptation' as it might first appear. First, no competition. Second, lots of wind (and lots of energy to put into copious amounts of pollen production, as there are no petals or leaves at this time of year- just shake a catkin-laden filbert in mid-winter, and try to escape without a yellow dusting). Third, lots of small, efficient, tufted female flowers to catch the wind. Fourth, the male catkins drop off to allow more nourishment to flow to the female. And finally, the tree goes immediately back into dormancy, so the fruit doesn't develop too soon, fall to the ground, and rot.

There are three ways to let hazelnuts grow. Left to their own preferences, they will form a dense shrub. Man has taken this natural preference in two separate directions. The original intervention was *coppicing,* cutting it down to the base, to ensure the annual ability to produce multiple new stems, used as material for woven fencing, and wattle-and-daub building construction. Coppiced hazels can live for several hundred years. The second human orchardist act was to train it into a tree, by removing the lower limbs. Hazels can grow to a height of ten metres, at the expense of a shortened lifespan of eighty years. The upside, of course, is the 20-25 pound of nuts per year that the tree produces, once established. Unfortunately, most of our hazelnuts are usually 'distributed and dispersed' by our Red Squirrels and Steller's Jays (someone in the neighbourhood has recently taken to feeding them peanuts this winter- we'll need to talk). There were so many in the orchard today, that I couldn't hear myself think for the squawking. (I imagine that the topic of conversation was mostly about distribution and dispersal.)
Historically, both the hazel's wood and nuts were made use of. The wood, because of its fine grain,

straight growth, absence of knots, light weight, durability, and pliability, was made into bows (and arrows), staffs, crooks, and walking sticks (sometimes bent into the desired shape while still on the tree), fishing rods, tool handles, whip handles, fencing, U-shaped stakes to hold down roofing thatch, hoops and rustic seats, hampers and baskets. In the coal pits of Durham, hazel baskets were called '*corves*'. Irish woven hazel hide-clad boats were known as '*coracles*'. Hazel charcoal made excellent crayons and gunpowder (and was eaten as a cure for stomach problems). Here in North America, the Ojibway and Chippewa used *Corylus Americana*, for baskets and drumsticks.

Two other traditional uses of coppiced hazel are especially significant. From the earliest Greek buildings until the early 19th century, house walls were constructed with panels ('*wattles*') of hazel wands woven between oak timber posts and then daubed with a mixture of straw and mud and lime. This was called '*wattle-and-daub.*' Coppiced hazel trees were often grown between oaks, so that both of the key construction elements could be found in close proximity. Wattle-and-daub disappeared in Ireland by the 16th century, because of landowner clearcutting, and in England two hundred years later, with the advent of cheap brick and iron.

The second special use of hazel wands was in rhabdomancy, the ancient art of divination. The divining rod is mentioned as far back as *Hosea 4:12* in the Old Testament *('My people ask counsel at their stocks, and their staff declareth unto them')*, albeit not as much as wine and whores in the same passage. The Romans had their '*Virgula Mercurialis*'. John Evelyn, the 17th century founder of the *Royal Society* wrote, in his '*Sylva: a Discourse of Forest Trees*', probably the best description of the mystery of hazel wand divination: *'It is very wonderful, by whatever occult virtue, the forked stick (so cut, and skilfully held) becomes impregnated with those invisible steams and exhalations, as by its spontaneous bending from a horizontal posture to discover not only mines and subterranean treasure and springs of water, but criminals guilty of murder, &c. . . Certainly next to a miracle, and requires a strong faith'.* This, then, is the practice of '*dowsing*' (from *Dousterswivel*, the charlatan in Sir Walter Scott's Gothic novel,*'The Antiquary'*, who used a forked hazel-rod in his magical performances- or maybe it was the other way around). In England, the rods were best cut on St. John's Eve. In Brandenberg, the tree needed to be approached in darkness, walking backwards, the fork cut silently, while reaching back between your legs. In Berlin, only an innocent child of true faith could cut a dowser and, even then, it would only have power for seven years. The power of a divining rod was tested underwater, where it was supposed to squeal like a pig. Only the truly gifted could become Dowsers, or *Rhabdomists*. At the moment of discovery, one apparently felt a quickening or slowing of the pulse, or a sensation of profound heat or cold. I still remember when an eighty-year-old friend of my father, Ike Edmundsen, had me hang on to his hazel dowsing wand as he walked over an underground stream. It pulled me to the ground.

If you have never tasted a hazelnut, there is no way I can describe it. It's one of those flavors that you use to describe other things you taste. Softly erotic, it's like making love in a sauna heated by burning birch. The chemistry of the primary flavor was only identified in 1990, by Roland Emberberger of the German fragrance company, Haarmann & Reimer, as *(E)-5-methyl-2-hepten-4-one filbertone*. Hazelnut texture is a product of the equally balanced fractions of protein, carbohydrate, and oil in the nut (acorns have more carbohydrate; walnuts more oil and protein). In Findik Esmesi, the crunchy burning birch sauna sex paste reaches its Pontus perfection.

Hazelnut paste is an important ingredient in Viennese tortes and is quickly attracting aficionados in the U.S., jumping away from salmonella-laden peanut butter. The filbertones are the basis of *Fra. Angelico* liquor, the namesake of a hermit monk who lived in the Piedmont hills in the 17th century. Iron Chef Masaharu Morimoto has produced a Hazelnut Ale, a more than gentle departure from his usual erudite culinary activities. Hazelnut oil is glorious in salad dressings and patisserie, and the right cooking.

Filbertone is complementary to the classic comestible combination Robyn and I grow and collect on the Island- the quintessential *umami* match of mushrooms, salmon and pinot noir (they're also brilliant on turmeric-flavoured cauliflower). The oil is also used in soaps and perfumes. Mashed filberts and figs were pasted on scorpion bites, to take away the pain. Filbertones go well with coffee, although I think that *Starbucks' Skinny Hazelnut Latte* is a bit over the top. Of all the possible flavor combinations out there, however, the most wonderful witchcraft, the fire in the filbert firmament, the reason there are so many hazelnut trees in the world, is chocolate. Even in Australia, 2000 tonnes per year are imported, just so the Cadbury company can produce its Hazelnut block, the third most popular brand in the country.

The combination was first constituted in the time of Napoleon's regnum, when the cost of importing raw cocoa from South America was very expensive. The addition of pieces of raw hazelnut sweetened the chocolate, and made it more affordable. The epicentre of this effort was in Piedmont. In 1826, Pier Paul Caffarel took over a small tannery in Turin, and converted it over to a chocolate confection laboratory. The Swiss chocolate industry got its start when Francois-Louis Cailler visited the lab, in a blatant act of industrial espionage. Twenty-six years later, Cafferel's partner-successor, Michele Prochet, created a new kind of dough, by blending sugar with cocoa, and ground *Tonda Gentile* hazelnuts. In 1865, he started producing a special chocolate, which he initially called *givu*, named after, and in the shape of a Piedmontese mask, with a tricorn hat and a little tail pointing upwards. (The mask, the symbol of the struggle for Piedmont independence in 1799, was invented by a heroic local farmer, Gian d'la Duja- John of the Mug.) During Carnival celebrations that year, Gianduja threw the delicious new chocolates into the celebrating crowds, and authorised Caffarel to use his name. Because of this honour, Caffarel decided to name his creation *'Gianduiotto 1865'*. You can still buy them individually wrapped in gold foil.

The granddaddy of Piedmontese and world hazelnut-chocolate combination production, however, was Pietro Ferrero, who originally owned a small patisserie in Alba. In 1946, he introduced 660 pounds of his own solid paste chocolate-hazelnut version of *'Pasta Gianduja,'* designed to be sliced and eaten on bread. Three years later, Pietro developed his first spread and, in 1951, released it as *Supercrema*. Because of the introduction of an Italian law prohibiting superlatives in product names, and because of the success of hazelnut cream overseas, Pietro's son, Michele Ferrero, reengineered Supercrema in 1963, intent on capturing a larger share of the international market. The first jar of *Nutella* left the Ferrero factory in Alba on April 20, 1964. It was an instant sensation, and became a cultural icon. In Nanni Moretti's *Bianca*, a character relieves his post-coital anxieties by eating a gigantic Nutella jar, during a dream scene. Chloé Doutre-Roussel's mother features, in her *The Chocolate Connoisseur*, flying into Mexico with several jars of Nutella and smearing it on her face, to convince a Customs Officer that it is a facial cosmetic, and not a prohibited food product. Today, the annual Italian production of Nutella is over 180,000 tons, the number one selling sweet spread in the world. The Ferrero Group also produces the chocolates *Ferrero Rocher, Pocket Coffee, Mon Chéri, Giotto, Confetteria Raffaello* coconut cream candy, and *Tic Tac* breath mints.

There are even uses for hazelnut shells, leaves, and roots. In the search for the answer as to why Eastern Filbert Blight hits some hazelnut cultivars harder than others, Angela Hoffman, at the University of Portland, discovered that the most resistant trees were making *paclitaxel*, the active ingredient in the anticancer drug, *taxol*, and in most of the drug-eluting coronary stents my patients come back with, from the Royal Jubilee Cath Lab. Hazel leaves were used to feed cattle, because they are the earliest to appear in the spring, and last to fall in the autumn; they were thought to increase a cow's milk yield. The liquor from boiled filbert leaves, was drunk as a blood purifier. Virginia Woolf's reference to *'all foliage and no filberts'*, discounts the promise of the roots, that hold the ultimate umami promise. If only I had known about the roots when we planted the orchard. The roots, my friend, can be the inoculum for the truffle. Not hazelnut chocolate truffles, but *Tuber melasporum*, the Black Queen, the Pearl of Perigord, real human sex pheromone truffles. Way beyond burning birch sauna oral gratification, black truffles are the culinary equivalent of love on a bearskin rug. I've recently found a Spanish method for succesfully inoculating established hazelnut orchards with Perigord truffle spore. And now I'm beginning to dream beyond Findik Ezmesi. In technicolor.

There's one more dimension to hazelnut wisdom, hinted at in John Clare's 1821 poem, *Autumn – 'The scrambling shepherd with his hook, 'mong Hazel-boughs of rusty brown, that overhang some gulping brook, drags the ripened clusters down'*. It's the wild link to the carefree joys of our childhood. Because, before magic and divination, honey and earth, mushrooms, salmon, pinot noir, chocolate, winter blooming, and burning birch sauna sex, there was the original, Love Potion Number Nine.

"Come, let's go
snow-viewing
till we're buried."

Basho

We sure as hell got buried today. It started to snow as I left work yesterday, and that party went on until dawn. Now, all our trees are weighed down, and wound up. Every so often one of them can't stand it anymore, and flings off a sugary cascade of wet, white anger. Spring may be just around the corner, but the G forces are deadly. The main problem here is that, in our original quest for the six sublime qualities, Robyn and I created a long secluded driveway that, on days like today, properly demonstrates solitude as a two-way valve. At the end of a five-minute knee-deep hike is an additional higher obstacle of grader-mounded snirt, blocking our access to the rest of the world. Our taxes at work are the only thing that will be working this morning. We're really snow-viewing now.

No mind. (I suppose that's a Buddhist concept, '*no mind*'. Probably different from '*never mind*', which is definitely not a good idea. Not any idea at all, actually). Since I can't go to work today, I've decided to write about my outside view, and how it got here. Before I describe the space, however, let's go back in time.

Late in the afternoon of September 30, 1983, twenty-five years ago, I set off to look for twenty-five hundred years ago. I kissed Robyn goodbye on the train station platform in Varanasi, India. There were drying clothes hanging out of sidetracked carriages, bands of thieving monkeys on the crosswalks, and a cow climbing the stairs on track number five. By the time my transport to Gaya pulled in, it was a swarming hive of humanity, in the shape of a slow train, that finally stopped in front of us. I had to squeeze into a crowd, where I thought the carriage door might be, until I eventually found myself scrunched up in a roof rack space that, not a moment before, had been a large jute bag of rice. I remember the big dragonfly caught in the light housing, and I wondered how much he had paid for the same amount of space. After three hours of yogic torture (all the more enjoyable with dysentery and nowhere for the cramps to go), I emerged onto a sea of sleeping pilgrims and a maze of turnstiles. In the station darkness, I could just make out the silhouettes of uniformed officials, sticking sharp objects into the arms of fellow disgorged passengers, in the line ahead of me. As the queue advanced, it became apparent that, while the syringes were occasionally changed, the needles were not. Then, all too soon, it was my turn. A hand grabbed my left arm. My right hand grabbed his.
"What's going on?" I inquired.
"Oh, nothing," he responded.
"Then why the injections?" says I.
"Only little problem," he offered.
"What little problem?" Because, I was now quite curious.
"Only little Cholera," he finally admitted.

"I probably already have Cholera," I said. And he let me go.

The next morning, after an omlette and chai, I was walking towards the bus station, when an old-fashioned rickshaw walla, with a crewcut and a ponytail, sidled up alongside me. He spoke no English, but we finally negotiated a price that I thought was designed to get me to the bus station. It seemed a little exorbitant, but he assured me that my destination was a long way off. I climbed up top, and he began to trot along the bumpy, rugged streets. The road smoothed out a bit, and I found myself looking up through the branches of sunlit, leafy mimosas, and cottonball clouds. There was just the perfect calm of little mechanical noises, warm air resistance, and gliding through the Bihar countryside. I awoke to the sight of my pony-tailed *walla*, having worked up quite a sweat, running around a sacred pool, along a river lined with coconut palms, umbrella'd monks, and the landscape of rice paddies against distant mountains. We pulled onto the main street of Bodhgaya, before I realized that he had run, not to the bus station in Gaya, but to my ultimate destination of the day, thirteen kilometers away. For seven rupees and a *Limca*, which he drained in one gulp.

I wandered the skyscaper temple complex, mesmerized by the frescoes, flower-laden, chanting pilgrims, birds, white-scarved serenity and the oldest, most venerated tree on the planet. *Ficus religiosa*, the descendent of the actual Bodhi tree, under which Siddartha Gautama had attained enlightenment in 528 BC. A priest handed me a handful of its leaves. They ultimately made the journey to my library, here on Westwood Lake. Two and a half millennia ago, the philosophy that was epitomized under that tree, made another. Across Asia, his lightness of being travelled through China, to Japan. Moving in the same space and time with Buddha's teachings, were more physical manifestations of his influence. The evolution of one in particular, the *Stupa*, will take us to our outside snow-viewing today.

The Stupa was originally a reliquary, a mound containing some of Buddha's ashes. Gradually, it morphed from a funerary monument, to an object of commemoration and, depending on where Buddhism went, its shape and form changed to accommodate local culture and materials. In China, the stupa evolved into the *pagoda*; in Indonesia, the latticed bells atop Borobadur; in Japan, the *Gorinto*, a five-story grave marker up to four metres high, and replete with Buddhist symbolism. The base stone is cubic, and represents Earth. The next level is spherical, and corresponds to Water. The third stone is triangular, Fire. The fourth story is a half moon, Wind, and the pinnacle is the jewel-shaped Symbol of the Void, the Ether. While Gorinto were the religious cenotaphs in Shinto shrines and unrelated in any way to lanterns, '*doro*', (which were originally made of metal). Somewhere along the way, Gorinto transformed into the stone lantern, '*ishi-doro*'. The first Japanese temple stone lantern dates from around 600 AD, and the oldest Shinto lantern from about 1300 AD. With a little imagination, one can see the third stone of the Gorinto hollowed out, and illuminated with the fire it represents (initially they likely had chimneys but no windows). Possibly used by monks to help heighten emotions during nightime rituals, the lantern may have taken on function as well as form.

There was likely little distinction between the original religious, and subsequent secular, use of Japanese stone lanterns. The transition may have been as simple as the thoughtful resourcefulness of recycling old stone lanterns from temples destroyed by war or earthquakes. The man who took the Japanese stone lantern from Buddhist gravestone to aesthetic icon, however, was tea master and warrior Oribe Furuta (1544-1615), a protégé of Sen no Rikyu. Before Sen-no-Rikyu committed ritual suicide in 1591, he had brought the '*Way of Tea*' to a new renaissance, and used old temple lanterns in his gardens to dimly light the way for his guests to the teahouse evening ceremonies. Oribe was bolder. He made his own lanterns (*Oribe-doro*) promoting '*the light of the self*', to illuminate the '*way of seeing*' the garden's teachings. Even the hidden Japanese Christian sects used Oribe lanterns, carving a figure of the Virgin Mary in the base of their *Krishtan-doros*. From the temple garden to the tea garden, it was just a small step for the stone lanterns to becoming an ornament in private residential gardens.

As a function of its varying strategic positioning requirements in the garden, *ishi-doro* continued to develop different design elements. Ultimately, there emerged four main styles of stone lantern: small and portable, *oki-doro*; pedestal lanterns, *Tachi-doro* ; the so-called 'buried lanterns,' *ikekomi-doro*; and the famous *yukimi-doro*. *Yukimi* are 'near water' lanterns characterized by their wide-brimmed roofs. Historically, these have three aesthetic attributes. The first is that the underside of the umbrella reflects and echoes the level and expanse of the water. Secondly, the roof is designed to collect a deep pile of snow, ideal for 'snow-viewing'. Finally the umbrella is often hexagonal (*hakkaku-dôrô*) and, because it casts light in several directions, is usually located at the crossroads of paths. On or near water reflected off the bottom, snow on the top, reflecting light in all directions, there is still more.

The Chinese defined the '*six sublime qualities*', or '*six design impossibilities*' that epitomize a perfect garden. There are inhererent contradictions in the desired combined qualities of vastness, solemnity, endeavor, venerability, abundant water, and vast views.

If one attempts to introduce an impression of vastness, the feeling of quietude and intimacy will be lost (spaciousness vs seclusion); if artificial elements are used, any sense of age will be undermined (artifice vs antiquity); if too much flowing water is employed, distant views become irrelevent (water-courses vs panoramas). They remained unresolved until 1676, when the 5th lord of Maeda Tsunanori of Kanazawa Castle, the *daimyo* who ruled the former Kaga Domain, began work on what was to become one of the three most beautiful gardens in Japan. Initially he had no water, but he commissioned Itaya Heishiro to build a siphon system to force a river to run up hill from 5 miles away. It still works today. The park was named '*Kenroku-en*' by feudal Lord Sadanobu Matsudaira, which literally means 'the garden that combines six characteristics'. Because it has them all. In winter, Kenroku-en is renowned for its *yukitsuri*- conical arrays of ropes carefully supporting tree branches in their classical shapes, protecting them from damage caused by heavy snows. We could certainly have used a few here yesterday.

The most famous contribution to the solution of the six impossibilities, however, is one lone Japanese lantern, my absolute favorite, the *Koto-ji Yukimi-doro.* The *koto* is a traditional Japanese instrument that most resembles a Western zither harp. The *ji* of the koto is the bridge or fret upon which the strings rest. The instrument tuning is altered by moving the *ji.* A *koto-ji* style lantern is a 2-legged stone lantern that resembles a harp tuner. The leg shape of the *yukimi-doro* was originally taken from the lotus, but these legs are longer and more elegant. For me, the supreme distillation of the Japanese garden is in the austere beauty of the *Koto-ji Yukimi-doro.* I'm looking at about a foot of snow-viewing stacked on the roof of ours right now.

In 1996, Robyn and I hired a young German landscaping *savant* to construct the Japanese Garden at the front of the house. He was razor sharp and, ultimately, a bit off his own edge. He brought in boulders, round stones from Mexico, rock bridges, preconstructed arbours, and a profusion of plants that included a twenty-five-year-old cherry tree that now sheds its white flowers all over the pea gravel every April. You have to be careful sitting on the bench under it when it's in full bloom because, among other hazards, the noise of the bees working will deafen you. For several years now, the garden has slowly developed, but I always felt there was a little something missing, something that needed to be added to provide a sense of the mystique, spirituality and tradition that I had always associated with formal Japanese gardens. The day Robyn and I assembled the *Koto-ji Yukimi-doro*, I heard the garden exhale. Beats gnomes and flamingoes, hands down.

I might just have to go to work tomorrow. But, for now, come, let's go snowviewing till we're buried.

A Good Thing on a Man 07 March

"Travel and society polish one, but a rolling stone gathers no moss, and a little moss is a good thing on a man."

John Burroughs

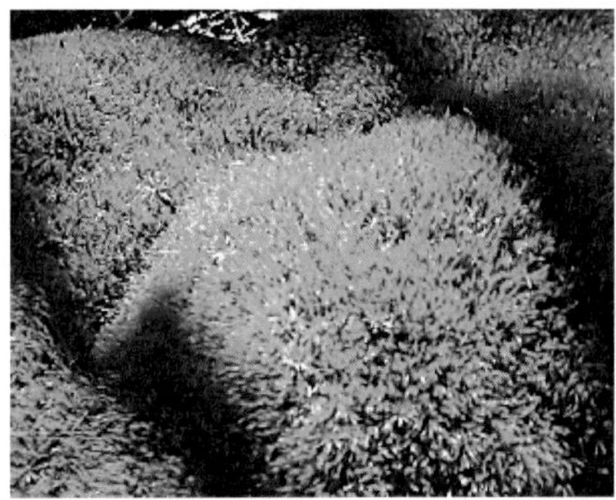

Enough already. Robyn and I have left the field of raised garden beds in defeat. Our rakes and pitchforks were no match for the sudden attack of side-on flurries. You'd think we'd have paid more than our fair share of Arctic reparations this year, for living in paradise the rest of our lives. Apparently not. Even the newly-arrived Canada geese on the lake are shaking their heads.

One more thing is going on right now, directly above us- even in this (hopefully) last storm of the season- an alchemic transformation, on the bluffs of the Westwood Ridges. The dessicated broomstraw green rock fur, that fills Benson's crags and crevices in the dry heat, is swelling into a luxuriant cashmere carpet of emerald ecstasy, in the warming wet. The moss is awake.

I never fully appreciated how beautiful and important these primitive plants were, until we moved to this rain forest. Mosses are the reason that all the monocultural industrial forestry advocates and rape-and-pillage developers (more and more the same invertebrate) are wrong. Mosses absorb a third of all rain into their mats. The main harvest, with their destruction, is severe flooding. Rivers become *eutrophicated* (i.e. slimy with algae), because the excess minerals that were previously held in moss carpets, are released all at once. And where do mosses get most of these minerals from? Why, from the salmon that migrate up those same rivers we are removing the mosses from, of course, through increased fishing and careless logging practices.

The ecology is an elegant Vivaldi *Four Seasons* masterwork. With early *Spring* rains, mosses leech minerals onto the deciduous trees they coevolved with, promoting new growth (conifers have bark that is too acidic, and their branches are shaped to shed snow-not very moss friendly). The dry, warm *Summer* forces the mosses into a period of dormancy. Nutrients that mosses have accumulated from summer dust once again leech onto the trees' branches and roots in the *Autumn* rains. Effective photosynthesis is impossible in freezing temperatures and low light conditions, so mosses once again shut down in *Winter,* until the cycle starts all over again in the spring. The ability of moss to act as a capacitor for large amounts of water and nutrients defines its essential ecological succession role, in the circumpolar boreal forests. It is the king of living carbon, covering 3% of the planet's surface. The moss layer is the only aerobic region where *methane oxidation* can occur. It houses an assorted collection of microbes and other animal life, and acts as a sensitive barometer of water and air pollution. It is the clear-cut canary in our increasingly contaminated coal mine.

Mosses are *bryophytes*, nonvascular plants, that differ from higher order vascular *tracheophytes* in several ways. They have half the number of chromosomes of their more evolved cousins (*haploid*) so they are more subject to severe natural selection. This also allows them to change their appearance and function more readily, in response to changes in their environment (*phenotypic plasticity*). Mosses can rapidly equilibrate to changes in their water content, and survive being air-dry at the cellular level (*poikilohydry* and *dessication tolerance*). Because they need water for sexual reproduction (*swimming sperm*), they have also heavily adapted to asexual self-cloning. Just reading about the complexity of their life cycles would push most of us towards an asexual option.

Mosses clump together as a *super-organism,* and communicate, as a group, with pheromones. Because of their small size, they are in close contact with only their immediate microhabitat (this may actually provide a mutational survival advantage when climate change really kicks in). Small is also relative. Our open canoe run, down Venezuela's Carrao river, was punctuated with religious gesticulations when we just missed the thrill of colliding with one of the gigantic midstream moss islands which, all by itself, could have played the leading role in Conan Doyle's *Lost World.* During the Carboniferous era, 300 million years ago, there was one 130-feet-high club moss covering 25,000 acres. More recently, however, their physical environment has provided more selective pressure than any of the other biology that surrounds them. Finally, their form and structure are known to evolve very, very slowly.

Despite this, they have obviously adapted well, or they wouldn't be here. They possess numerous reproductive strategies (one *Splachnum* subspecies makes use of flies to convey its spores from one pile of dung to the next). It is the one plant that decays at the bottom while the top is green and continues to grow. When intact cultures of the Common Roof

Moss (*Ceratodon purpureus*) were recovered, after the Space Shuttle Columbia tragically disintegrated upon reentry in 2003, researchers were astounded. Rather than finding the typical random chaotic cell growth that occurred in other plants exposed to a zero gravity environment, scientists were surprised to find that the moss grew in striking, clockwise spirals (from specialized tip cells that respond to both gravity and light).

In drought conditions, moss metabolism can slow down to almost zero. They shut down at 21 C, max out their photosynthesis at 10 degrees C, but can still grow in temperatures just above freezing. How can they do this? The answer is found by looking at why certain animals would even consider eating the stuff, given that mosses taste awful (bitter only begins to describe it), and have little nutritional value. The answer is *antifreeze*. Barnacle geese, migrating north, begin to consume moss as soon as they arrive in their arctic breeding grounds. Reindeer and bog lemmings fill up with moss. Why? Mosses are composed of up to 35% *arachidonic acid*, a highly unsaturated fatty acid, which allows cells to keep working at low temperatures. Moss adaptability also employs arachidonic acid to make certain *oxylipins*, used as a form of defensive chemical mimicry. Examples include ®-*1-octen-3-ol* (which smells of mushrooms), and *(E)-non-2-enal* (found in higher plants, and smelling of cucumber).

The adaptability of mosses is more than surpassed by their utility to our own species, despite the taste. The evidence is in the virtual strip mining, rapidly increasing in various ecosystems around the world. From disappearing New Zealand peatlands, Malaysian high mountain devastation (for pillow fillers), to truckloads of National Forest removal in the U.S., mosses are being mobilized *en masse,* right off their skinny rhizomes. The scale of the current exploitation is geometric but humans have always employed bryophytes in diverse ways. Mosses were used in pottery making in the French Stone Age as we now use sand. Siberian Eskimos slathered rolled- up skins frozen into the shape of sled runners with a moss mixture, to shape and protect them. Even now, the Pangnirtung Inuit run electrical extension cords to summer tents for their electric guitars, while the tent is heated by ancient *kudliks,* that burn with a wick of moss. In India, mosses have been used as *pharki* doormats, smoke filters, door covers, and as *sirona* cushions, to carry water on their heads. When we're camping, we use moss as fire kindling, camp scouring pads, and fishing worm containers. The Romans used it for toilet paper. Moss has served as an absorbent (hiking boots, *Johnson & Johnson* diaper linings, sanitary napkins, contraceptives, Himalayan cigarette filters, beer clarifying, livestock and pet litter urine collection), insulation (clothing, baby cradle liners in Lapland, crocodile egg incubation in the Philippines, and to keep milk and other foodstuffs warm or cool), decoration (Maori cloaks, New Guinea masks, bracelets and red plaited rope, ladies' hats in London and Boston, and compressed into embossed buttons), and as a stuffing material (dolls, balls, pillows, and mattresses).

One type of moss became so popular as a pillow stuffing that, in 1741, Dillenius named it *Hypnum* because of its association with sleep. Linnaeus, the Grand Namer himself, copied the bears in choosing the moss *Polytrichum commune* for his bedding. An important reason, other than soft comfort, for using mosses as stuffing, is their resistance to mold and hungry insects, possibly due to their content of *ferulic* and *coumaric acids*. This property has been exploited to several uses. In the Himalayas, grains and other containerized foods were covered over with a coarse powder of dried moss to repel insects. Both there and in the Pacific Northwest, mosses are used to pack mushrooms. Apples, plums, carrots, and young trees can be shipped or winter-stored in mosses. Alaskan Natives used to cover processed fish and sea mammals in a wood or skin-lined shallow pit with moss, and leave the flesh to ferment for a couple of months. More recently, when they switched to plastic bags to line the pits and enclosed the food, they created the anaerobic conditions, perfect for the resultant 12-fold increase in *botulism* noted by Public Health Officials. They've now, apparently, gone back to more traditional methods.

Mosses have utility in taxidermy (they're safer than the *arsenic* now more commonly employed), and in shipping small amphibians from biological supply houses. In the Russo-Japanese War, bandages were made from *Sphagnum* peat moss, to conserve precious cotton for packing gunpowder. In WWI, the *Canadian Red Cross* went through about 200,000 pounds per month, during the last six months of the war. It was cheaper than sterile dressings and wounds healed faster due not only to its ability to absorb 3-4 times as much liquid as a cotton bandage (at a rate three times as fast), but because it contains *sphagnan,* an antimicrobial polysaccharide that binds the enzymes of acid-sensitive bacteria, and the minerals they rely on (there may have also been some *penicillin* from some other fungal elements hanging around). Our Nitinaht native neighbours, just down the road, used Maidenhair moss (*Fissidens adianthoides)* to bandage wounds, and *Sphagnum* as a disinfectant. Their women chewed on *Polytrichum commune,* to speed up the labor process in pregnancy. The Chinese also use it as a diuretic, laxative, hemostatic agent, a medium for dissolving gall and kidney stones, and tea, for treating the common cold.

Bryophytes have been used to treat fevers (*Fontinalis antipyretica* was recorded in Linnaeus' journal), diseases of the liver and lung (*liverwort* and *lungwort*), heart conditions (*Rhodobryum giganteum*), and skin disorders (*Sphagnol* is used to treat boils and mosquito bites). Many are being investigated for other antimicrobial, antifungal, antiviral, and anti-tumor effects. Huperzine A is a moss-derived *'nootropic agent,'* which counteracts the neurochemical abnormalities underlying learning and memory losses linked to Alzheimer's. The most promising uses of bryophytes in medicine, however, are in genetic engineering. Since the entire genome of *Physcomitrella patens* was first mapped, and we are now able to culture it in a bioreactor, it has been recognized as the perfect model for studying the molecular development not only of mosses, but also vascular plants, and all the way up the evolutionary chain, to us. The man to watch here is Ralf Reski, Professor of Plant Biotechnology at the University of Freiburg and who, in 1999, founded, on the strength of his bryological 'lab rat', *Physcomitrella patens,* the Greenovation Company. By 2002, his biotech company was already employing 30 people, to produce recombinant blood-clotting *factor IX,* for pharmaceutical use. Professor Reski's next trick may well be an agricultural one. *Physcomitrella patens* could serve as a mechanism for genetic transfer to vascular plants, in order to increase their tolerance to salt, drought, osmotic stress, cold, and insect predation.

Because that will still taste better than eating moss the way it is. Even the Chinese considered moss as famine food only. Granted, *Sphagnum* was once used by Laplanders as an ingredient in bread, and Native Americans once used Camas bulbs, simmered in blood with moss, to make a soup, but the only truly wonderful flavors that have ever come out of a moss, is the sphagnum peat of my favorite single malt (*Marchantia polymorpha* has also been added to wine as a 'crunchy treat', but this should have been declared a capital offense).

Mosses have almost as many other applications as your own imagination can think of. They are used in floral arrangements, container gardening, 19th century mosseries and Victoria hanging baskets, topiary, horticultural soil mixes, orchid and mushroom culture, store window displays, aquaria and terraria, chinking, fire retardant insulation, green roof construction, peatwood, peatcrete, peatfoam, peatcork, waxes, resins, dyes, varnish, leather treatments, cranberry farms, heavy metal detection and cation exchange, organic compound filtration, forensics, oil spill cleanup (*SpillSorb, Oclansorb Plus, Peat Sorb* and Newfoundland *Hydro-Weed*), erosion control (*Procédé BRYOTEC*), and mining spoil revegetation. And fuel. Peat could help our problem with waning oil supplies. It is clean-burning with a low sulfur content, and provides more than 8,000 BTU per dry pound.

In Canada, the peat deposits store more energy than do all the natural gas and forest reserves combined. Half the world's peat production is used for fuel, generating the equivalent of 100-200 million tons of oil. In Ireland alone, shorn of her trees centuries ago, 25% of the fuel source is moss, over 100 million tons each year. Yet, there are the usual dangers I eventually get around to describing for you. Harvesting peat moss is not the same as the harvesting of moss peat, and peatland 'harvesting' has increasingly become peatland 'mining'. Most of the loss of peatlands is due to agriculture (France) and forestry (Finland), although peat harvesting for fuel is a growing problem in northern Europe. Loss of peatlands affects the original forestry species, from microbes to caribou and, with more carbon coming out of the carbon sink, results in more greenhouse gases, and more global warming. It takes at least twenty years to replace the moss that was taken.

Peatlands are history books- of our planet's past vegetation and climate, and of us. They are renowned for their ability to preserve the dead. In 1991, an

11,000-year-old giant mastodon was found in Ohio, with its last meal of flowers and seeds, there for all to see. The horrors of the lives and deaths of famous bogmen continue to fascinate. In 1952, in Tollund Fen, Denmark, two brothers (peat cutters) were surprised by the discovery of a 2000-year-old man, with a twisted leather noose around his neck. There were grains in his stomach, and a grin on his face, as if his death had somehow saved him. That same year, *Grauballe man* was found, also by peat cutters. His skull was fractured and his throat had been cut. Unlike Tollund man, his face was all pain and terror. His stomach was full of a porridge, containing 63 different grains. He was dated to about 210-410 AD. In England, thirty-two years later, 2000-year-old *Lindow man* was found, well-preserved by the sphagnan in the peat. He had also died a violent death, with two blows to the head, a thong for hanging, and his throat cut. He was not a laborer, but a man of high rank. There are now over 1500 such bodies, that have been exhumed from the moss. They may have been Druid priests sacrificed to the Earth Goddess. Or maybe not. Two thousand years later, police in Macclesfield, England, investigated Peter Reyn-Bardt, overheard boasting of the murder of his wife, Malika, 23 years previously. They had found no evidence of the crime. The excavation of a peat bog, adjacent to Reyn-Bardt's back yard, uncovered a well-preserved skull of a female. Immediately after Peter confessed to the murder of his wife, the *Oxford University Archaeology Research Lab* determined that the skull was 1700 years old. A little moss is a good thing on a man.

In February 1845, the eight-eyelashed Tasmanian moss *Splachnum octoblepharum* was found by W. Valentine, growing on the bones and decayed clothing of a bushranger, at the base of the Western Mountains.

Two double-barrelled guns and pistols lay by his side. A little moss is a good thing on a man.

The sun has just come out on Westwood Lake. And I think about that luxuriant cashmere carpet of emerald ecstasy, awakening in the warming wet. When I was a rolling stone, I spent five years hitchhiking around the world, getting polished by travel and society. Then I met Robyn. A little moss is a good thing on a man.

> *"This is farewell. I shall wait beneath the moss*
> *Until the flowers are fragrant*
> *In this island country..."*
>
> Hideki Tojo

In Between 08 March

"We come from the earth, we return to the earth, and in between we garden."

Anon

There's a wonderful joy in turning over the hibernating soil in our raised beds today. I can smell chocolate promise, pungent with Pasternak ozone, with every twist and lift of my pitchfork. This is not one of those life and death activities. It's much more important than that, the big hand on my clock. Cicero said that *'if you have a garden and a library, you have everything you need'*. In the garden section of my library, I have a collection of seed catalogues, full of spring anticipation. Gardening begins with the dreams in January, and I dream bigger than emperors.

The garden is never so good as it will be next year and, every March, when it's still Summer in the light and Winter in the shade, my favorite mail-order seeds start arriving, in little coloured envelopes. They find their way into the alphabet of my accordion file box in the shed and, when the right moment in the right week of the right month arrives, claim their own personalized paydirt: Arugula, Basil ('*Genovese*' and '*Thai*'), Beans (fava '*Superaguadulce*', asparagus yard-long *'Bacello'*, bush-green *'Balong,'* and yellow wax *'Rocquencourt'*), Beets (*'Detroit Red'*- although I prefer to plant a mix of *'Chioggia'*, *'Cylindrica'* and *'Touchstone Gold'*, Robyn's pickling recipe from Nana Pitcon seems to work best with a more rustic approach, Broccoli (*'Comet'*), Cabbage (*'Savoy'* and *'Red'*), Carrots (*'Nantes'* or *'Mokum'*), Corn (*'Bodacious'*), Chard (*'Riccia da Taglio'* and *'Fordhook Giant'*), Ching Chiang, Cilantro, Cucumbers (*'Cool Breeze'*), Dill, Eggplant (Japanese *'Kamo'*), Escarole, Fennel (*'Romanesco'*), Kale (*'Black Tuscan Lacinato'*), Lettuce (too numerous to list, but oh I do love *'Amish Deer Tongue'*), Mesclun, Parsley, Parsnips (*'Gladiator'*), Peas (*'Sugar Snap'*), Radicchio (*'Palla Rossa'*), Radishes (*'French Breakfast'*), Spinach (*'Bloomsdale'*, *'Olympia'* and New Zealand), Squash (I usually plant *'Waltham'* butternut and South African *'Gem'*, but this year I'm going out on a limb with *'Marina Di Chioggia'*), Sunflowers, Tomatillos, and Zucchini (*'Aristocrat'*- only two plants, only two plants, only two plants...). These are just the seeds. Out in the raised beds, back under the snow (it's the vernal equinox for Chrissake), lie subterranean asparagus spears, strawberry rhizomes, and a buried bulb ballet of Russian garlic and French shallots. Woven through the unique architecture of our raised beds, are small boxes of blueberries, black currants, gooseberries, and rhubarb, and a central arbor of kiwifruit and table grapes (*'Interlaken'* is Robyn's favorite, but we also have *'Flame'* and *'Himrod'*, actually a turnip masquerading as a grape).

Just to the left of the raised bed Pagoda are the fruit trees. There is a small orchard of cherries, peaches, pears, plums (our favorite fig jam *'Greengage,'* and an F1 hybrid that reverted to its wild-type the minute it was planted), and apples- including a *'Cox Orange Pippin'* for the vintage Port in the cellar. To the right of the Pagoda is our Berry Run, compleat with golden raspberries, boysenberries, tayberries, and a Himalayan blackberry that got in with a fake ID.

You may have noticed that there are some wonderful things that are not present on this list of planned composted comestibles. There are no peppers (no Jalapenos- this is unfortunate), no tomatoes (no '*Sungold*'- this is a tragedy), and no potatoes (no '*Yukon Gold*'- this is a catastrophe). The reasons are simple and diverse. First, I just can't seem to grow peppers. Maybe it's the magnesium, maybe it's the lack of a greenhouse. I get them to their shape but not their show business. This is a great source of personal shame (and a retirement project). Second, I used to grow great tomatoes but, in recent years, the blight has been getting straight 'A's' in Natural Selection class. Nothing is more frustrating than watching your heirlooms make it all the way through the summer until, just before their sugar hits escape velocity, it's a Black Death party and you're the caterer. Third, there is one thing that is even more frustrating- the black tie coon supper club that nails our Yukon Gold every single time. I'll still plant them this year, because I'm an eternal optimist with a failing memory.

The Gardener's Dictionary defines a garden as '*one of a vast number of free outdoor restaurants operated by charity-minded amateurs in an effort to provide healthful, balanced meals for insects, birds and animals.*' Among the deer, the rabbits, the raccons, the mice, the birds, and the slugs, there is hardly room enough for the stuff I'm trying to grow. And in those remaining spaces live the weeds, which differ from non weeds by how much more easily non weeds come out of the ground when you pull on them *('While better men than we go out, and start their working lives, by grubbing weeds from garden paths with broken dinner knives'* -Kipling). Nature doesn't just abhor a vacuum; she blows. Even my faithful hound, Shiva, has repeatedly been caught red-handed eating grapes on her tiptoes, or standing in the raised bed boxes, pulling carrots out by their tops with her bared teeth, and a flamboyant toss over her shoulder. It's the jungle out there, and there are no property rights. What I can't fathom, is how cabbage butterflies find my cabbages? How does the carrot fly get under the reemay to our carrots? John Ruskin once offered: '*the highest reward for a person's toil is not what they get for it, but what they become by it.*' Well, I'm becoming a little choked. In 1798, William Wordsworth opined that '*wisdom is oftentimes nearer when we stoop than when we soar*' and, more recently, even Martha Stewart has acknowledged gardening as a '*humbling experience*' (from the humbling experience herself). My garden may be a thing of beauty, but it is also an unforgiving arena of sex and death.

The word *garden* is from both the Old English *geard* ('fence or enclosure') and *garth* ('yard or a piece of enclosed ground'). The Oxford Dictionary defines it as 'enclosed cultivated ground'. Enclosure is essential to gardening. That is something we thought we did well and, initially, we did.

In the beginning, there was Mike Gogo. In 1993, I rode out Nanaimo Lakes Road, with a plan in my head, and a list in my hand. I needed untreated cedar, enough to build fourteen 12x3 ft. raised beds, two feet high. There would be seven pairs of raised beds, all connected by a long central 'hallway' of as many *torii.* It was very Shinto, and *tres chic.* The middle path would be covered with grapes and Kiwifruit-the *Hanging Gardens of Westwood.* On either side of this centre aisle would sit various fruit-bearing shrubs and, external to that, elevated fields of chocolate earth studded emerald green. I had designed it, with some foresight, as a labyrinth of wheelchair friendliness. No cast-iron back with a hinge destiny for me. Mike would charge me a King's ransom for his timber and, determined to know beans, I paid it.

Hungry to begin, I was waiting with my belt sander, retro-aural pencil, skill saw, T-square, bubble level, and nuts, bolts, and nails, when the truck came down the driveway. A flurry of activity ensued. On one sunny, Spring day, Robyn and I assembled the pagoda and, a few short weeks later, I had filled the fourteen boxes with topsoil and hope. And grape-vines, and Kiwifruit, and rhubarb, and berry bushes. The first year, I couldn't walk outside without tripping over the joy of my own cleverness. Then I realized that I needed more garden space, for those things that didn't like living two feet off the ground. A plot was opened up for the *three sisters* (corn, pole beans, and squash), and some second cousins, the following Spring. We were heading, inexorably, towards the Illyrian goal of a small house and a large (and enlarging) garden, when I realized we had...varmints.

One of my patients was a fisherman, who provided us with enough thick nylon netting to make a true 'enclosure'. Every year required the employment of new defensive strategies, as Mother Nature invited more of her friends to the picnic. Interior netting, mulch, polyester row covers and, this year, slug bait for the first time. This escalation of technology is designed only to retain some portion of the vegetables and fruits of our labour. The ephemeral is of lasting value only if the ravenous appetites in our back yard would back off. Just a bit. Please.

The measure of a great society is when old men plant trees whose shade they know they shall never sit in, and I am, despite all my efforts both ways, getting old. I look to other old men who gardened. There was gardening wisdom in abundance, in the Founding Fathers of our southern neighbour. George Washington hoped to spend the remainder of his days '*in peaceful retirement, making political pursuits yield to the more rational amusement of cultivating the earth*'. Thomas Jefferson recognized that '*Though an old man, I am but a young gardener*'. And Benjamin Franklin observed that '*man receives a real increase of the seed thrown into the ground, in a kind of continual miracle, wrought by the hand of God in his favor, as reward for his innocent life and his virtuous industry*'. Ralph Waldo Emerson nodded to his vegetables and they nodded back. His garden spade healed all his hurts.

And that's why we garden, isn't it? It's not about the multicoloured chard, or the braised home grown radicchio, or the size of your beefsteak tomatoes. *Too many people spend money they haven't earned, to buy things they don't want, to impress people they don't like.* The essential elements of being happy are having something to do, something to love, and something to hope for. I have all three, every day as a gardener. That man is richest whose pleasures are the cheapest, and gardening is the purest of these. You can bury a lot of troubles digging in the dirt. Gardening is a medicine with no toxic dose. However, there is no hiding your inadequacies. I can tell who you are by looking at your garden. You must love your garden, even if you don't like it.

For part of the year now, Robyn and I are looking forward to gardening in New Zealand. This will be a new adventure for us, learning about soil, pests, and novel plants to grow (tamarillos, feijoas, passion fruit, kumara,...). Sometimes New Zealand seems so very far away as we get older. But we come from the earth, we return to the earth and, in between, we garden. So many seeds and so much space, and so little thyme in between.

"The best place to seek God is in a garden. You can dig for him there."

George Bernard Shaw

Shiva the Wonder Dog 18 March

"If I have any beliefs about immortality, it is that certain dogs I have known will go to heaven, and very, very few persons."

James Thurber

She is beginning to show her 10 years. There is something wrong with her right back hind leg, and this means no more hikes up the ridges (or anywhere else for that matter). When a strange car glides down the driveway these days, she no longer sling-shots around the house, in patriotic defense of her country. Sometimes, she doesn't even hear them coming. She likes her living room mat, and she lets you know if dinner is late by trying to meet your eyes, instead of prancing. Snoring while asleep, she doesn't chase as many virtual varmints these days. Shiva is getting old.

We almost didn't get Shiva. As responsible citizens, we first went to look for a dog at our local SPCA. After some deliberation, Robyn and I settled on an energetic mutt, and were invited in to meet the matron. A grey-haired woman, with rimmed glasses (chained around her neck with too much chain), showed us to our seats, across from a cluttered desk. You just knew there were ten cats at home. She asked why we thought we would make good parents to the dog in the cage. I told her that we both loved dogs (we still had Kali, our brindle lab-terrier cross), that we had a piece of land on a lake, that there were tennis balls from next door, and that there were lots of rabbits to chase. *Strike one.*

"Where will the dog sleep?" she inquired.
"In the garage", I said. *Strike two.*
"We consider our clients as family members, and we would expect them to be allowed inside," she said.

Robyn, who grew up in New Zealand, dog tapeworm heaven, and always had outside dogs (Kali had spent her first few years outside in a doghouse, buried in winter snowdrifts), was not impressed. "So, if we don't take this dog home, you'll just kill it?" she asked. *Outta there.*

That evening, while reading through what passes for a newspaper in our town, Robyn found an ad for Akita-Lab puppies (I knew what a Lab was, but I wasn't as sure what an Akita did). We made the phone call and, the next weekend, we drove out Extension Road to the farmhouse where the doggies lived. The owner turned out to be one of my old patients. She raised purebred Akitas but, on one night of slack vigilance, a friend's male Labrador jumped the fence, and her best laid plans (so to speak) came undone. There were six pups, five black ones, and one white one, with beautiful kohl black eyes and muzzle. *Wag Wag Wag.* Shiva hooked Robyn like a spring steelhead. I was perfectly happy to go with one of the dogs-of-colour, but my wife's determined Antipodean attitude is never to be trifled with. Shiva was spoken for, but the prospective owner hadn't shown up, as arranged. We ended up driving home with a white bundle of separation anxiety, in the crook of my Cowichan sweater.

Shiva spilled into Kali's life like a Dixieland band spills into a monastery. She was greeted with much growling, and averting of the eyes. By nightfall, however, they were getting along. There was one large dog blanket in the garage. When I said goodnight to them, Kali was on the mat, and Shiva was on the concrete floor. When I checked back a little later, they were both sharing the mat. How adorable, I thought. Just before I went to bed, I couldn't resist one last look. Shiva was on the mat, and Kali was on the concrete. And that's the way it went, for the rest of Kali's unnatural life. Kali played *omega* to Shiva's *alpha.* If Kali fetched a ball, Shiva fetched it out of Kali's mouth. If Kali came over for an ear scratch, Shiva hip-checked her into next week. When Kali finally passed on, Shiva pretended not to notice.

Shiva was sharp as a samurai sword, from day one. Robyn had driven out to buy Shiva a few hundred chew toys one morning, and I took both dogs out to the fenced vineyard. Merrily pruning away, I looked up, with dread. No Shiva. I scoured the vineyard. The gods were frowning. Frantically, I ran out onto the road, images of what Robyn would do to me, if I actually found her there, rattling around in my brain. No Shiva. Finally, in full panic mode, I opened the gate back to the house, and ran to the garage. There, on the concrete, smiling and wagging her metronome tail, was Shiva, comfortably pleased with her first big outing.

As the years went by, Shiva picked up all of Kali's knowledge, and then went on to grad school. Unlike Kali, she loved to meet new people, and they loved her back. She refined her cuteness into a ninja weapon, bashfully stroking her muzzle with her paws, throwing her big head against visitors thighs, checking their pockets for treats (she knew how to count). Unlike Kali, again, she was easily distracted. She would swim precisely halfway across the lake, and then turn around. She would fetch a ball twice, but you had to retrieve it the third time. She would go all the way to the end of our drive to get the paper, but then drop it twenty yards from the house. She'd roll over to let you rub her stomach, but you could tell she was only cooperating with the concept.

Shiva has different reactions towards other animals. The first is her usual short-lived bemusement. She always runs after deer in the vineyard but, measuring her options as to what she would do if she caught one, inevitably reconsiders. Red squirrels are chased and treed but, after awhile, she lets the little rodents share the deck, leaving them to eat my hazelnuts in peace. Her second response is fascination. She sometimes sits with head cocked for hours, mesmerized by the llamas next door, or a snake in the compost. Finally, she is the consummate Big Game rabbit hunter. Even motoring down our driveway with Shiva in the back is great fun, with her big head bobbing right beside mine, ears cocked, eyes wide, whining uncontrollably, when a big one hops in front of the truck.

The Akita part of Shiva is very Japanese. She watches me like a hawk, alternately raising one black *Ainu* eyebrow, and then the other. She knows if we are going somewhere by how thick the socks are that I bring downstairs. She knows that '*go*' is a verb. She feigns disinterest by yawning, or blinking, and looking in the other direction, but her laughing tail gives it all away. She'd make a lousy poker player. Down at the lake, between the two big fir trees, she sits like a sphinx, collecting sunbeams, and compliments. She runs a *Yakuza* extortion racket along the lakefront, barking loudly at passing walkers to give up their treats. Whenever we returned from a long trek up

Mount Benson, I would open the gate to find a treasure trove of various brands of dog biscuits, thrown over the fence by her many admirers.

Akitas are not supposed to bark and, for the first year, Shiva didn't. One summer afternoon, Robyn and I heard a spine-chilling wolf howl come out of the back yard. She had found her voice. Now she talks to me, in low grunts and grumbles, but I have never heard her utter a bad word about anyone. She loves to lick my ears and face (depending upon what she has last eaten, this is not necessarily a benediction). She is insanely loyal, and quick to plant herself in the middle of any interest I show in other dogs or people. Like me, Shiva hates noise, and has little time for the fence border hi-jinks of adolescent males. She doesn't seek out the company of others of her species. As she has matured, she has become a creature of habit. From her early morning neighbourhood food forays, until she taps on the living room sliding door windows after her supper (wanting in to lie on her mat), you can time Shiva's planetary position to the second.

One morning, one of my colleagues, on a *vow of silence* Buddhist retreat two doors down, opened her eyes from cross-legged meditation on the front lawn, to find Shiva performing her morning ablutions, only a few feet in front of her.
"It's a koan," I said.

When Shiva was able to climb up the ridges with me, there was nothing more peaceful in the world than sitting together on a mossy hilltop in the sunlight, saying nothing, linked to paradise. So gloriously uncomplicated, Shiva lets me do her worrying; she accepts me unconditionally, but I could never be as good as she thinks I already am. The most famous statue in the Shibuya train station in Tokyo commemorates an Akita named *Hachiko*, the faithful pet of Imperial University Professor Eisaburo Uyeno, in the mid 1920's. Every day Hachiko would walk with his master to the station, and wait all day until he returned. One day Professor Uyeno died, before he could return home. Every successive day, for more than ten years, Hachiko continued to wait at the train station. He died there, waiting. Shiva would wait like that. And unlike very, very few persons, Shiva would go to heaven.

> *"To sit with a dog on a hillside on a glorious afternoon is to be back in Eden, where doing nothing was not boring - it was peace."*
>
> Milan Kundera

Ducks Unlimited 22 March

"It does not cluck.
A cluck it lacks.
It quacks.
It is specially fond
Of a puddle or pond.
When it dines or sups,
It bottoms ups.

Ogden Nash

They should be arriving any day now. I've cleaned around the main pond to welcome them, and Robyn and I have already seen Buffleheads diving on the lake. The sun is beginning to flicker feebly, like it's on battery backup. Soon they will literally drop out of the sky, back into our spring rituals.

For the last few years, we have had Mallard mating pairs in residence. Our first seasonal clue that they have arrived is a heart-stopping fright, from their single-winged swoosh straight-up, vertical takeoff, out of the pond, thirty-five feet into the air and over the trees, when we have surprised them. A slow cautious détente resumes, as the season progresses. They need the pond to bill and coo; we need to swoon over their ducklings. Even Shiva has accepted them as extended family (although she loves to literally scare the crap out of the spring paddlings, in the nearby reserve- bowling for Mallards).

The word 'duck' derives from the Anglo-Saxon '*dūcan,*' meaning '*to bend down low, as if to get under something*', because of the way they feed by upending. There are seven different subspecies of duck: perching, pintail, pochard, teal, whistling, widgeon, and dabbling, the tribe to which our denizen Mallards (*Anas platyrhynchos*) belong.

Mallards originally evolved in Siberia, and their bones are found in Stone Age archeological sites throughout Eurasia. They are now the most numerous water birds in the world. It is a precarious equilibrium. While the total North American duck population is thought to number nearly ten million, eleven million ducks are killed in Europe every year, due to hunting, poisoning from lead shot, avian botulism, agricultural run-off, direct habitat loss, and predators (in Alberta, we have the tar sand toxic tailing ponds). Ducklings, unable to fly, are particularly vulnerable in their nests (to raiding foxes, eagles, and hawks), and on the water (to pike, muskies, crocodiles, and herons). None of this susceptibility is aided by the fact that Mallards have the longest migration of any duck, extending from late Summer to early Winter. From Westwood Lake, our snowbird pair flies on down to Mexico, Central America, and the Caribbean, where the male Mallard, filled with carnival spirit, molts into his iridescent green-headed, chestnut-chested, purple wing-patched Calypso costume. Oh, look at me, and she does.

It's the female that brings a male to breed near the place she was hatched, or the previous year's breeding site. They will be monogamous for the year but, because male ducks never breed in the same area twice, she will return home to our main pond this year with a new mate. The only sound he will ever make is the whistling of his wings in flight, and a soft humble rasping '*raeb-raeb*', from his syrinx (the *'conversation-call'* of *Lorentz*). Female dabbling ducks do all the loud '*quack*' ing and, not unlike the other couple on the property, she is clearly in charge. During courtship, the drake dips his bill into the pond, and tosses it into the air, covering the female with water. If everything goes well, she will lay up to a dozen buffish-green eggs, and 28 days later, right after hatching, she will lead them to the pond (the drake takes no part in caring for the eggs or young).

The ducklings are *precocial*. They can swim and feed themselves on insects, as soon as they hatch, but they stay close to their mother, for protection. If all this sounds like traditional family values, it ain't. While the main pond could be a scene from a Robert Bateman painting, the pond near the vineyard more resembles a San Quentin prison gang. This is where all the rejected Mallard males hang out, and their behaviour is incomprehensible. These drake derelicts sometimes target an isolated female duck, until she succumbs to a phenomenon known as *rape flight* (I won't elaborate). There is also an unusually high number (19%) of male-male homosexual pair relationships, among Mallard males. Finally (truly final), the first reported case of Mallard homosexual necrophilia was documented by Dutch researcher Kees Moeliker. On June 5, 1995, the duck was killed on impact, after flying into the glass façade of the *Rotterdam Natuurmuseum*, about three metres from the ground. The male chasing him copulated with the corpse for 75 minutes, dismounting only twice the entire duration. The determined drake wandered off, but returned later, calling '*raeb-raeb*' repeatedly, long after his victim was already in the freezer. Herr Moeliker has photographs. I don't especially want to see them. This aggressive rapacity of the Mallard is spoiling the genetic biodiversity of the world's other endemic ducks, having now already crossbred with 63 other species.

Other than some minor Muscovy exceptions, all domestic ducks are descended from the wild Mallard. These are found throughout the temperate and subtropical areas of North America, Europe, Asia, and New Zealand (where the most common duck, like the Canada goose, is currently considered a pest). In 1867, the year Canada became a Dominion, Mallard game farm stock was introduced to New Zealand from Australia. Once established, they learned how to eat the blue-bottle blowfly (*Calliphora vicina Robineau-Desvoidy*). Robyn's father, and his brother Bill, used to hunt them (the ducks, not the blowflies-although you would likely need the same weaponry).

Mallards have other adaptations, that at least partially compensate for the deadly list of survival pressures I've described to you earlier. Once they straight-up vertically clear the treetops, they have been clocked at over 45 miles per hour. Their wing muscles are extraordinarily strong, as they would have to be, using such short, fast, continuous strokes. They follow both *Allen's Rule* and *Bergmann's Rule* of birds. Allen's Rule requires that appendages need to be smaller in polar forms, to minimize heat loss, (and larger in desert and tropical equivalents to facilitate heat diffusion). Bergmann's Rule states that polar forms tend to be larger than related ones from warmer climates. The average life expectancy of the Mallard is 5-10 years in the wild, but some individuals have lived for as long as thirty years. Even beyond blue-bottle blowflies, mallards are opportunistically omnivorous. If a frog gets caught in their beak lamellae, he gets to stay.

And for reasons that I am sure are unrelated to cases of homosexual necrophilia, of all the animals in the arc, ducks are an inexhaustible source of human mirth and silliness. Donald Duck, Daffy Duck, Darkwing Duck, Howard the Duck, rubber duck, weird duck, sitting ducks, lame duck, duck soup, and

Groucho Marx: *'Now here is a little peninsula, and here is a viaduct leading over to the mainland.'*
Chico: *'All right, why a duck? Why a duck, why-a no chicken?'*
Groucho: *'Well, I don't know why-a no chicken. I'm a stranger here myself.'*
Groucho was also quoted as saying: *'Yes, I do concur. That thing, indeed, is a duck. And it's dead.'*

Which brings us back to dead ducks. For a dead duck is, above all, as my neice, Rita, would say, 'tasty.' Further bonus points are scored with the wine that is perfectly matched to duck, pinot noir (We've definitely come a long way from the lambrusca *'Cold Duck'* pop wines of the 1970s, that we confused with sparkling wine: *'Baby Duck', 'Canada Duck', 'Fuddle Duck', 'Kool Duck', 'Love-A Duck'*. What a misspent youth that was). The quintessential French duck dish is *canard a l'orange* (*canard* is also often used in English to refer to a deliberately false story, from the old French idiom, *'vendre un canard à moitié'*, meaning to 'half-sell a duck'), but there is a Middle Kingdom recipe from the other side of the planet that is at least equally exquisite. Peking Duck has been prepared in China since the Southern and Northern Dynasties of 420-589 AD. The dish, originally named *Shaoyazi* (燒鴨子), was included in Hu Sihui's (忽思慧) *Complete Recipes for Dishes and Beverages* (飲膳正要) in 1330, by an Imperial kitchen inspector. The first restaurant specialising in Peking Duck, *Bianyifang*, was established in the Xianyukou, Qianmen area of Beijing, in 1416. It was the *Quanjude restaurant* (全聚德), however, in 1864, that developed the hung oven to roast ducks, and introduced the Peking Duck to the rest of the world. It became the favorite dish of Fidel Castro, Helmut Kohl, and Henry Kissinger (it was one of the important factors responsible for the U.S.-China rapprochement in the 1970s).

I knew all of this when I took my friend, Ben Ho, out for dinner one night in Singapore. We ordered the Peking Duck. We got a stack of thin pancakes, some scallions, and some skin. And a bill for $40. I asked the waiter where the rest of the duck went. He brought giblets and a bill for another $40. Ben, who should have known better (but he'd had a *Singapore Sling* at the *Long Bar* over at *Raffles* before dinner, and was plum out of alcohol dehydrogenase) told me that what we had eaten was all Peking Duck. After $80 and a realization that I wasn't going to walk on any duck bones on the floor, I conceded defeat, and we returned to the hotel to rest up, for an early flight to Kathmandu. Somewhere in Singapore today walks a naked duck, with an electrolarynx and a gastric feeding tube, relating the story of his heroic escape from a crazed *Gweilo*, with a duck meat fetish. I have made a vow to forgive Ben. Someday.

There is one more dead duck Mallard story worthy of relating. In 1437, Archbishop Henry Chichele founded Oxford's *All Souls College* in memory of *'the souls of all faithfully departed',* who had died in the *Hundred Years War* with France. When his builders were digging the foundation, an enormous Mallard flew up out of a drain, where it had been trapped for many years. This gave inspiration to the strange *Mallard Hunt Ritual* which occurs every January 14 of the first year of every century. On that night, Fellows abandon their dinner to take up sticks and torches, and wander round the quadrangles and over the rooftops, in search of the ghost of the Mallard. These '*Mallardyzers*' or *Mallardians,* carry their '*Lord of the Mallard',* on a chair, and a dead Mallard on a pole (hoisted on his own canard, so to speak), singing their 'Mallard song' *('Then lett us drink and dance a Galliard in ye Remembrance of ye Mallard, And as ye Mallard doth in Poole, Lett's dabble, dive & duck in Boule')*. The procession is customarily followed by '*a lot of drinking and a fireworks display*'.

But, for now, we're waiting for live ducks. Today is good weather for ducks, and we have all our ducks in a row. Furiously flapping from over the horizon, they'll hit the main pond, like a duck to water, like water off a duck's back, like the duck's guts. And, well, if it looks like a duck...

The Last Shubunkin 01 April

"No human being, however great, or powerful, was ever so free as a fish."

John Ruskin

I honestly don't know what or if he thinks or feels, but I do know he has been down there a long time. Nineteen years to be exact. Almost two decades of avoiding the predation horror that gobbled his friends, within three months of their arriving. He sees only shadows, hears only the sound of Shiva's tongue lapping a few times a day, and feels only...well, that's the question then, isn't it? What does a twenty-year-old Japanese goldfish feel? If I feel for him, am I feeling my anthropomorphic projection, or his suffering? Can he truly appreciate his plight, or is he just a collection of primitive sensory transducers and reflexes? Why does this question bother my consciousness so intensely, every time I go by his pond? And what makes it his pond, anyway?

I once asked an aquarium owner if it wasn't cruel to keep his fish confined in a space they had never evolved to be constrained by. He told me that his fish only had a memory of four seconds, and that everything was always new for them. He was a liar, of course. I could read their faces.

Don't misunderstand. I have slain my share of fish. Except for the odd squeamish moment of dispatch, using either the Canadian *concussion baton technique,* or the New Zealand *brain spike method*, I have always viewed the fish *murder-death-kill* ritual as integral to the sport of angling, and morally neutral. Before I considered the situation of the Last Shubunkin, I had no second thoughts about this worldview. Fish are cold-blooded, I reasoned. Bruce '*we'd-rather-go-too-far-than-not-far-enough*' Friedrich, PETA's director of vegan outreach, has apparently renamed all perfectly good fish as the more politically-correct '*Sea Kittens*'. Bruce, like all fish, has no neocortex. And '*terrorism*' is now a '*man-made disaster*'. James Rose, at the University of Wyoming, had already confirmed the unfeeling nature of the species in his *Neurobehavioral Nature of Fishes and the Question of Awareness and Pain.* Killing fish should be just like pulling carrots.

Except that, as one gets older, the meaning of every dead fish and pulled carrot intensifies, just as the senses, used to acquire that art, science, and memory, lose their scintillation. The early years of catching walleye, bass, and pike in Northwestern Ontario were crude, in comparison to my first steelhead on a fly in the middle of the Stamp River, here on the Island. Thoreau had observed that many men go fishing all of their lives, without knowing that it is not fish they are after. Even if fish suffer (and I haven't conceded the point yet), what is it about fishing that balances off that knowledge, and makes it okay? It may be a bit like bullfighting, although we know that the bull really does have an existential appreciation for his pain. The transcendent nature of the fishing experience is more than the parts of the art we bring to the murder-death-kill ritual. It's more about the canvas than the paint. It's the solitude or the rare camaraderie, the wind and the water, the birds and the moss or the sun and the coral. It's the contact drama of death or escape with the primeval, and not the protein. It is a cosmic experience. When fish die, they fall toward the sky for a reason.

There is increasing evidence that fish are more than a collection of primitive receptors, however. Dr. Lynne Sneddon, and her group in Scotland, published the results of her torture of 20 rainbow trout, in the *Proceedings of the Royal Society*. She identified 58 specialized receptors on their head, 22 of which look virtually identical to corresponding human pain receptors, both under the microscope, and in terms of their mechanical and thermal thresholds. These receptors send signals to the trout's brain via nerves. When '*nasty stimuli*' were applied to their lips, their heart rate went up by 30%, they dramatically increased the rate at which they beat their gills, and they began to exhibit a '*rocking*' behaviour, refused to feed for a long time after the injury, and rubbed their lips in the gravel of the tank, a most uncharacteristic behavior. There is old movie footage of WWI shell-shocked soldiers clasping their arms to their chest, rocking back and forth, rubbing their wounds incessantly, and not eating. We now call this *Post Traumatic Stress Syndrome*. When Dr. Sneddon gave the traumatized trout morphine, their behaviour instantly returned to normal. Without a neocortex. Fishes do have opiate receptors in their brainstems, and structures similar to our own limbic system.

In other studies, older fish have been shown to teach younger fish about predators (including the sound of trawler engines). Kristopher Paul Chandroo, of Guelph University, has proposed that there may be forms of primary consciousness that exist with neural systems other than those which include a neocortex (*'An evaluation of current perspectives on con-*

sciousness and pain in fishes'). Maybe our 19- year-old Last Shubunkin is hardwired in such a way that he can still mentally construct and integrate, remember and, not just feel, but feel a feeling. Surely the best evidence that he possesses some intellect, is his very survival. *Outwit. Outplay. Outlast.* Indeed. My friend, Mikie, and I are going fishing on the weekend. In addition to the harvesting of sentient mussels, oysters, clams, prawns, and crabs from the shores and depths of Barkley Sound, we're going to slay some extremely intelligent Chinook. As humanely as possible.

Postscript: Despite all protestations by the uninformed and unenlightened to the contrary, there are no trout in Westwood Lake. Stay away.

Lighting up a Swamp Lantern 20 April

"I still have my lantern."

Diogenes

The smell is one of the most lurid signs of Spring at Westwood. Shiva likely gets it before I do, coming around this corner of the lake but, when I do pick it up, it does a sharp acrid dance in my sinuses. The aroma is toxic culinary- black rubber sautéed in garlic butter with aromatic *herbes de Provence, escargots de Bourgogne* in rotten eggs, or spinach and matchbook onion *quiche.* As an original good ol' boy from Northwestern Ontario, it smells like only one thing to me- skunk. The whole brimstone, bear-blinding, sulfur-spraying, striped weasel experience. The kind you can taste and smell at the same time, and wish you couldn't.

It's an alien life form, this Western Skunk Cabbage (*Lysichiton americanum*). Every aspect of its personality is high Gothic. *Lysichiton* is, literally translated, a loose-fitting *ancient Greek tunic,* which accurately describes the dramatic, large, canary- yellow, leafy bract (*spathe*) that encloses the fleshy, club-like spike, bearing the skunk cabbage's minute flowers (*spadix*). An Aboriginal legend accounts for the origin of the skunk cabbage spathe: *'Long ago, there were no Salmon. The People ate Skunk Cabbage leaves and roots. Finally, the Salmon came up the river and Skunk Cabbage, in human form, stood up and alerted the People to their arrival. In return, Skunk Cabbage was given an elk-skin blanket and a war club*'.

These unique flowering structures place it in the *Arum* plant family, from the Arabic word for fire, *ar*, the two burning reasons for which I will allude to later. There is an Eastern Skunk Cabbage (*Symplocarpus foetidus*) with purple, rather than crayon yellow, spathes. In Quebec, it is called *tabac du diable* ('devil's tobacco') or *chou puant* ('stinking cabbage'). Other Arum tribal members include the poisonous corn lily, or false hellebore (*Veratrum californicum*), the pious Jack-in-the-Pulpit (*Arisaema triphyllum*) that we used to call *Indian Turnip* in Northwestern Ontario, the flesh-pink Dead-Horse Arum of Corsica (*Helicodiceros muscivorus*), the graceful Calla lily (*Zantedeschia aethiopica*), and the elegant Dieffenbachia. In Japan, there are massive Spring pilgrimages to bogs in the Hokkaido region, to view the flowering White Skunk Cabbage (*Lysichiton camtschatcensis*). Its sacred name, *Mizu Basho*, translates as *'water' plus 'banana-like plant,'* also associated with the revered 15th century poet of the same name. Western Skunk Cabbage grows from Kodiak Island, Alaska, south along the west coast to Northern California, with isolated populations also found in northeastern Washington, northern Idaho, Montana, Wyoming, and in some wild, marshy areas of England and Scotland.

Henry David Thoreau called skunk cabbage the '*Hermit of the Bog*'. It has also been referred to as the '*Eye of Spring*'.

Wherever it lives, once rooted, it's impossible to dig out of the ground (I've tried). Despite the lack of a taproot, skunk cabbage has a massive contractile root system designed to anchor the plant deeper and deeper into the muck, with each passing year. *Just when I thought I was out...they pull me back in.* There is a thick, round, central rhizome, out of which hundreds of pencil-thin ring-wrinkled roots grow in all directions. Near the end tips of each of them are many tiny, fibrous rootlets, pulling for the alien team. Large, older plants lie deeper than younger ones. Maybe they know something the younger ones don't for, in the early spring, bears, coming out of hibernation, seek out skunk cabbage roots as a cathartic, to jump start their digestion. This bear borborygmi beginning comes from powerful stuff, the first of the two Arabic fires, *calcium oxalate.*

If you are foolish enough to ingest any part of Western Skunk Cabbage, irritating needle-like crystals of calcium oxalate will puncture the mucous membranes of your mouth and throat immediately. Even small amounts of calcium oxalate are enough to cause intense oral burning, swelling, and choking. Larger doses result in profound indigestion, nausea, vomiting, and diarrhea (alright if you're a bear fresh out of hibernation, perhaps), breathing difficulties, convulsions, unconsciousness, and death. Recovery can occur, but usually at the expense of permanent liver and kidney damage (or at least kidney stones).

Early First Nations people knew that cooking Skunk Cabbage leaves and roots in many changes of water removed enough calcium oxalate to provide a reliable, but not very choice, source of calories, when food was scarce. Here's a good rule. If you have to boil anything multiple times to make it safe to eat... don't eat it. The Meskwaki Indians mixed *Jack-in-the-Pulpit* with game, and left the meat out for their enemies to find. The taste of the oxalate was undetectable because of the flavored meat, but swallowing it painfully tortured, and ultimately killed, their foes. Inorganic sources of calcium oxalate exist (*ethylene glycol* antifreeze, and beer stone left over from the brewing process, the most notable examples), but you just can't beat plant sources of poison for sheer entertainment value. Calcium oxalate is also found in rhubarb, taro, kiwifruit, agave (and therefore *tequila*), and spinach. It's almost enough to make you skip the next salad bar. *Dieffenbachia* stalks have the highest concentrations of all flora, but our humble Western Skunk Cabbage is not far behind.

This is not to say that Native Americans did not exploit the plant. Skunk cabbage's waxy leaves were used to wrap, carry, dry and store many foods. Meat and fish and vegetables were steamed separately in its leaves, just as the Polynesians used taro or Africans used banana leaves. Skunk Cabbage leaves were also employed as berry basket liners, and rolled to make conical disposable drinking cups. Dried roots were used for cramps, convulsions, whooping cough, and toothaches; root poultices were applied to wounds. The Haida used its white-fingered tubers as lures for their yew fish hooks, and halibut were fooled into thinking they were vacuuming down an octopus. First Nations even used Skunk Cabbage as an underarm deodorant, difficult as it is to believe that armpits smelling of burnt rubber, garlic, and rotten eggs constituted an improvement. In the 19th century, the *U. S. Pharmacopoeia* listed Eastern Skunk Cabbage as the drug *dracontium*, recommended in the treatment of heart failure, respiratory diseases, nervous disorders, and rheumatism.

The second and principal inspiration for the igneous appellation derives from Skunk Cabbage's peculiar ability to generate heat, enough to melt surrounding snow. They are thermogenic, and the how and why are enthralling. Generating heat requires two processes, production and retention.
Root starch is broken down to glucose, and transported to the flower clusters. Normally, glucose is

broken down by oxygen-dependent cell respiration, to produce ATP (adenosine triphosphate), the biochemical currency of most metabolic processes, in most life forms on this planet. The pathway is known as the *Krebs cycle,* and occurs in small cellular organelles, called mitochondria. The reactions are efficient, but not perfect, and some heat is simply lost from the reacting molecules. Heat loss is, therefore, usually viewed as an unavoidable casualty of burning sugar to make ATP. We know that this biochemistry can be poisoned by *cyanide.* In the cells of the Skunk Cabbage spadix, however, nobody's making ATP. This elk-skin blanket and war club flower cluster uses a different, cyanide-resistant pathway, to make metabolic heat as a primary product, ATP be damned. How much heat? As much as a small mammal, or a hummingbird (in all it's bejeweled parabolic splendor). As much as 15 to 35 C above ambient temperature for two weeks, more than enough to melt snow.

Why does it do this? Skunk Cabbage lavishly revs its metabolic engine more like a lizard than a lettuce. The thermogenesis advantage must be worth it, however, because the energy demands on the plant are huge. It melts snow to get itself pollinated before other flowering plants can. By vaporizing scents into the chilly spring air. And what could you possibly be able to attract that is awake enough to pollinate you, at this time of year? The warmth and unique smell of the Skunk Cabbage have evolved together to mimic a dead animal, in which microbial processes have raised the carcass temperature. What pollinates an imitation dead carcass? Flies. And a beetle called *Peelecomalius testaceum*, which feeds on the pollen, and uses the inflorescences as a mating site. This plant thermogenesis phenomenon is quite rare. Certain South American night-blooming water lilies can elevate flower temperatures, as part of a complicated pollination tango with scarab beetles. The Titan Arum of Sumatra (*Amorphophallus titanum*) has the most horrible scent in the world. It has been named the *Corpse Flower,* and its bouquet can be detected more than a mile away. Its spadia makes up the largest floral structure in the plant world- up to three meters tall (compared to the Western Skunk Cabbage spadia height of 18 inches- but the cabbage can outburn the titan in heat production, any day of the week).

There is one final extraterrestrial quality to this unusual Gothic green swamp lantern. It vanishes. The brilliant, leathery, green leaves of the Skunk Cabbage are the largest of any native plant in Canada. They unfold in a beautiful spiraling pattern. In late July, the leaves develop small holes, begin to droop, and then turn black and slimy. Then, they rapidly dissolve away. The Lords of the Wetlands in May have melted away by August. Skunk Cabbage is mostly water and air, and a little fire. Goethe once invited us to become 'as flexible and mobile as nature herself'. In the early Spring at our place, nature is busy, lighting up the swamp lanterns around Westwood Lake.

Sliding Down the Razor Blade 04 May

"There is a slippery step at every man's door."

H. W. Thompson

White cherry blossoms blew sideways, outside the old house kitchen window, on a May morning like this one, twenty years ago. I kissed Robyn, and walked out the front door, off to work. What I saw, hanging off the end of the left wooden handrail, froze me solid- a squirming, deforming mass, half a foot around, a writhing dream catcher wheel of slime strands, some elongating and some growing shorter and thicker, at different speeds. It was a ballet of rubber cement. On cautious close inspection, I noticed two fat black spotted yellow apostrophes, suspended in a perfect *yin-yang* symbol off the railing. Unwittingly, I had interrupted a private moment in the bizarre mating ritual of two of Westwood's most unusual residents. Prior to this incident, whenever I had encountered them on the trail, I had simply walked on, disregarding them as some dull species of slow-moving primordial poo. Since that morning in May, however, I slow down to study these land snails, at each encounter.

Dr Augustus Addison Gould, an American conchologist, and President of the *Massachusetts Medical Society,* first gave our Pacific Banana Slug its scientific name (*Ariolimax columbianus*), in 1851. 'Will' Cuppy, an American satirist and recluse (who committed suicide with sleeping pills after being evicted from his apartment), described their origins in 1949: '*Land snails used to live in the ocean, but moved ashore. Since nobody told them otherwise, they expected the land to be as wet as the water. We all make mistakes*'. He was right.

Approximately 550 million years ago, in what we now call the Cambrian Period of the Paleozoic era, large wormlike molluscs, with exoskeletons of lime, frolicked in the primordial oceans. We know this because we have found their fossilized shells, much easier than finding surviving remnants of half-billion-year-old dead slugs. During the Devonian period, 100 million years later, invertebrates began to leave the ocean, because of increased solar radiation in the water, and warmer, wet conditions on land. Upwardly mobile molluscs evolved divergently, into two distinct species: Land Snails retained their external shells, which protected and contained their bodies quite effectively, although at the cost of having to exist in calcium-rich soils, in order to be able to maintain their chemical armour. Slugs, on the other hand, traded increased mobility in a broader range of environments, for an increased susceptibility to dessication and predation. Of predators, there is no shortage. Garter snakes, ducks, geese, shrews, moles, racoons, beetles, crows, and salamanders, all get their share. Banana slugs were a food source for the Yurok natives of northern California, and the German settlers from Humboldt county, who came later:

Banana Slugs Sautéed

12 large banana slugs
White vinegar
Butter

Drop the banana slugs into a container of white vinegar for about an hour. This both kills them and congeals their slime. Use plenty of running water to rinse the slime and vinegar off their bodies, Gut and clean them as you would a fish. Then, using your thumbnail, pop out the small hidden shell from the head area. The shell will be about the thickness of a fingernail and about the size of a dime.
Cut the slugs into bite-sized or smaller pieces and sauté in butter. Serve over rice. They would go well in sushi.

Banana slugs are the second-largest species of terrestrial slug in the world, growing up to 10 inches long (compared to the European *Limax cinereoniger*, which can reach a foot in length). They are able to stretch out to 11 times their normal length. The Pacific Banana Slug is found from Alaska to California, but there is also a California Banana Slug (*Ariolimax californicus*) and a Slender Banana Slug (*Ariolimax dolichophallus*), discovered only as recently as 1943. Pacific Banana Slugs have yellow, green, brown, or white bodies, a hump on their back and a mantle, a leathery saddle remnant of what used to carry their shells. On the right side of their mantle, there is a hole called a *pneumostome*, through which their lungs connect to the outside. Banana slugs have two pairs of tentacles. The larger, upper eyestalk pair is used to detect light or movement. The second, lower pair is the olfactory organ, sensing chemicals and 'smells'. Both pairs of tentacles are retractable, to protect them from the surrounding environment. The Banana Slug's jaw is a solid structure, that can drop like a guillotine. Its mouth is called a *radula*, containing several rows of up to 27,000 sharp, backward-pointing teeth, which rasp and grind at leaves, mosses, dead plant material, wild flowers, ferns, animal droppings and, especially, mushrooms (they can smell a mushroom 10 yards away with their lower antennae). Like sharks, they routinely lose and replace their teeth. Banana Slugs are *detritivores*, recycling decomposers. They have evolved into a symbiotic relationship with California Redwoods (the tree that also originally covered Vancouver Island, millions of years ago), providing nitrogen-rich scat, and eliminating any plant that tries to compete with these red giants.

Banana Slugs clean the forest floor and spread spores and seeds, as they move forward slowly on their single muscular foot. How slowly? Very slowly, about .007 miles an hour. Doing the math, it takes an hour for a Banana Slug to reach that mushroom he can smell. In the 100 yard dash, a Banana Slug would take over nine hours to cross the finish line.

Slugs mark their homes with their own scent, so they can find their way home in the dark. When the temperature drops, Slugs have the ability to hibernate. In mid-summer, when conditions in the woods get hot and dry, Banana Slugs bury themselves in forest debris, secrete a protective layer of mucus, and become inactive, a process known as *estivation*. The Banana Slugs' additional mucus production during this season is enough to help protect the Sow Bug (*Porcellio scaber*), against the same death by dessication, a relationship known as *temporary commensalism*.

The Banana Slug's seemingly vulnerable nakedness is more than compensated for by the evolutionary adaptation that glues together its entire world. *Slime*. Mollusc Mucus. Slug slime has five main functions.

The first is *respiration.* Gas exchange occurs partially on the skin of Slugs and can only take place in the presence of moisture.

Second, already alluded to, are the *protective benefits* of slime. When Banana Slug mucus comes in contact with a moist surface, an anesthetic compound is produced, which causes membranes to go numb. This is the quintessential predator deterrent, and the reason why Banana Slugs aren't prominent menu items in Vancouver Island eateries. Raccoons have learned to roll the Slugs in dirt, to coat and neutralize the slime, but this would still not likely make it anyone's favorite amuse-bouche. As a useful side effect, slug slime *can take away the sting* from nettles. There are other forms of protection afforded by slime. It allows slugs to *travel unharmed,* across the sharp edge of a razor blade or piece of glass. When the slug humps its body up with its glazed layer of thick mucus, it appears more formidable and larger in size (as formidable and ferocious as any Banana Slug could possibly hope to appear). Slime also helps them *retain moisture* (dry slug slime, on the other hand, is very flammable, and slime trails are thought to be a contributing factor in forest fires, during the dry season).

Third, slime is critical to Banana Slug *mobility,* a high artform of lubrication locomotion. However, there are physical and physiological limits to the locomotion lubrication. The slime's adhesive strength must be overcome by the slug; and the slug has to replace the slime it uses as it moves. Speed is not an option, if you have to continually manufacture the slippery highway on which you cruise. The highway material itself needs special properties. Slime is 96 percent water, the reason we tend to encounter slugs when it's raining or damp. Scientists originally thought that the molecular structure of slug slime was like a plate of spaghetti- with thicker mucus having more tangled strands. But in 1993, Verdugo and Viney demonstrated that slug mucus is a highly organized polymeric substance, which can rapidly absorb up to 100 times its initial volume of water. The slug cells cleverly package up this polymer in granules, coated with a layer of cell membrane material, keeping it dry, until well outside the cell. When these packets break open, upon contact with extracellular ATP, the results are explosive. The thickness of mucus is controlled by the swelling of the polymer network, and that swelling, in turn, is proportional to the saltiness of the water it picks up. (This discovery also turned out to be the missing link between thick mucus and the faulty transport of chloride ions, that characterize the disease Cystic Fibrosis.)

Different surface parts on the slug produce different types of slime. The pedal gland, in the foot, secretes a thick, sticky mucus. When the slug wants to move, it starts sliding the back end of its foot. The *shear stresses* produced by this sliding motion cause the slime underneath that section to become slippery, and that section can then move forward. When the rear end of the foot stops moving, the slime underneath it turns solid, making it stick. At the same time, a section of foot, just in front of the rear section, starts to move, creating slippery slime, which pushes that part of the animal forward. In this wave-like way, the slug creeps along, with just one part of its foot moving at a time. This process even allows a Banana Slug to travel upside-down. When a slug is stationary, it glues itself to surfaces with the solid form of its slime. The physical properties of this versatile polymer allow the slug both to move on liquid, and to stick to solid surfaces, simultaneously.

While the pedal gland makes thick slime, other glands produce thin slime, the stuff that makes up the 'slime trails' you see early in the morning. Slugs can also move vertically (like very limited fat spiders), on a string of thin slime, produced at the end of their 'tails'. Researchers dream of applying slug slime technology in medicine (e.g. drug delivery systems) and bioengineering, materials science (eg. adhesives, glues, and water-based lubricants), and sewage treatment plant pollutant traps but, so far at least, attempts to reproduce slug slime in the lab have been unsuccessful.

The fourth use the Banana Slug sometimes has for its slime is nutritional, in times of damp deprivation and absolute necessity.

The ultimate Banana Slug mucus use is for sex- and here it has a diversity of function. Slug slime contains pheromones to attract other slugs for mating. Couples lay down a thick layer of slime as a blanket to mate on. They taste and eat each other's slime, either as a way to obtain hormonal information, or a convenient snack to fuel them up for the rubber cement ritual I found on the old house handrail that May morning, twenty years ago. Mating occurs at night. Banana Slugs are hermaphrodites, and have their genital openings near their heads. They Yin and Yang for up to twelve hours straight (comparable to a continuous ten day copulation for a sixty-year-old human in slug years), exchanging sperm that fertilize the eggs internally. There is no monogamous fidelity. Slugs are capable of storing sperm for weeks. Some form sperm plugs that prevent other male sperm from getting into the female reproductive tract, but some tricky females will remove this plug, and mate again. As if all of this wasn't bizarre enough, when the Banana Slug disengages from his twelve hours of sex, he happily gnaws off his penis. As Sugar Ray Robinson said, "*You always say 'I'll quit when I start to slide' and then one morning you wake up and realize you've done slid.*"

Banana Slugs lay up to twenty pinky-nail size pearly, opalescent eggs, in clusters, under rocks, logs and in soil. Most slugs die after laying their eggs. Parental guidance is not their strong suit.

And then there was Captain Beefheart, who apparently didn't think much of Bob Dylan- '*Bob Dylan impresses me about as much as... well, I was gonna say a slug but I like slugs.*' But I think the Bard knew a whole lot more about Banana Slugs than Beefheat. You only have to look at what he wrote:

A Hard Rain's A-Gonna Fall, Buckets Of Rain, Let's Stick Together, Wiggle Wiggle, All Over You, In The Garden, Foot Of Pride, Walkin' Down The Line, You Ain't Goin' Nowhere, Endless Highway, Quit Your Low Down Ways, Most Likely You Go Your Way (And I'll Go Mine)

The Voice of Protest, just like the rest of us- sliding down the razor blade of life.

The Ponds 16 May

"A fool can throw a stone in a pond that 100 wise men can not get out."

Saul Bellow

Robyn and I have been increasingly lured into taking our lunch on a bench, under the cottonwood canopy that enfolds us, beside the big pond. After a morning of happy gardening and vineyard debudding, we consume our sandwiches quietly. Shiva stalks the last morsels, cocking her head one way and then another, lying across the cedar chip mulch path, blocking all means of escape. There is a sparrow that chirps brazenly for his share of the spoils, in the alder immediately above our heads. We take our last bites, and reach for the watermelon slices. The skimmia reflected across the pond, is a mustard fireworks explosion of yellow watercolour. Striders leave streaks on the oily rich liquor. A tree frog *c-r-r-icks* from his hidden cove. We are all at peace, in a forest that was only a cow paddock, twenty years earlier.

When we dug the foundation for our house, Ray the Excavator asked me if I wanted him to *'carve out a couple of ponds'*, while he was still sitting way up there in his guru cab.

"Sure," I said, trying to imagine picking up a few trout on my way back from the vineyard, at the end of long day.

"How about an island in the middle of the big one?" he inquired.

"That would be great, Ray."

Now, I'm sitting on my own private island, with a fly rod and a glass of my own Pinot Noir. *Two o'clock. Ten o'clock. Two o'clock. Ten o'clock. Snap-Zzzzzzzz*, spilling my wine so as not to lose this trophy rainbow. Ray immediately got stuck into digging out the first pond, and I trundled off to work.

I couldn't wait to get home that evening and, when I did, I ran down the paddock to look at my first new pond. Robyn came with me.

"Wow!" was my initial reaction. Then, "Hey, wait a minute. Where's my island?" I puzzled out loud.

"You don't need an island." came from Robyn's direction. I protested, conjuring up how the conversation with Ray must have gone: "*Still want an island?*" "*Island? We don't need no stinkin' island.*" Seeing my disappointment, Robyn offered an olive branch.

"Just get him to put it back," she said. Which prompted the short discussion about geology.

I needn't have bothered. As it turned out, she was right (as usual). We didn't need an island. It would have been out of proportion. Besides, several years later, Robyn put in a small Japanese pier to nowhere- which looks *subarashi*.

The two ponds have very different personalities. The first pond, the smaller one, adjacent to the vineyard and closer to the road, is a dark brooding oval lagoon, with encroaching alders. The tree frogs love it but, other than for a blast of white from the hawthorn in the spring, we seldom linger on its path. The big second kidney basin pool is a warm, serene brush painting, a Matsuo Basho haiku. *'An old pond A frog jumps in The sound of water'*. Here we can look into the depths of our own nature, or just eat a sandwich. We hope to live long enough that, many years from now, it will have transformed into our *Golden Pond.*

One Summer several years ago, the kids from next door put sunfish in the big pond. A few Summers later, a marine biologist friend from Mauritius stocked it with crayfish. I still throw my crab carapaces and fish skeletons in, when Robyn's not looking. On one occasion, she asked me what I was going to do with the head and bones of a particularly large halibut. I told her I was going to bury it in the garden. She told me the dog would dig it up. I buried it anyway. An hour later, I watched Shiva sneak by the living room window, dragging her exhumed trophy. That's when I started using the pond. It's not Saul Bellow's hundred wise men I have to worry about.

The origin of the word *'pond'* is from *'pound,'* meaning a man-made confined enclosure, for cattle, water, or whatever. When the British arrived in New England, they applied the term to natural pools as well. When I arrived in New England from Northwestern Ontario, at the ripe old age of sixteen, I couldn't understand why bodies of water, that we would have called lakes, were called *'ponds'* by local convention. I had always thought that ponds were much smaller, and had different plants and animals, but these guys either didn't seem to understand this, or didn't care.

Is a pond defined by its biology, or its size? The freshwater biologists would have you believe that a pond is a body of water where light penetrates to the bottom, is shallow enough for rooted water plants to grow throughout its deepest part, and lacks wave action on the shoreline. These criteria can be entirely undermined, however, with seasonal change, pollution, algae blooms or shade from large trees. Perhaps a more practical definition of a pond should be based on size (e.g. smaller than would require a boat to cross, or where a human can walk across the entire body of water without being submerged). But here, again, there are problems of standardization. In the UK, the charity, *Pond Conservation*, has defined a pond as *'a man-made or natural waterbody which is between 10 square feet and 5 acres in area, which holds water for four months of the year or more'*. Some regions of the U.S. define a pond as a body of water with a surface area of less than 10 acres. The *International Ramsar Wetland Convention* sets the upper size limit for ponds at 20 acres. So why is the most inspirational pond in history, Walden Pond in Concord, Massachusetts, 62 acres? Because there is, as yet, no internationally- recognized pond size cutoff, because this nomenclature is a historical and cultural determinant, and because Walden is... Walden. Just as I have dessicated Bo tree leaves from Bodgaya bookmarking the Buddhist writings in my library at Westwood Lake, I have dried maple leaves from Henry David Thoreau's cabin bookmarking my copy of *Walden*. It has not acquired one permanent wrinkle after all its ripples.

It is no dream of mine,
To ornament a line;
I cannot come nearer to God and Heaven
Than I live to Walden even.
I am its stony shore,
And the breeze that passes o'er;
In the hollow of my hand
Are its water and its sand,
And its deepest resort
Lies high in my thought.

Whenever the calculus began to hurt my head at MIT, I would head out to Walden Pond, for a little Thoreau. Whenever even that wasn't enough, I would hitchhike to Vermont, and trek into Stratton Pond. And float.

Ten years later, I met a Kiwi girl in the Cairo Airport, at three o'clock in the morning. We went to the Himalayas. Three years after that, she flew across the Big Pond, and we were married. And now we have two ponds. And we eat our lunch on a bench, under the cottonwood canopy that enfolds us.

Sum Antics 20 May

"The ant has made himself illustrious;
Through constant industry industrious;
So what? Would you be calm and placid;
If you were full of formic acid?"

Ogden Nash, The Ant

He's mocking me again with those beady little red squirrel eyes. Perched on the long bird feeder, up the Douglas fir just outside our kitchen window, he extends his tiny paws, to show me the next breakfast hazelnut on the menu, from his previous year's harvest. I'm thinking that the huge boiling nest of insects right below him, would be perfect for breaking the fall of any thieving rodent, accidentally blown off his podium. But I put away my imaginary slingshot, and shift my attention to my attention to the mound, transfixed.

Robyn & I have two of these convex colonies of Western Thatching Ants (*(Formica obscuripes),* here at Westwood. One is up at the top of the vineyard, and the other is sitting in the bush under the Red Bomber. They may be part of the same *supercolony,* or not. They were here when we arrived, and they will be here when we're gone.

While some ants do not form permanent colonies (South American Army Ants and African Driver Ants alternate between nomadism and masses of workers forming temporary nests with their bodies, holding each other together), our Western Thatching Ants form elaborate flood-resistant air-conditioned nests, populated by fleeting generations of workers, that take on more dangerous and more expendable jobs as they get older- from babysitting to trailblazing to dead in just a few short weeks.

Thatchers are large humpbacked red and black ants, with two other rather distinguishing characteristics. They farm aphids and, because they immediately spray their hard bites with *formic acid*, they are painfully displeasing in any chance encounter. How painful has been semiquantified by Justin O. Schmidt, an entomologist at the *Carl Hayden Bee Research Center.* His *Schmidt Sting Pain Index* is an attempt to characterize the bites of various insects. Reading like personalized wine-tasting notes, his tiers of torment evoke a peculiar masochistic aesthetic. Scoring ranges from the lowly Sweat Bee at 1.0 *(light, ephemeral, almost fruity. A tiny spark has singed a single hair on your arm*), all the way up to the 4.0+ Bullet Ant *(pure, intense, brilliant pain. Like fire-walking over flaming charcoal with a 3-inch rusty nail in your heel*). Our Thatching Ants are, thankfully, somewhere in the middle.

There are limitations to this simple chile pepper *Scoville Scale* metric to describe the effects of ant bites, however. Fire ants score only 1.2 on Schmidt's Index *('sharp, sudden, mildly alarming. Like walking across a shag carpet and reaching for the light switch'*), but they have a poison sac containing piperidine alkaloids, that can be very dangerous to hypersensitive individuals. The sting of Jumper Ants can be fatal. There are also Trap-jaw Ants, which can snap their large spring-loaded mandibles shut at over 200 km/hr. I'll keep the Thatchers, at my picnics.

Our word *ant* comes from Middle English *ante,* through Old English *æmette,* from West Germanic *amaitjo*, the original meaning of which was, in fact, '*the biter*'. They've been biting a very long time. Ants evolved from vespoid wasps in the mid-Cretaceous period, about 130 million years ago. After the appearance of flowering plants about 100 million years ago, they diversified to become ecologically dominant, around 40 million years later. Today, on the planet, we have 12,000 classified species out of about 14,000 total, with only approximately 580 species in North America (compare us to the tropics, where one can collect 300 species within 25 acres, and more than 40 species can be found in a single tree). Ants have colonised almost every landmass on Earth, except Antarctica, and some remote islands. They are the most successful insects of all time.

Ants form 20% of the animal biomass in our temperate forest, 10 times that of moose biomass in B.C.'s Central Interior. This is still not as much as the one-third of biomass in the Brazilian rain forest attributable to ants. The mass of all the ants on our planet easily exceeds that of people (so far). Only one millionth the size of humans, for every human in the world, there are also one million ants. An ant brain has about 250,000 brain cells. A human brain has 10,000 million- so a colony of 40,000 ants has collectively the same size brain as a human (although ant brains are the largest amongst insects, individually, ants are stupid. Collectively, however, they are a formidable force of adaptation). Right here is where the ant-human proportionality game ends. Ants don't sleep. If a man could run as fast for his size as an ant, he would be as fast as a racehorse. Ants can carry 10 to 20 times their body weight which, as Ron Darian points out, is *'useful information if you're mov-*

ing out and you need help getting a potato chip across town'.

To move extremely heavy things, they work collectively. For ants, there is no 'I' in team. Their social structure is, like our own, the reason they co-dominate the Earth. Unlike human higher cortical socialization, however, each individual ant is a chemical microswitch, a gasoline tanker of behavioural pheromones. The vehicle itself weighs less than 5 mg but consists of various compartmentalized factories (i.e. *Dufour's glands,* poison glands and glands on the hindgut, pygidium, rectum, sternum and hind tibia) that produce up to twenty different communication chemicals. These pheromone vapors follow *Graham's Law of Effusion,* and can act quickly, slowly, briefly, or with perseverance. The diversity of behaviour that this chemical alphabet can elicit is magnificent. A crushed ant emits alarm pheromones (*citral, citronellal, 4- methyl-3-heptanone* and *limonene*-terpenoids, related to the essential oils contained in cloves, roses, peppermint, camphor, cedar, and eucalyptus) that send nearby ants into an attack frenzy, and recruit more ants from further away. The release of *limonene* also causes a circling response in attacking ants. Blends of pheromones, produced and released as a symphony of Graham's Law of Effusion, are necessary for successful, coordinated attacks. In the African Weaver Ant, for example, the mandibular gland secretion produces serial behaviour based on the sequential release of four pheromones. Initially, *hexanal* causes an alert response, followed by an attraction response of *1-hexanol.* As the ants approach the droplet, *3-undecanone* initiates further attraction and biting, and *2-butyl-2-octenal* stimulates more intense biting behaviour. Only men and ants indulge in such highly organized mass warfare. Their foreign policy consists of relentless aggression, territorial conquest, and genocidal annihilation of neighbouring colonies, whenever possible. As Bert Holldobler and Edward Wilson remarked in their *Journey to the Ants*: 'If ants had nuclear weapons, they would probably end the world in a week'. Self-defense pheromones are usually carboxylic acids (e.g. *formic acid,* but also *tridecane, 2-tridecanone, pentadecane,* and 2-*pentadecane*), which even some birds will use to control lice by crushing ants in their bills and rubbing them through their feathers.

Some ants employ *propaganda pheromones* (a mixture of *decyl, dodecyl,* and *tetradecyl* acetates), to confuse enemy ants into fighting among themselves, until they can be enslaved. One of these specific pheromones (*anabaseine*), used to lead nest mates back to prey they intend to kill, is currently undergoing trials as possible Alzheimer's therapy. The nuptial flights and mating of the carpenter ant are governed by *methyl 6-methylsalicylate,* a winged wintergeen waltz. Colony workers begin to raise new queens when the dominant queen stops producing a specific pheromone. Even in death, ants release *oleic acid,* which not only results in the removal of corpses but, also, if dabbed on living ants, the compulsory expulsion of the healthy. By far the most ephemeral and powerful of chemical controls are the trail pheromones. Just 1 milligram of *methyl 4-methylpyrrole-2-carboxylate,* is enough to lead a column of ants, three times around the world. If you've ever watched ant behaviour, after you've interrupted a trail with a swipe of your finger, you know it doesn't take long, before they've found the shortest way around the obstacle. Some of these trails will endure for 10 months and many rainfalls, after their original production. Some deter other insect herbivores from crashing the neighbourhood.

Beyond the chemistry of ants making trails, lies the Artificial Intelligence applications of trail-making ants. It starts with the 51° angle that every ant uses to split off a trail, walking away from the colony. The famed foraging answer to the *Travelling Salesman Problem* (the salesman can travel from any city to any other city, but must visit each city once and only once using the most efficient path possible) is known as the '*Ant Solution*', and has been successfully employed in routing telecommunications. *Ant Colony Optimization* and *Swarm Robotics* are newer branches of AI, which will further develop our collective intelligence algorithms.

The ecological impact of ants is profound. Ants surpass earthworms in the amount of soil they transport to the surface, mixing, mineral cycling, aerating, and changing the chemistry and drainage of the dirt they live in, and we live on. Many plants have their seeds dispersed by ants. In South Africa, black ants collect and store Rooibos tea seeds in their nest, where humans can gather up to half a pound of seeds from one ant-heap. Stick Insect eggs mimic seeds, and are taken into ant colonies and inadvertently protected. Ants prey on insects and spiders, and account for an 85% reduction in the caterpillars of Pacific Northwest defoliating moths.

Just as our Thatchers farm aphids, Leafcutting Ants farm gardens of fungi. One type of ant even has a three-way association with a host plant and a sticky fungus, which is used to trap their insect prey. They eat and are eaten. Pileated woodpeckers, bears, antbirds, poison dart frogs (whose skin toxins come from the ants they ingest), flies, fungi, anteaters, pangolins, and several Australian marsupial species eat ants. Humans eat ant egg soup, honey ants, chocolate covered ants and more. There is even a worm (*Myrmeconema neotropicum*) that infects a certain canopy ant, and causes their black abdomens to turn red. The behaviour of the ant is changed and, climbing high into the trees, they are mistaken by birds for ripe fruits, and eaten. The droppings of the bird are collected by other ants and fed to their young, which continues the cycle.

Finally, because they are such an important part of our natural world, ants are an integral part of our imagination and culture. To us, they represent industriousness and cooperative effort. The Chinese character for ant (蟻/蚁) is a combination of logograms that may be interpreted as *'insect* (虫) *which behaves properly* (義/义)'. In the Bible's *Book of Proverbs*, it is written: *'Go to the ant, thou sluggard; consider her ways and be wise: which having no guide, overseer or ruler, provideth her meat in the summer and gathereth her food in the harvest'.* Aesop alludes to the same attributes in his fable of *The Ant and the Grasshopper.*

In Hopi mythology, ants are considered the very first animals. Other First Nations used ant bites in initiation ceremonies as a test of will. In some parts of Africa, ants are the messengers of the gods. Ants are still with us in more recent popular culture. They appear in Mark Twain's *A Tramp Abroad*, Robert Frost's *Departmental,* and T. H. White's *The Once and Future King.*

If you ever sent away for an ant farm, in the back of an Atom Ant comic book in the 1960s, you learned the meaning of disappointment, when the shipping failed to happen across the U.S.-Canadian border.

Beyond *Antz, A Bug's Life, The Ant Bully, The Ant and the Aardvark,* and *Ant-Man,* ants are ensconced in the fertile firmament of Science Fiction evil. From the giant ants in the movie *Them!,* to the insect inspiration for the bugs of *Starship Troopers,* there is nothing quite like a colony of alien ants, to raise the hairs on the back of your neck. Except for one thing, perhaps. The sight of a single winged carpenter ant, crawling along your maple floor, in the early spring. Dragging sawdust.

> “The ants are my friends, they're blowin' in the wind. The ant, sir, is blowin' in the wind.”
>
> Bob Dylan

An Ill-Shaped Thing 05 July

"From far out in the center of the naked lake
The loon's cry rose.
It was the cry of someone who owns very little"

Robert Bly

The moon is not quite full but pretty damn close. I couldn't sleep. Taking up a position in one of the Adirondack chairs on the deck, I sat and watched the lunar light ghost dance inside a trapezoid on the lake. Shiva lay at my feet, head cradled between her front paws. A plaintive howl sat us up. The shivers that rippled up our marrow knocked out our wind. Loonacy.

I remember when Robyn first heard a loonatic wail. It was just after we were first married. It seems like yesterday, but my bones know I'm lying. On Lake of the Woods, in Northwestern Ontario, my parents owned a cabin out past a Native Reserve (we used to call them *reservations,* but that apparently sounded too much like doubt, or dinner). They insisted we come down from Winnipeg on weekends, and have it all to ourselves. The first time there, near dusk, sitting on the dock, amid the vast expanse of water, rocks and reeds, Robyn took the full brunt of an echoing loon tremolo. She almost cried with the intensity of it. Lightning crackled down her spine. Like the first time she heard a trio of pan flutes, charango, and drum, in a hole-in-the-wall café, our first night in Cusco, or the marin and in the courtyard of our *hospedaje,* in a highland town in Guatemala. Except this was better.

The Common Loon is anything but. An ancient bird according to some; experts disagree on how old loons are. If the first bird progenitor that flew off the dinosaur evolutionary tree was an *archaeopteryx,* 150 million years ago, the first loon may have appeared 80 to 125 million years later. He was about six feet, from head to tail.

Here in British Columbia, we have all five species of his descendants (Common Loon (*Gavia immer*), Yellow-billed Loon (*Gavia adamsii*), Pacific Loon (*Gavia pacifica*), Arctic Loon (*Gavia arctica*), and the Red-throated Loon (*Gavia stellata*)), and only the Yellow-billed doesn't come to Westwood Lake.

Also called a *Great Northern Diver* (or *arsefoot, call-up-a-storm, ember-goose, greenhead, guinea duck*, or *walloon*), its more usual name may be derived from the old Norse *luenn,* meaning 'beaten, benumbed, weary or exhausted', or a 15th century Scottish expression for 'rogue' or 'scamp'. A *loon-slatt* was the name of a coin, worth a hangman's fee. It's quite a stretch, but a perfect match- a word without a proper definition, for a bird without a proper name.

Wherever it came from, there is a definite connection with the moon- lunatic in the looney bin, as crazy as a loon. In some Native legends, the loon is the creator of the world, a bird of magical powers, a predictor of rain, or an omen of death. The Inuit called it *tuutlick* or 'having a tusk', the Cree *mookwa* or '*Spirit of the North',* and the Ojibwa called the loon *Mang* or 'the most handsome of birds'. With their black and white sleekness, elongated bill, red eyes, striped necklace and speckled back, they are stunningly beautiful.

The loon's elegant appearance, however, does not completely translate into all-terrain locomotion. Of land, air, and water, their design is way too clumsy for the first two. Loons are poorly adapted for moving on land, because their feet are too far back on their body. In 1634, William Wood, in a New England Prospectus, wrote, *'The Loone is an ill-shaped thing like a cormorant'*. They avoid Terra Firma, except during nesting season.

Loons have difficulty getting airborne, and must swim into the wind, across up to 50 metres of open water, to pick up enough velocity for take off. They can become stranded on a pond that is too small. This is a particularly vexing problem if they mistake wet parking lots or highways for lakes and rivers. Once aloft, however, they are excellent fliers, and pilots have clocked them at speeds up to 80 miles per hour. Why do they have so much trouble getting off the ground? Because they have bones that are solid. Why do they have bones that are solid? Because their metier is not going up, it's going down.

The loon can dive to depths of 80 metres, staying underwater for almost a minute. They are a not-so-distant relative of the penguin and, like penguins, their main food source is fish, about two pounds a day (although they also eat frogs, salamanders, snails, crayfish, and leeches). As well as solid bones, Loons have three other adaptations for fish diving. Their 54-inch wingspan propulsion system allows them to dive quickly. Their 3-inch pointy bill is used to stab or grip prey. Everything is eaten headfirst and whole, so the loon swallows small pebbles (*gastroliths*), to aid in crushing the hard bits.

One of the most endearing images of *Loonworld,* is the way that chicks ride on their parents' backs. This allows them to conserve heat and to rest but, most importantly, to avoid the copious predators that lurk in all the land, water and air interfaces of their nursery. Eagles, gulls, crows, racoons and carnivorous fish are all waiting for a careless chick, and an inattentive mother. Loons are ferocious defenders of their nesting area. They will aggressively bayonet any perceived threat, and have been known to kill ducks, and even Canada Geese, that got too close. Loons have special dances to warn off potential threats. One involves kicking their feet so fast, that they walk on water. Another is called the *penguin dance,* when the parent tucks its wings against its body, and swims upright, until you leave, or it dies of exhaustion.

The Loon may well be able to dance a bit of *Bojangles* but nothing, nothing in this world, is anything like what comes out of its mouth. Its cries are penetrating, mesmerizing, primitive, bereft of any decent adjectives to give one any sense of their sheer visceral power. They are the essence of wilderness solitude, the ultimate zen koan of one hand clapping awareness, a registered letter from the Universe, that your life and your troubles are so small as to be ridiculous. Whenever some American filmmaker wants to evoke being remote in Nature, anywhere in the world (even in the Amazon), a loon call goes off in the distance. They may be the official state bird of Minnesota, and Mercer, Wisconsin may call itself the '*Loon Capital of the World*', and on and on and *On Golden Pond,* but those sounds are the sounds of the essence of Canada. Pierre Burton couldn't have felt anything like a Canadian, even making love in a canoe, without loonsong in the background. Even our money is named for it.

There are four distinctive Loon calls: the *Hoot*, the *Yodel*, the *Wail* and the *Tremolo.* The Hoot is a series of short, single notes, given among individuals in close proximity, as a sign of curiosity or happiness, that allows them to keep in contact. Nothing special.

The Yodel is a male call, an expression of aggression during a confrontation. A little bit more interesting perhaps. The Wail is a long mournful moan, like a wolf howling in the distance. It is a cry to a separated chick or mate to 'come back, I'm here'. A Wail is answered with another Wail. The Cree thought that this was the sound of dead warriors calling back to us. It sends chills. Finally, beyond all the haunting melancholy, is the rapid, five-beat high-pitched Tremolo, an alarm call that we have often associated with the idiot laughter of a loonatic. It is not. It is the sound of you waking from your sleepwalking, the echo of all it means to exist.

Sadly, again, that echo is receding quickly. We have never made good companions. Back in 1766, Jonathan Carver, a Mississippi River explorer, noted that the Common Loon '*was ill-favored flesh but excellent sport*'. When William Brewster's boat steamed up New Hampshire's Umbagog Lake in 1824 '*the progress was indicated and proclaimed by the frequent popping of guns fired from her decks at the Loons*'. We don't actually have to shoot them now. The smallest piece of small lead split shot released by anglers and hunters, once ingested, can poison and kill a Loon within two weeks. Collisions with boats and jet skis kill more. Loons need lakes with absolutely clear water to see their prey- but try to find one. Even if the water is clear, the acid rainfall in it now kills off more than half the Loon chicks hatched in any given year.

The moon is a little higher now, and I think I'll go back to bed. There is one more disconsolate call off the water, and an old John Prine song starts up in my head.

"So I'm up here in the north woods
Just staring at a lake
Wondering just exactly how much
They think a man can take
I eat fish to pass the time away
'Neath this blue Canadian moon
This old world has made me crazy
Crazy as a loon
Lord, this world will make you crazy
Crazy as a loon."

Clacking Stick 20 July

"Today I saw the dragon-fly
Come from the wells where he did lie.
An inner impulse rent the veil
Of his old husk: from head to tail
Came out clear plates of sapphire mail.
He dried his wings: like gauze they grew;
Thro' crofts and pastures wet with dew
A living flash of light he flew."

Alfred Lord Tennyson, *The Dragon-fly*

There are two kinds of light on the ghost trees in my peripheral vision, as I swim to the other side of the lake today. Approaching the opposite bank, the elongated, gnarled spires of long dead cedars soar with a heavenly white luminescence, when I glance to the left. Bobbing in the rhythm of my breast stroke, are their dark matter black tower relatives, off to the right. The sun, in setting, is setting up this optical glide path. I'm on another dog day heat wave late afternoon water crossing, except Shiva is getting too old to paddle it with me. A trout leaves a bullseye over there, and the air suddenly crackles electric. The dry rattle wing zapping of a Sapphire Dragonfly, which alights on the log in front of me. *Clack clack.* The silence returns, and I know I have reached the far Westwood shore.

I've always loved Dragonflies. Through the years, they have escorted me on my swim sojourns, but only after I was well away from land. They *tictac* around the garden in the midsummer heat. My affection for dragonflies is not universally shared by other members of my species, however, as their many ambivalent names through European history might indicate- *Ear cutter, Adder Bolt, Devil's Riding Horse, Horse Stinger* and my favorite, *Devil's Darning Needle* (because it was believed that they would sew the lips of wicked children together while they were sleeping).
The earliest written reference to 'Dragonfly' was in Francis Bacon's *Sylva Sylvarum: or a Naturall Historie in Ten Centuries,* in 1626. Its scientific naming came from Johann Christian Fabricius, an 18th century entymologist, who coined the term Odonata, meaning '*tooth-jawed*', a reference to the mouth parts of the nymph. There are about 5,000 different species of dragonflies all over the world (except Antarctica). Most of these are found in remote, tropical areas. In British Columbia we have 64 species, all with formal taxonomic names. But the common ones are more evocative, sounding like sports teams or motorcycle gangs:- Darners (Green and Mosaic), Clubtails (Snaketails, Grappletails, Common Clubtails, Hanging Clubtails), Spiketails (Cruisers), Emeralds (Baskettails, Striped Emeralds, Common Emeralds) and Skimmers (King Skimmers, Pond Hawks, Blue Dashers, Meadowhawks, White Faces, Saddleback Gliders and Rainpool Gliders). Common Dragonfly names elsewher, are not quite so New World. In England they were known as '*water dippers*', in China '*old glassy*', and the ancient Celts called them '*big needle of wings*'.

The oldest fossilized record of a Dragonfly is over 300 million years old. *Meganeuropsis permiana* lived 300 million years ago, in the steamy swamps of the Carboniferous period. He had a 2½-foot wingspan, and took no prisoners. His was the only insect body plan other than the cockroach, that has survived intact through the millennia, since the dinosaur extinction. Today, they range in size from the 7½- inch wing-span Dragonflies in Costa Rica, to their tiny 20-mm-wide East Asian cousins, *Nannophya pygmaea.*

Any creature that has survived almost unaltered for so long should be a marvel of adaptation, form and function translated into altitude and attitude. My shore-hugging swim companions are mostly eyes, wings and mouthparts, on a long aerodynamic body. The large compound eyes take up two-thirds of their head. Each eye consists of about 30,000 tiny lenses, positioned to provide 360 degree vision. The eyes are so big they touch each other. Although 80% of the brain is devoted to sight, they see detail less well than we do. But this hardly matters at all. On a brute hunting machine, the only function of vision is to detect and localize predators and prey. The head the eyes sit on is, in itself, an amazing piece of design wizardry. It is an inertial guidance system suspended in an upright position, on the pointed end of the thorax, and has sensory hairs that allow it to act as a gyroscope. If the body strays in pitch, yaw or roll, there is a negative feedback loop, that moves two pairs of strong transparent wings back into alignment.

No other insect devotes such a large amount of its body weight to flight. Wing muscles account for up to 40-60% of its weight, compared to 13% for the honey bee. Chest wall muscles attach directly to each of the four lightweight, stiff and flexible wings, contract and lever them in any direction, and allow each to move independently. This direct muscular control of each wing makes the Dragonfly one of the most agile of insect aerialists. Because their wings beat slowly, at a rate of approximately 20-90 beats per second (compared to 300 beats per second for our honey bee friend), they have no buzzing noise, another excellent hunting advantage. Their wings can move in four distinct patterns, depending on the need of the circumstance. They routinely fly *asynchronously,* with the hind wings downthrusting first, followed by the front wings, lagging a quarter of a beat behind (they can only generate thrust on the downstroke). When it needs to move up and back quickly, the Dragonfly will blast both sets of wings simultaneously. To hover, the dragonfly can counterstroke front and hind wings, and fly like a Damselfly. Finally, to execute a sharp turn, the individual wings can move *asymmetrically*, like they're paddling a flying canoe. The clacking sound is a forewing hitting a hindwing, on a turn. Dragonflies can take off vertically, hover like a helicopter for more than a minute, fly backwards or sideways, zigzag and turn, and stop on a dime. They have been clocked at 100 km./hr. As a former aeronautical engineer, they give me goosebumps. All of this flight finesse has a cost, of course. Dragonflies are incapable of walking.

How do these winged eyeballs actually catch their prey? In one of two ways: by briefly hovering over vegetation and picking insects up with their legs (*gleaning*), or in midair (*hawking*). Sometimes hawkers will catch their small prey, like mosquitoes and midges, in their biting mouthparts on the fly (so to speak), and chew them down headfirst; sometimes they will catch larger prey like flies, bees, ants, and butterflies, in a basket they make with their suspended legs. They will follow mammals, to prey on the insects also following mammals- which is why they are my swim buddies only so far out onto the lake.

The reason these buzzbombs are in such a frenetic hurry, is because adult Dragonflies only live about two months. In that solitary, poor, nasty, brutish, and short *Hobbsian* interval, they must grow strong enough to mate and then die, and not the other way around (for that way is impossible of course). Many Dragonflies do die before mating- from accidents and predation, and from starvation. If they are unfortunate enough to have two months of poor weather, neither they nor their prey can fly, although they can still be eaten by birds, spiders, frogs, and larger species of dragonflies. Adult Dragonflies are also a minor human food item in some countries- they are a delicacy in Indonesia, where they are caught on poles made sticky with birdlime, and then fried in oil.

If they are lucky enough to mate, it is still all a little surreal. Before a male Dragonfly can mate with a female, he must mate with himself. He transfers sperm from the primary genitalia at the tip of his abdomen to the secondary set at the base. When he finds a female, he grabs her by her head and she curves her abdomen around in a circle, to acquire his sperm. You have likely seen dragonflies flying in either this '*wheel position*', or in tandem. This is because it is a long process. This is because the male is making sure that he has removed the sperm of other males with specialized organs called *hamules*. This is because Dragonfly mating is not about romance.

After the eggs hatch, most of the five year life cycle of the Dragonfly is spent as a *nymph*, living just beneath the water's surface, using extendable jaws to catch other invertebrates, tadpoles and fish. They breathe through gills in their rectum, and can rapidly propel themselves, by suddenly expelling water out their backside. Unlike their adult forms, they can deliver a painful bite. Nymphs undergo approximately 10-20 moults over their long larval life, until exposure to air causes them to begin to begin breathing. When the back of its head finally splits open, at the weakest point in its most recent skin, the adult Dragonfly crawls out, pumps up its wings, and flies off, to clack along the shoreline.

Dragonflies have symbolic significance in many world cultures, but they definitely have a more evil reputation in the West. A Romanian folk tale describes the origin of the Dragonfly as a horse once possessed by the devil. The Maltese word for Dragonfly is also 'Hell's mare' (*Debba ta' l-infern*). Swedish legends tell of the devil employing Dragonflies to weigh people's souls, and trolls using them as spindles to weave clothes (*trollslända*). In Norway, they are called 'eye pokers' (*Øyenstikker*), and in Portugal, 'eye snatcher' (*Tira-olhos*). In the southern U.S., they used to think that Dragonflies followed snakes around, and stitched them back together if they were injured ('snake doctor'). They made a hobby of collecting Dragonflies ('*oding*'), especially in Texas. Further south, Dragonflies are called *matacaballos* (horse killers), or *caballitos del diablo* (Devil's little horses).

Among Native Americans and in East Asia, Dragonflies have a better reputation (in the same way as its namesake, the dragon, has a positive image in the East, but an association with evil in the West). Some Native Americans believe Dragonflies represent swiftness and activity, are a symbol of renewal after a time of great hardship, or are the souls of the dead. To the Navajo they symbolize pure water. Dragonflies are a common motif in Hopi rock art, on Pueblo necklaces, and appear as a double-barred cross on Zuni pottery. Robyn and I have a painted tin Dragonfly in the garlic bed. He's very territorial.

The Chinese sometimes refer to Dragonflies as the *typhoon-fly*, due to their large numbers appearing before storms. In Vietnam, Dragonfly behavior is used to forecast rain: 'Dragonflies fly at low level, it is rainy; Dragonflies fly at high level, it is sunny; Dragonflies fly at medium level, it is shadowy' (*Chuồn chuồn bay thấp thì mưa, bay cao thì nắng, bay vừa thì râm*). But it is in Japan where the Dragonfly enjoys the most reverence of anywhere on Earth. In ancient mythology, Japan was known as *Akitsushima*, which means 'Land of the Dragonflies'. In 792 AD, Poem 98 relays the inspiration, the story of the Emperor being bitten by a horsefly, which was subsequently eaten by a Dragonfly. Dragonflies often appear in art and literature, especially haiku ('The red dragonfly -In some way or another He likes the evening too.'). With their short intense lives, they are symbols of new light and joy, swiftness, happiness, love (two Dragonflies paired together), good luck, prosperity, purity, harmony and, above all, strength and courage- the word for 'victory' and 'Dragonfly' sound similar in Japanese. Traditionally known as *katsumushi* or the 'invincible insect', the Dragonfly sometimes adorned Samurai helmets as a favored symbol of martial success.

They are not always successful, however. Many years ago, Robyn and I were walking the path around Blue Lake, near Rotorua, in New Zealand. We came across a pitched battle between a Dragonfly and a wasp, a fraction of the size of the larger insect. The wasp, deliberately and without haste, calmly severed the Dragonfly's head from its body, and flew away with it. To what purpose was unclear. There must also be some symbolic meaning to this experience but, although it continues to haunt us, we are still unaware of what it might have been.

Every hot summer day after work, I swim across Westwood Lake. Immersing myself in the cool water, I leave behind the daily inferno of patient suffering, pushing gently and rhythmically against the watery resistance. The Nootka word for Dragonfly is '*clacking stick'*, named after the cedar tongs used to remove coals from the fire. *Clack clack*. And he comes again.

"Time is for dragonflies and angels.
The former live too little and the latter live too long."

James Thurber

Heaven's Gate 08 August

"Soon silence will have passed into legend. Man has turned his back on silence. Day after day he invents machines and devices that increase noise and distract humanity from the essence of life, contemplation, meditation....."

Henry David Thoreau

Until now, you would be forgiven, if you thought you were reading some latter-day Westwood *Walden*, or backyard bird guide. You might have assumed, wrongly, that Robyn, Shiva and I are untouched by the more mundane and unsavory experiences that affect all lives. Today I'll take you to the dark side's factory floor, for a pastoral polemic.

We were awakened three times last night, by a rabble of drunken louts, proclaiming along the boardwalk. Their noise was at worst, profane and, at best, a cogent argument against ten million years of human evolution. They cursed Shiva for her protective barking, and later, the sound of squealing tires echoed down the lake as they departed. And returned, and departed. When I awoke this morning, it was from too little sleep. I wandered out to the garden with my coffee, to sit and reflect. Even that effort was doomed.

Less than a minute after I found my favorite garden Adirondack chair, I was out of it.

Even waving my arms, he didn't see me. I knew he couldn't hear me. Plugged into the iPod earphones under his earmuffs, the leaf-blower danced and screamed in six-eight time. He was three acoustic layers down, and a world away. On my other side, one of our other neighbours started the riding mower she resides on, accompanied by the whining *thrum* of her weed-whacking helper. A motocross biker gang emerged along the ridge across the lake, like a swarm of chainsaws. The garbage truck combine-harvester began emptying bins two doors down. A helicopter flew directly overhead, and the kid at the top of the drive powered up his grunge garage band. It was a summer Saturday, after a long summer Friday night. In order for sound to become noise, somewhere along the trail, the physical must travel through the physiological, to exit through the psychological and the philosophical.

Sound is just sound when it is just physics, a simple form of energy, expressed in units called *joules*. The rate of production of energy, or power, is expressed in *watts*, a watt being one joule per second. But it is not the number of watts of acoustical power generated that is the problem, it is the rate of flow (i.e. flux), measured in watts per square metre, where the area of concentration is your eardrum. When the engineers got hold of the unit of acoustical energy flux, F, they made it complicated, by converting into a base 10 logorithmic decibel (dB), so that

$$D = 10 \log F + 120$$

meaning that, for every increase of 10 dB, there is a tenfold increase in energy flux. The only real facts you need to know are these- the louts last night were shouting at 60 dB; quiet conversation occurs at 55 dB and if you complain about '*noise*', a Bylaw Official in Saanich accepts 58 dB (the level at which you can't hear what I am saying in the same room), as a perfectly acceptable background 'sound' level. By civic ordinance, it is entirely legal for someone to interfere with your ability to hear conversation, with twice as much acoustic energy as you are adequately communicating with.

Bylaw Bob would have determined you were mistaken that it could have been annoying you. The leaf blower terrorism next door operates at over 75 dB, legal between the hours of 0700 and 2300. All of those hours, inclusive. But clearly, then, the difference between sound and noise is more than just about physics. Could it, more accurately, be about physiology?

Moving from the physical energy flux to measurements of acoustic perception, physiologists have recruited human subjects to evaluate pure tones of different frequencies and intensities, for the same '*perceived loudness*', calling them '*phons*,' and '*sones*'. For sounds that are not pure tones and have a wide frequency range, physiologists have used analogous units of the '*noy*' (suggesting both noise and annoyance), and its logarithmic counterpart, PNdB, (short for perceived noise in decibels). One problem is that the human ear is not equally sensitive to all frequencies, at one frequency with varying amplitudes in all individuals, or in the same individual at different ages.

None of this matters to Bylaw Bob. He has a picnic basket full of his own metrics, to help him decide what constitutes an acceptable sound level for various activities: LAeq,T for the assessment of residential development sites, LA10,T for road traffic noise monitoring, LA90,T for the background noise level, LAmax for the maximum noise level, LEP,d the daily personal workplace noise exposure level, and that all-important Vibration Dose Value (VDV), the fourth root of the integral of the fourth power of acceleration, after it has been frequency-weighted. But none of this, Virginia- not the physics nor the physiology, tells us anything at all about how annoying an intrusive sound actually is. Which would bother you more? 58 dB for 3 seconds or 55 dB for 3 hours? 58 dB at 2:00 pm or 55 dB at 2:00 am? Vivaldi at 58 dB or squealing tires at 55 dB? Rain on your roof or a dripping tap? Random thunder or regular pile driving?

To get finally from sound to noise, we need to ascend to the next level, the psychological, riding those sound waves into the external ear canal, vibrating the eardrum, sending the resultant neuroelectrical signals from the inner ear to the auditory cortex, and on to the frontal cortex and the deep hippocampal and other visceral centres of the brain, where our emotions live. Where our rage resides.

Annoyance is contextual, not mathematical. It's not about the decibels, its about the dumbbells. Noise is unwanted sound. Noise is trespassing. Quiet is good. And disappearing.

The unfortunate truth is that one man's noise is another man's music. Witness the moronic motorcycle engine-revving madness that goes on for hours down our street. The backwards baseball-capped adolescent, so offended by the use of the high-pitched mosquito deterrent at the local convenience store, boombox thump-thumps behind closed truck windows down Arbot Road, breaking an otherwise quiet Sunday without remorse. The whine of the mitre skillsaw addict in the trailer park continues, unabated, for so many weeks on end, that he could have built a dozen real houses by now. I know these people are enjoying themselves, but if they were producing proportional smells instead of sounds, they would all have been tasered by a Hazmat S.W.A.T. team in a heartbeat. We need to know what is happening here, why it is happening and why it matters.

What is happening is that we are making more noise than ever before. This is not because there are more of us living in greater proximity (I've been in some pretty crowded monasteries). This is our desert-derived monotheistic heritage run amok, with two stroke *Germs, Guns, and Steel.* Nature needs to be tamed, yea, verily, vanquished. Progress is measured by a process of acquiring more and more petroleum-powered weapons, to do just that. The ninety-year-old Buddhist monk, Diasetz T. Suzuki, told the mythologist Joseph Campbell, after reading the Old Testament: *'God against man. Man against God. Man against nature. Nature against man. Nature against God. God against nature. Very funny religion'*. And a very noisy one.

Now I'm not such a Luddite that I can't see that some unwanted acoustic poisoning is unavoidable. As a society we all individually, implicitly, agree to tolerate a certain amount of noise, for benefits that we think are worth the annoyance- motorized transportation, labor-saving machinery, karaoke (strike that last one). In fairness, there is continuous quality improvement going on, designed to make our machines quieter, and I can't wait for the real advent of the electric car. However, along with the right to make some noise, should come the responsibility of keeping the intrusiveness to a minimum, to make no *unnecessary* noise. The leaf blower is the hands-down antithesis of this principle, an irrational instrument of questionable utility, operating at the cost of self-immolation and social isolation, that exists solely because it can. My father used to say that a man has the right to throw his fist as far as he wants, as long as it doesn't touch the nose of his neighbour. With that kind of noise, we have failed this vital societal principle.

Surveys of high school students demonstrate that the majority believe they have an unlimited right to make as much noise as they want, anytime they want. They have become the apotheotic synthesis of parental indulgence, hormones, and leisure. No longer are they seen and not heard. Growing older rather than up, they regale us with their chopped motocross dirt bike recreational excavators, boom cars, all-terrain vehicular mechanized fun toys, speed boats, jet skis, power tools, and ghetto blasters ('cause they like to share Depeche Mode's *Enjoy the Silence*, Delerium's *Silence*, and Queensryche's *Silent Lucidity,* at full volume). Their lives are one big party-hearty in Surroundsound.

We have reached a point where it is almost unimaginable for all our activities to be unaccompanied by some form of noise. Some of this derives from our Western cultural tradition of feeling uneasy in the company of others who are quiet. We can misinterpret their silence as anger, hostility, disinterest, or any number of other emotions. Muzak evolved as a comfortable narcotic sound barrier to conversation and it's now louder than ever. More sadly, we have also reached that further point of having a culture of total inconsideration for anyone else in, or even the actual environment, itself. In these intolerant times, if you put your finger to your lips, you're more than likely to get another one back. To what depths have we sunk, when we cannot even abide the quiet of the countryside? Even in Calcutta, Mother Teresa had noted: *'See how nature--trees, flowers, grass--grows in silence; see the stars, the moon and the sun, how they move in silence...we need silence to be able to touch souls'*. But not on the ridge trails these days, where I can hear the iPods coming, by the tinny sounds leaking from their earbuds. When joggers run by our bedroom window at 5 a.m., their animated conversations can be easily heard across the lake, when they should be listening to the sounds of their own bodies instead.

So, why does it matter? Well, one of the reasons is that there are negative health effects from noise. For several decades, we have been aware of noise-induced hearing loss, but it's not about the volume. Most 'convenience' power tools bypass physical exertion, but it's not about the loss of exercise opportunity either. The real life-killing effects start with disturbed sleep. More than 30% of people living in the EU are exposed to nighttime equivalent sound pressure levels exceeding 55 dB, mostly because of aircraft noise and traffic. This can be up to 80 dB in cities of developing countries. The primary sleep disturbance effects consist of difficulty in falling asleep, awakenings, and a reduction in REM sleep. Stress hormones surge into the bloodstream, leading to primary visceral effects like increased blood pressure, heart rhythm disturbances, and an increased propensity to diabetes. But it is the secondary, or after-effects, where the evil begins in earnest. People who even perceive the quality of their sleep to be impaired are more tired, depressed and irritable. They use more sedatives and sleeping pills. They have trouble learning and, when it happens all night long, every night of every year, the more susceptible will develop mental disorders. They close their bedroom windows and have to use earplugs instead of their balconies, turn up their radios and television volumes, write petitions, and complain to authorities, usually with no results. They begin to use alcohol and drugs to get away. They become unfriendly, aggressive, and disengaged. And then...they snap. In August 1995, the *Daily Mirror* published a report on more than 16 people in Britain who had committed murder or suicide in the preceding six years, because of noise.

The victims included: Julie Harvey, from Manchester, who overdosed on painkillers after she moved to avoid noisy neighbours, only to find herself near the friends of her previous tormentors; Valerie Edwards, from Bristol, who died of pneumonia after sitting in a park for several nights in the cold and rain, to avoid her neighbour's loud music; Jack Gott from Bradford, who killed himself after noise from a teenage neighbour drove him insane; James Bourke, from Birmingham, who was battered to death, after neighbours became sick of his loud classical music; and Harry Stephenson, from South Glamorgan, stabbed 22 times, for complaining to a neighbour who incessantly revved his car in the early morning.

Another reason it matters is because we have lost the right to enjoy our own property, without the intrusion of noise, especially the unnecessary leisure lamentations of louts. Alexander Pope knew them ('*It is with narrow-souled people as with narrow-necked bottles; the less they have in them, the more noise they make in pouring out*') as did Ben Franklin ('*The worst wheel of the cart makes the most noise*').

If noise, and especially loud noise, belongs to the street and the vulgar, what company does silence keep? Pretty impressive, actually. Nature's silence allows us to '*come to our senses*'. We speak (or don't have to) of '*peace and quiet*'. '*Inner peace*' is a spiritual goal that is meant to bring us in contact with reality, ourselves or, if you're a believer, the divine. This is found in Christianity (especially Quakerism), Sufism, Buddhism, and in Hindu yoga. Silence is wonderfully represented in proverbs ('*We must have reasons for speech but we need none for silence*'; '*One coin in the money-box makes more noise than when it is full*'; '*When the river is deepest it makes least noise*') and people. From Lao Tzu ('*Silence is a source of great strength*') through Gandhi ('*In the attitude of silence the soul finds the path in a clearer light, and what is elusive and deceptive resolves itself into crystal clearness'*) to Einstein (*'I lived in solitude in the country and noticed how the monotony of a quiet life stimulates the creative mind'*), they got it right. And the Max Ehrman parchment that many of us hung on our dorm room walls at University? *'Go placidly amid the noise and haste, and remember what peace there may be in silence'*, during the years we were anything but. Silence can be commemorative, as in *'a moment of'*, or respectful, as in *'you have the right to remain'*.

Silence is Golden but total silence is not. In laboratory experiments, animals that have been subjected to complete silence show behavioral change and aggression. What to make of prospective deaf parents, who consider themselves a *'linguistic minority',* and demand a selective form of IVF to ensure that their child will also be born deaf? After last night, I don't judge them too harshly.

But what can we do, and what hope is there? We do have rules about noise. We've had them a long time. The ancient Romans enforced rules about the noise emitted from iron-wheeled wagons which, battering the pavement stones, caused annoyance and disruption of their sleep. Horse carriages were not allowed in certain Medieval European cities at night, to ensure a restful sleep for the inhabitants. However, those were different times. In our 21st century, we will bear a shortage of water and of silence. Let's start global and work local.

The *World Health Organization* has proposed guidelines for community noise, in the categories of annoyance, speech intelligibility and communication interference, disturbance of information extraction, and sleep disturbance. Their *Guideline 4.3.7,* regarding Parkland and conservation areas, invokes keeping the *signal to noise ratio* low (whatever the hell that means) using three principles: the *Precautionary prin-*

ciple, the *Polluter Pays principle*, and the *Prevention principle*. Only one big problem: the *Enforcement principle*. Noise is not like chemical effluent that sticks around and invites inspection. Noise violates you at night, on weekends, and on weekend nights 'cause the louts are out when the lights are out.' Noise may be transitory- a motorcycle, for example, roaring along on the other side of the lake for thirty minutes after midnight. Bylaw Bob and his decibel meter is currently unavailable, but your call is important to us. And then the noise, after causing its damage, is gone, no slick to be found. *'Dadadadada, vroom, putt, putt, dadadadada. WRAAAaaaaAAAHH. WRAAAaaaaAAAHH.'* Gone.

Working our way down the food chain, we pass the Federal and Provincial governments who have no interest, and land where the rubber literally meets the road- the municipality. One needs to remember that there is money in noise. Case in point was a communication from a certain Sandy Currie, Executive Director of the Toronto-based Marine Manufacturers Association who, in 1996, took umbrage at Saanich Council's decision to ban jet skis on Prospect Lake. Ms. Currie called the ban '*a virus which must be snuffed out before it spreads... The Municipality has basically thumbed its nose at all procedures. They have taken it on themselves to pass a bylaw which seems punitive, arbitrary, and very discriminatory... We haven't yet decided to throw in the troops and high-priced lawyers. I hope that if they have a look at the report and really think about what they are doing, cooler heads will prevail.*' Hey, jobs at stake here. To get to the finish line you need to begin with our local Noise Bylaw:

City of Nanaimo Noise Control Bylaw 1994, No. 4750 is a bylaw that regulates or prohibits making or causing noises or sounds that disturb the quiet, rest, peace, enjoyment or convenience of individuals or the public. The most common complaints received by the Bylaw Services include barking dogs, loud music, and noise caused by heavy machinery and construction activity. The playing of radios and stereophonic equipment or any apparatus used for the amplification of sound where the noise is disturbing and clearly audible is prohibited before 9:00 a.m. and after 11:00 p.m. Noise due to construction shall not be caused before 7:00 a.m. and after 9:00 p.m. Monday to Saturday and before 9:00 a.m. and after 9:00 p.m. on Sundays and Statutory holidays. Noise caused by any domestic animal or bird that is persistent and creates a disturbance by its cries, barks, or howls is prohibited at any time. Depending on the nature of the complaint, a City representative may be dispatched to the scene of difficulty, or a letter may be sent to the individual or company that is alleged to be causing the noise, advising them of the complaint and requesting compliance. Failure to comply will result in the issuance of a municipal ticket. If a ticket is issued, the complainant(s) may be required to testify in court if the allegation is disputed. Should you wish to report a loud and/or disturbing noise outside of normal office hours, please contact the local R.C.M.P. office at (250) 754-2345.

To its credit is the absence of any arbitrary decibel level, a dismal failure of a criterion in any jurisdiction that chooses to use it. It recognizes that, not only the public, but also individuals who are annoyed, can have their grievances addressed. Its simplicity and general interpretability is to be admired. But then it falls flat on its face, by restricting enforcement to after 11:00 p.m. and before 09:00 a.m. The Bylaw was obviously designed for residential and commercial areas, but it may as well not exist, if noise is not more rigorously controlled around natural reserves like Westwood Lake. The animal life doesn't know it's 11:00 p.m. (not the four-legged kind, anyway).

Which brings us to the hooliganism of last night. Because of the worsening squeeze from the nightly revelers, and the early morning coffee chat joggers, (both of whom are in the Park long after and long before the signs indicate the trail is closed and open), residents along the trail had met with representatives from the *Parks and Recreation Department,* to discuss issues of noise, vandalism, littering, and personal security. We have always had an excellent relationship with the City. In the early years, we contributed funds to help build the boardwalk that now graces the trail along the lakeshore, finally solving the problem of the incessant, insistent interloping declarations of riparian rights. This year, when the abuse hit critical, the city acceded to our request for gates, to be placed at either end of the inhabited part of the trail. The plan was to close them when the Park was closed, and open them when the Park was open. The gates went in and the venom came out. The rage was swift, and predictably irrational. The local rag (*'somewhat undernourished',* according to Mark Steyn) ran a blog question, inviting bile for the gates and blood for the gangthink. There was denial ('I don't think early morning joggers tend to chat a lot'; 'the sounds of a group out hiking would be welcome'; 'birds chirp in the morning... shoot them'), class warfare ('complaints of a few wealthy landowners'; 'buyer beware'; 'If this isnt NIMBY-ism'; 'they want to have their cake and eat it too'; 'Give us ordinary people a chance to enjoy this lake'; 'Wouldn't it be a novel idea to have people worry about others rather than themselves'; 'if you buy a house next to a park, YOU HAVE NO RIGHT TO BITCH ABOUT THE NOISE!'; 'my tax $$'s are paying for these gates to appease a few complainers'), participaction ('way to encourage fitness Nanaimo!'; 'buy some ear plugs and get a life.....or perhaps get up and go and enjoy the trails yourself....ya bunch of'), and vengefulness ('I need to go start my Harley'; 'I will bring along a ghetto-blaster as well, cranked to volume 10'; 'What I would like to see is a ring road around Westwood Lake'). It was only a matter of time. We knew this. Last night they went around the gates.

There are only three things that could save us from this evil. The first is nostalgia. What if we started to hear the whirr of reel mowers, clicking across lawns again. Or the sound of a bamboo rake. The rustle of a broom. The whoosh of a handsaw. That's not going to happen. There used to be an old guy that stood up in the back of his canoe and sang Italian arias while he paddled. It was rather charming- now he has a boombox playing Top 40. We live in inexorable times.

The second idea is the Dutch Solution. In Holland, individual provincial authorities can designate certain areas as 'silent zones' (*Stiltegebeid*), areas of 'at least several square kilometres or more, in which the sound load caused by human activity is not high enough to disturb the natural sounds in the area'. I like this one very much. There is no reason why it shouldn't happen here.

Then, there is a third option. In the Early 1970's, a nutbar named Marshall Applewhite formed a cult whose 39 members believed that the planet Earth was about to be recycled (wiped clean, renewed, refurbished and rejuvenated), and that the only chance to survive was to leave it immediately. They called themselves '*Heaven's Gate*', and on March 26,1997, they committed suicide in shifts, the remaining members cleaning up after each prior group's death. All 39 were dressed in identical black shirts and sweat pants, brand new black-and-white Nike Windrunner athletic shoes, and armband patches reading '*Heaven's Gate Away Team*'. Now there's some participaction you can believe in.

Shiva's barking at some spandex on his cell phone down at the lake.

"Honey!" He shouts. "You wouldn't believe how quiet it is up here."

"Silence is a fence around wisdom"

German proverb

You can download 2 minutes of silence here

Domaine Renegade   01 September

"God made Cabernet Sauvignon.
The Devil made Pinot Noir."

André Tchelistcheff

Robyn will tell you that I never really liked wine, before that night at the College. When she first arrived from New Zealand, back in 1986, I brought her back to the little walk-up apartment I had just renovated, above the convenience store on Arbuthnot, in Winnipeg. I had bought a $3 bottle of Hungarian *Szekszárdi,* to go with the white vinegar-soaked Greek salad I made, and let her know that this extravagance was an unusual indulgence, for very special occasions only. How far we have come!

The epiphany came six years later, when a colleague approached me in a hospital hallway.

"What are you doing tomorrow night?" he inquired. I asked what he had in mind.

"I signed up for a wine course at Malaspina, but I can't make it this week." Would I like to go in his place? I protested, out of real disinterest at first but, seeing that he didn't really want his seat at the table to stay empty, I agreed to attend.

The following evening, I found the *Discovery Room,* and took my place, sheepishly, among the local *cognescenti.* The instructor's name was Gord. After a brief blackboard lecture on the geography of Burgundy (I had previously believed it only referred to the detestable colour of the corduroy pants my mother always bought me, to start the next school year), he disappeared. When he returned, it was with seven carafes of brick-coloured liquid. The rest of the experience knocked me off my perch, like a space shuttle launch. The atmosphere filled with an indescribable bouquet of violets and cherries and roses and allspice and pepper and mushrooms and raspberries, and shit. A naked young girl in a mink coat had entered the room, and Gord poured her out into my six glasses. I looked back at the blackboard to read what he had just written. '*1990 Cote du Nuit Grand Cru Burgundy*'. I had, unwittingly, arrived at a tasting of historical quality. The first sip filled the back of my mouth, and hooked me right through the gills.

The cold spring rains that year were no obstacle to my wheelbarrow and shovel. My every spare moment was taken up with trench warfare among the battlements, digging raised mounds for my patrician pinot plan. The first rootstock arrived by Greyhound bus, in early May. A little rooting hormone, more bonemeal; a lot of labour, more love. There were buds, then leaves, then hope, then dashed.

The problem was that I had chosen to plant the most difficult vine to grow, and the most difficult wine to make. *Heartbreak Grape.* Even if everything else in the vineyard was ideal (and it wasn't), growing pinot noir is molten masochism. The vine does not like new dirt and climate- it sure didn't like mine. It mutates anytime, and can degenerate and die in a heartbreak heartbeat, for no good reason it will ever communicate to you. It buds early, just in time for lethal spring frosts. Its grapes don't care about your dreams either. They are thin-skinned and unpredictable, with an exceptional physical predispositon to burn in the sun and rot in the rain. Our autumn weather is a fungal festival, and each harvest is a moving target of necessary variations in pruning, thinning, picking, moon phases, personal philosophy, and varmints.

Every year has taught me about a new something not to do. The first year was a hornucopia of big game. At four a.m. one morning, I sat bolt upright in bed, ran naked out the front door, screaming for Kali to follow. I made it all the way down to the vineyard, in time to see my dog howl past the two five-point bucks that were breakfasting in Bambi's café. We were all half asleep, and I hated to wake them. Deer-fencing went in pronto. The second year, I discovered the local birdlife. All of it, all at once. Bird-netting now works most of the time (although you haven't lived until you've seen a robin dive bomb through a nylon net for lunch). The third year, I realized that wasps require innumerable ingenious little beer-filled traps, to distract them from chomping on the grapes. And then there's powdery mildew and bunch rot and, just when I thought I had it all covered, and nothing could possibly assail the fruit fortress, I drove down the driveway, on my way to the hospital one night about three o'clock in the morning, to find a family of racoons, climbing the birdnets to Paradise.

So it took a few years to get grapes, and we weren't even halfway through the heartbreaks. Pinot noir has 18 amino acids which cause it to ferment violently. It is prone to off-flavours and outright spoilage. It will suddenly, and unbelievably, change radically, for no apparent reason. You might think you bottled Audrey Hepburn, and then she runs off with another winemaker.

And that is, after all, why pinot noir winemakers 'walk into the valley of the shadow'. Because, after years of bad weather, blemished grapes, and flawed fermentations, even after years of good but ordinary winemaking, there may be that one time you hit the sweet spot. The Holy Grail. The chimeric, sensual, hedonistic Noir Nirvana. Matt Kramer, the Burgundy Brainiac professional taster, described great pinot noir as *'like having sex and the fantasy of sex at the same time...you never break out of the sip-dream sip-dream mode.'* She's the elusive, ephemeral, haunting, irrational, temperamental princess minx, a femme fatale in a glass– curling her subtle smoke from a lip, crossing her long glycerol legs down a curve, an untamable, erotic, sweet-perfumed corruption, breaking the heart of ninety-eight percent of those of us who try, misguided by the immoral compass of her liquid geography, with false promises of transcendence.

And no matter what else you've accomplished in your short sojourn on the planet, there can be no better epitaph on your headstone than *'He made great pinot noir'*.

Yesterday, we pulled the bird netting over the grapes, with straw brooms. As I ran the front nylon curtain along the *Sexy 'S'* of upright posts facing the hazelnut orchard, I felt the excitement of knowing that there were only a few more weeks to go before showtime. In the cold predawn dark in late October, after praying for no rain and taking daily refractometer measurements, the curtain will get pulled back the other way. Friends will arrive, secateurs handed out, and the harvest will begin. Carts of purple promise will be wheeled into the basement for crushing and destemming, their ultimate destination only a few feet away in the fermentation barrels. When we are finished, just after noon, we will all gather in the kitchen for a hearty repast, and samples of the year's previous production. And maybe a little of the famous *2006 Domain Renegade Reserve,* as well.

People ask me where the name of the winery came from. It came from a local MLA with an unrestrained fondness for the sound of his own inane banter. They asked him once, about a physician who was consistently critical of the medical care reform inertia of his governing party.

"Oh, him," he said. "He's a Renegade." It was the only thing he ever got right. The only way to live life. When they asked Marlon Brando what he was rebelling against, he gave the correct answer. *Whaddaya got?* What I got are two things- the first is a story.

In 1979, an American named David Lett, poured his *Eyrie Vineyards 1975 South Block Reserve Pinot Noir,* into the *Vine Olympiad* in Paris- he electrified the wine world there, and again in Burgundy the following year. In 1993, Robyn and I camped out, in the dorms of Linfield College in McMinnville, Oregon, for the *8th International Pinot Noir Celebration.* We were sitting in a small group session, discussing the sensory dimensions of pinot noir. I mentioned that I liked the barnyard *sauvage* of some Burgundies, a quality of debatable worth. Suddenly there was an eruption from the other side of the table. "Shit!" one participant exclaimed, "If I wanted to make shit, I'd make shit!" I begged to differ, and the temperature in the room began to rise perceptibly. Strangely and suddenly, my shins were aching, because Robyn was kicking them under the table. It appears that I was arguing with David Lett.

The second thing I've got, now, is *veraison.* The grapes have changed colour. The acid is falling, and the sugar and flavour content rising. What started as a long rainy Spring, has developed into the best vintage year, ever. So far. This is how legends begin. If nothing bad happens, we'll be swooning over this wine with our duck and salmon and wild mushrooms for a very long time. Robyn and I have come this far, from a $3 bottle of Hungarian *Szekszárdi,* and a vinegar-soaked Greek salad. *Whaddaya got?*

One Man's Trash 08 September

"Suburbia is where the developer bulldozes out the trees, then names the streets after them."

Bill Vaughn

Robyn was unimpressed from the first encounter. "What are you, some kind of tree hugger?" he said. Like it was some form of spiritual infirmity. She could barely hear him, over the angry deep-throated growl of heavy metal-on-metal excavator carnage, ripping up the forest around them. The smell of diesel, dirt, and cedar accompanied the visual devastation. A gigantic chipper-shredder sprayed a long continuous plume of ground forest, high into the air. "I just want to know if it's possible to save some of it," she said. It wasn't.

None of the characters in this story were inherently evil. But some of them may have been carriers. The first was the original owner. He had bought the 12-acre property, two lots over, a few years before we arrived. After clearing a large site on the water, he built a modest, white, plastic-sided two-story house for his family, but fretted about whether he would have enough money to live on, in retirement. Nice enough guy. We used to visit each other, for barbeques, and bluegrass jam sessions. He planted a redwood grove down near the lake, and even gave us a couple of saplings, to plant on our own property. We took them home, along the short path and with the long view I thought we all shared. In 1994, Robyn and I noticed too many cars, parked down and the lights up, at his house, every night in a row, for a week. A few days later he came over, to tell us he had sold out...*Foggy Mountain Breakdown.* His plan was 'to buy a woodlot somewhere'. The day the trees fell, another neighbor asked if he could rescue some firewood, but was told it was 'spoken for'.

I've never been a big fan of Prince Charles, but this one he got right: "Somehow, we have to find the courage to re-assert the once commonplace belief that human beings have a duty to act as the stewards of creation," he said. Somehow, and unfortunately for Westwood Lake and creation, Banjo skipped class that day.

Enter the developer. No tree hugger, he, despite a subsequent local award for 'Environmental Sustainability'. In 1994, he was still more grin than granola. The trees came down, all of them. Two whole years of metal-on-metal grating noise, from 7 am to 11 pm, rubbed the neighbourhood's nerve endings raw. Not satisfied with a standard-density residential housing project, he set out to extract as much profit out of his clearcut as possible. The result was a 12- acre paved paradise of hydrocarbon runoff into Westwood Lake. Automatic gates were added and locked, further isolating his asphalt sea from the rest of the community. Because of the property's 'Agricultural Zoning' designation, he was able to call it a '*campground*'. Because of influence, an ol' boy City Councillor referred to the new 150-lot carpark as 'a *hell of a job*'. He got the first part right.

There was even an ingenious name devised for the '*campground*'. The sign outside says '*Luxury Resort*'. A '*campground*' is defined as '*a site where people on holiday can pitch a tent*'. But no tents were allowed at the luxury resort, only *'Recreational Vehicles',* on 150 tiny asphalt rectangles of sumptuous parking luxury. Nonetheless, the developer surmounted one semantic obstacle after another. When he was blocked from selling these parking spots as freehold real estate, he sold *'Lifetime Memberships'.* In 1998, when he realized that City bylaws restricted living in tin cans to six months out of the year, he applied for a *'Permanent Residence'* exemption to the rule. The Westwood Neighbourhood Association gathered 500 signatures on a petition, opposing the creation of this ghetto. City Hall equivocated. They assigned the ol' boy Councillor to strike a *'Campground Committee',* under the guise of conflict resolution. The committee was contaminated with conflict of interest, and the result was unprecedented in the history of provincial municipal legislation. A *'New RV Zoning'* was created, allowing year-round residency in recreational vehicles, and the proliferation of bylaw-exempt outbuildings, and other structures (with the grandfathering of those already erected).

Still the blacktop investors struggled. In 2005, The developer applied again to rezone the property, in an attempt to allow strata ownership. Once more into the breech. The public hearing was a fiasco. Flag-waving, *'Save our Strata'*-buttoned RV troglodytes, flooded in en masse, in support of this vital low cost housing *'lifestyle choice'*. The chanting drowned out the debate.

To this day, the strata has not yet been realized, because of the cost involved in *'upgrading'*. The property is now for sale, and a recent offer is said to have fallen through. The self-induced handicap of *'lifetime members',* and the history of incessant zoning brinksmanship, neighbourhood alienation, and environmental degradation (with the loss of wildlife and the natural aesthetic that used to grace our area), may make some prospective buyers cautious, for a while longer. Whoever that next fictitious character may be, the likelihood is that he will continue the inexorable tradition of devastation, that characterizes the species. We can look forward to another two years of metal-on-metal '*improvements*'. As long as we reward the misguided ethos that consumers are more important than citizens, our contempt for responsible stewardship will go on forever. For how could we ever conceive of an alternative to creating yet another place not worth caring about?

Actually, I walk through it quite regularly. The other day I met a lovely lady I know on the trail there. Her name is Vi. She has no plans to extract the most profit from anything. We spoke of the ducks and the rain and the forest. And we spoke of Bill Morrell, her companion, before he died in 2003. Bill was a contractor but, unlike some environmental sustainability prize-winners, thirty years before he died, Bill donated 275 acres of forest to the public. For their enjoyment, year round from dawn to dusk. No automatic gates. No lifetime memberships. No rezoning roulette. It's called Morrell Nature Sanctuary, now owned by the Nature Trust of British Columbia. It's also on a lake.

You can take refuge in a sanctuary. I like that. Robyn and I now have two giant redwoods. They touch the sky. I like that too.

"A man is rich in proportion to the number of things he can afford to let alone."

Henry David Thoreau

"Never forget that everything Hitler did in Germany was legal."

Martin Luther King

Other Lives 13 September

"What is life? It is the flash of a firefly in the night. It is the breath of a buffalo in the wintertime.
It is the little shadow which runs across the grass and loses itself in the sunset."

Crowfoot

The wind is up. Orange fir needles blow sideways, at the end of a parched Summer. Their branches bow deferentially as they go by. A grey coolness has settled over Mount Benson. Autumn rain smell.
Some Westwood spirits that don't have their own chapter still make a contribution. The hundreds of trees that Robyn and I planted in this cow pasture over the years, and the ones that are now gone, have their own unwritten stories- the big, solitary Garry Oak, and the twin Tamaracks. The magnificent Bigleaf Maple that we chopped down to build our house haunts me. The loss of the Chilean Cedar I grew from smuggled dust, saddens me. The elegance of the Japanese Snowbell and Hemlocks enchants me. Beneath them, the Red Huckleberry, Snowberry and Salmonberry; and beneath them, the Kinnikin-nick.

There are bees and wasps with preordained flight-paths. A Western Painted Turtle swims in the oval pond. The Great Blue Heron squawking at dawn, and the kookaburra kingfisher, cleaned out all but the last shubunkin. We have doves that coo in the branches of the alders, and occasional osprey and peregrine falcons that don't. One morning, a Ring-necked pheasant strutted between our fruit trees. There are field mice in our compost, and bats that fly over the garden at dusk.

Some other lives are human visitors, some invited, some not. The Japanese tourists, picking blackberries down our driveway, only spoke Japanese. What could we say? There are family and friends, now gone, who used to taste wine and laugh at our table. There are those, still with us, warmly welcome.

There were other lives here before Robyn and me. The old red and white *Coca-Cola* cooler that we found in the bush twenty years ago was an artifact of Venutti family picnics on the shores of Westwood Lake. There was dancing under the stars, and the strings of electric lights and violins. Toy soldiers still surface out of the vineyard soil, when the snow melts in the Spring. When I first dug the garden, I pulled out fragments of burnt wood and charcoal, rare old blown glass bottles and porcelain shards with Chinese characters.

A hundred years from now, there may be no red huckleberry or kinnkinnick left. The herons and kingfishers may be gone. Other lives may find remnants of a vineyard, or a hazelnut orchard, or a raised bed garden. Or maybe not. It could be all buried under cement and steel. I don't really know what they might find.

But I know this. For a few fantastic years, on the western edge of civilization and the shores of Westwood Lake, we had it all.

Afterward

Robyn and I face forward on the *Coastal Renaissance* ferry, on our way back to Vancouver Island. We're returning from a tranquil weekend in Washington State, collecting fall memories and wine. Our own crop of pinot noir is still on the vines, but we hope to harvest next Sunday. In a couple of hours we should be turning into the gravel drive of Domaine Renegade, past the vineyard and hazelnut orchard and cottonwood canopied ponds, decelerating for the quail and rabbits, stopping around the last corner in front of the big dogwood tree. Shiva will come barking around the house, to welcome us home.

In a few weeks the days will shorten. The weather will chill and the rains begin. As the pulse of Westwood slows, the big teak doors will jam shut once again.

With continued good fortune, we will all survive another Winter until, one night a few months from now, out of the cold and the dark, it can all begin again. *Krek-ek.*

Biology

Chemistry

Literati

Special thanks to Markus Gislet, Dan Ward, and Linda Kukulski for their artwork, and Christine Whitelaw for her help with editing

Other books by Lawrence Winkler:

Orion's Cartwheel
Between the Cartwheels
Hind Cartwheel
The Final Cartwheel

www.lawrencewinkler.com

Markus 93

Lawrence Winkler lives at Westwood Lake
with Robyn and Shiva.